Praise for Alpine Rising

"*Alpine Rising* is a wonderfully written account of the truly unsung heroes of Himalayan climbing. The Indigenous Sherpa, Balti, and others of the region have for many years shouldered the brunt of burden and broken trail, often with little recognition, which led to the success of Western-based expeditions. Their tenacity and drive have allowed them to finally step out from the shadows, take the lead, and come to the forefront of alpine ascents and guiding across the globe. I'm honored to have worked with some of these climbers as teammates."

—Ed Viesturs, author of *No Shortcuts to the Top*

"Giving voice to local climbers from Tibet, Pakistan, Nepal, and India who have long enabled Westerners to tackle the world's highest peaks, Bernadette McDonald shares their histories, perspectives, and present-day realities—including the high rate of attrition and the suffering of those left behind. Gripping, thought-provoking, and often shocking, *Alpine Rising* is an important addition to the canon of mountain literature."

—Maria Coffey, author of *Where the Mountain Casts its Shadow*

"Timely and important, *Alpine Rising* is an authoritative and nuanced addition to mountaineering history. It evokes precious personal memories of time spent in the hills with Pertemba, Ang Phu, Little Karim, and so many others whose contributions are finally being fully acknowledged and celebrated."

—Sir Chris Bonington, author and mountaineer

"Bernadette McDonald has shown once again that she is the best equipped mountaineering author to give these irreplaceable people the credit they so fully deserve. *Alpine Rising* is a brilliant read and fills an important gap in the rich history of mountaineering literature."

—Bob A. Schelfhout Aubertijn, mountaineering historian

"In this courageous book, McDonald documents how significant contributions by local climbers in the Greater Ranges have been consistently underappreciated, and underreported, throughout mountaineering history. She skillfully shows how relationships and dynamics between local and foreign climbers have evolved, creating a compelling, impactful, and long overdue story."

—Steve Swenson, author of *Karakoram*

Alpine Rising

Sherpas, Baltis, and the **Triumph** of **Local Climbers** in the **Greater Ranges**

Bernadette McDonald

MOUNTAINEERS
BOOKS

MOUNTAINEERS BOOKS is dedicated
to the exploration, preservation, and enjoyment
of outdoor and wilderness areas.

1001 SW Klickitat Way, Suite 201, Seattle, WA 98134
800-553-4453, www.mountaineersbooks.org

Printed in Canada
Distributed in the United Kingdom by Cordee, www.cordee.co.uk

First edition, 2024
27 26 25 24   1 2 3 4 5

Design and layout: Kate Basart/unionpageworks.com
Cover illustration: Jeremy Collins

Library of Congress Cataloging-in-Publication data is on file for this title at
https://lccn.loc.gov/2023028030. Library of Congress record for the ebook edition
is available at https://lccn.loc.gov/2023028031.

Mountaineers Books titles may be purchased for corporate, educational, or other
promotional sales, and our authors are available for a wide range of events. For
information on special discounts or booking an author, contact our customer service at
800-553-4453 or mbooks@mountaineersbooks.org.

♻ Printed on FSC-certified and 100% recycled materials

ISBN (hardcover): 978-1-68051-578-7
ISBN (ebook): 978-1-68051-579-4

An independent nonprofit publisher since 1960

Contents

Author's Note

ONE OF MY GOALS IN WRITING THIS BOOK IS TO HONOR THE PEOPLE I've profiled by recognizing the differences in their cultures and roles. The mountainous regions of Pakistan, India, Tibet, and Nepal are rich in complexity, with many unique ethnic groups. Although I frequently refer to "local" climbers in order to differentiate those who were born and live in the high mountains of Asia from "foreign" climbers, it's important to say up front that these local climbers do not belong to a single, interchangeable group.

Readers of this book will undoubtedly have varying levels of familiarity with this part of the world and the people who dwell there. But even the most knowledgeable mountain history buff can be confused by terms now widely used. *Sherpa*, for example, is a word that has probably been co-opted more than any other name in the world. (If you google "Sherpa," the first five links are for businesses and services completely unrelated to the people.)

I hope that these brief notes will provide background and context for the distinct peoples and roles that fill the following pages.

GEOGRAPHIC DISTINCTIONS

Ladakhi: a person from Ladakh, the northernmost region of India. Coming from an arid and mountainous region, many Ladakhis were involved in early Himalayan exploration, and they continue to take part in expeditioning to this day.

Balti: a resident of Baltistan, which is in the eastern part of Gilgit Baltistan, a vast region in Northern Pakistan, home of the Karakoram range, the Hindu

Kush, and the Hindu Raj, as well as the western end of the Greater Himalaya south of the Indus River. The 28,000-square-mile area has a population
of around two million people and shares borders with China, Afghanistan,
and India. Many Balti people have become known for their mountaineering
exploits.

Hunza: At the far northern edge of Gilgit Baltistan, west of Baltistan, is the
Hunza region. Residents of this high-altitude region are recognized as excel-
lent climbers and have been supporting foreign expeditions since outsiders
began coming to the Karakoram. It's not unusual to see the terms Hunza and
Balti used interchangeably, but they are from different regions within Gilgit
Baltistan.

Astori: The Astor Valley is located near the Himalayan giant Nanga Parbat.
Local climbers from this region are referred to as Astoris.

Magar: The term Magar refers to the third-largest ethnolinguistic group in
Nepal. They come from western Nepal and have traditionally provided the
largest number of Gurkha soldiers within the country.

Bhotia: Bhotias are ethnolinguistically related Tibetans who now live in
many regions bordering Tibet. Bhotias who settled in Darjeeling were often
hired as porters by the early exploratory expeditions that came through
the area.

Sherpa: Another ethnic group that emigrated from Tibet were Sherpas,
many of whom moved into Nepal via the Khumbu region. The term Sherpa
means "people of the east," referring to the geographical area of Tibet where
they originated.

As early as 1906, Sherpas living in the Khumbu area began relocating to
Darjeeling, the Indian hill station where foreign expeditions hired porters
and high-altitude porters. They soon distinguished themselves as excellent
mountain workers. So much so, in fact, that some people believe that to be a
mountain worker is to be a Sherpa. This is not necessarily the case, although
many members of this ethnic group still work in the mountains. Today, many
mountain workers, particularly in the Everest area, are ethnic minorities
from other groups who migrate to the Khumbu region for seasonal jobs. As
Shae A. Frydenlund, a scholar who studies the climbing industry in the Everest region, points out, many of these people pass as Sherpa in a practice she
defines as becoming "situationally Sherpa."

Rai and *Gurung*: Although Sherpas constitute the most recognizable and
well known of Nepali climbers working in the high mountains of Asia, there
are also an increasing number of Rai and Gurung climbers. Rai people are a

distinct ethnolinguistic group found mainly in the eastern parts of Nepal, as well as mountainous areas of India and in western Bhutan. Gurung people are a distinct group that hails from the Annapurna region of Nepal.

······

With Sherpas, Gurungs, and Rais, it is traditional to include their ethnic origin within their names: Tenji Sherpa, Abiral Rai, Prakash Gurung.

In Balti villages such as Hushe and Sadpara, it is customary for residents to include the name of the village: Sajid Sadpara, Taqi Hushe.

Sherpa names often indicate the day of the week on which they were born: Nima—Sunday, Dawa—Monday, Mingma—Tuesday, Lhakpa—Wednesday, Phurba—Thursday, Pasang—Friday, and Pemba—Saturday. This tradition can create confusion since there can be multiple Nimas or Mingmas on one expedition. They are sometimes referred to by their village or their lodge combined with their first name—Khunde Nima or Panorama Mingma. There are also alternate spellings for many names, depending on how they are transliterated into English: for example, Tsering or Tshering, Dorj or Dorjee.

PROFESSIONAL DISTINCTIONS

Porter: This term doesn't refer to an ethnic group but is rather a job description. Since much of the terrain in the Himalayan and Karakoram ranges was—and in many cases, still is—without roads, almost everything is transported on the backs of porters. These men and women are the backbone of expeditioning in these remote areas, and they have been carrying massive loads on rocky trails, across rubble-strewn glaciers, and over snow-covered passes for as long as foreigners have been exploring the regions. Porters come from many ethnic groups within all the Himalayan ranges.

Early in the history of Himalayan exploration, porters were often referred to as "coolies." A coolie is most simply defined as a hired laborer, but the term is now considered demeaning, in part because it harkens back to the poorly paid local laborers routinely hired by Europeans who lived and traveled in Asia in the seventeenth century. In this book, "coolie" is a term used only when quoting a primary source.

Another kind of porter has emerged in the evolution of climbing—the high-altitude porter, sometimes referred to as "HAP." As porters gained more experience moving over vertiginous ground, they began carrying foreign climbers' loads ever higher. In Nepal, they were generally called "high-altitude porters," but the abbreviation HAP became synonymous with Pakistani porters working at elevations above 7,000 meters. These porters had greater climbing skills than regular porters did, were generally better equipped by their employers, and better paid. Many became highly proficient climbers with successful and independent climbing careers, and eventually preferred to be called "climbers" rather than "porters." The term HAP has become out-dated as a result.

Gurkha: These are professional soldiers, originally recruited from the Indian subcontinent, but now only from Nepal. Ever since the Anglo-Nepali War of 1814–16, when the British East India Company fought Nepali Gurkha soldiers, the Nepalis became renowned for their skills, their endurance, and their bravery. Gurkha regiments have taken part in many famous battles: Gallipoli, Baghdad, Afghanistan, and more. In addition to fighting wars, the strong and disciplined Gurkhas were often recruited by foreigners to assist them with exploration and mountaineering expeditions to the Greater Ranges of Asia.

Sahib: Foreign explorers and climbers were traditionally referred to as "sahibs" by their local companions. Sahib was used as a term of respect for anyone of higher social or official status. In this book the term is used only in historical context, since it has largely fallen out of use when Sherpas speak with foreigners, an indication of their ongoing efforts to be recognized as mountaineering equals.

One Summit—Two Centuries

TEN NEPALI CLIMBERS CREPT OUT OF THEIR TENTS AT CAMP 3. IN THE early morning hours, the sky above K2 was clear, heavy with stars. The otherworldly temperatures that hovered near −75°F felt like a punch in the face. Bent over and stiff from the uncomfortable night, the silent figures relied on instinct and experience as they attached their crampons and hoisted their packs. In twos and threes, the bobbing orbs of their headlamps began ascending toward Camp 4.

The ten climbers had coalesced as a team almost by accident. But now they were one unstoppable force.

There were four separate groups on K2 in January 2021, including over sixty climbers from nineteen countries. From three of those teams emerged a single group determined to make the first winter ascent of K2. Their presence signaled a growing trend: independent Sherpas with no client responsibilities. Sherpas climbing for themselves.

The highly respected Mingma Gyalje Sherpa (known as Mingma G) and his partners Dawa Tenjin Sherpa and Kilu Pemba Sherpa were among them. Born in Rolwaling, Mingma G had so many 8,000ers to his name it was hard to keep track, including two ascents of K2 in summer and one previous winter attempt. Serious, and at times blunt, he was clear about his intentions: "My dream, and my only real mission, was to see the Nepalese flag on the 8000 Meter Winter First Ascent list."

Also at K2 was Nepali climber Nirmal Purja, known as "Nimsdai," or simply "Nims." He described the climb on his blog with his customary flamboyance as "one of the last remaining grand prizes in mountaineering, a feat regarded as impossible." The smooth-skinned, baby-faced Nims had risen to fame in 2019 after claiming all fourteen 8,000-meter summits in just over six months. Even though he'd accomplished all his previous ascents with supplemental oxygen, Nims made it clear he intended to make the first winter ascent of K2 without it. And then to paraglide off the summit. As he tweeted upon his arrival in base camp: "Game is on, folks."

Nims brought with him five high-altitude specialists: Mingma David Sherpa, Dawa Temba Sherpa, Pem Chhiri Sherpa, Gelje Sherpa, and Mingma Tenzi Sherpa.

The final member of the summit team was Sona Sherpa, a professional climber employed by Seven Summit Treks (SST), based in Kathmandu. By far the largest group on the mountain, the SST team offered a fully commercialized approach to winter climbing on K2.

The Nepali climbers stopped to rest at Camp 4 and wait for the sun's warming rays. As expected, their spirits rose with the temperature. Mingma Tenzi was out front, fixing lines. By 3 p.m. they had climbed through a steep ice gully known as the Bottleneck and were inching up the traverse toward the summit. Ten meters below the top, the men in front stopped, waiting to regroup so that all ten climbers could touch the summit together; this historic climb would be a shared experience. Somehow, they found the energy to belt out the Nepali national anthem as they stepped onto the pinnacle of K2 at 4:43 p.m., January 16, 2021.

Their triumphant video sped around the world, delighting millions. Slanting low in the sky, the sun lit their high-altitude suits like beacons of hope: brilliant red, shimmering gold. Their upturned faces defied exhaustion as they took those final steps to the top. Singing, yelling, whooping, and hollering. Sixty seconds of joy.

In the days and months that followed, social media was flooded with images of the climb, with some viewers speculating about the use of supplemental oxygen, and with many others posting congratulatory messages from every corner of the globe. Ten Nepali climbers became ten global superstars.

Turn back the clock to July 1954. There is only one team on K2, an Italian expedition led by Ardito Desio. Despite multiple attempts, the "Savage Mountain" had yet to be climbed in any season. Desio's expedition began with eleven Italian mountaineers and thirteen Hunzas, accompanied by a "battalion of Balti porters" who carried thirteen tons of gear to base camp. By late July, only four men were in serious contention for the summit. Desio chose Achille Compagnoni and Lino Lacedelli as the A team. Supporting them was the youngest and strongest member of the team, the impossibly handsome, twenty-four-year-old Walter Bonatti.

Desio, who was in base camp, ordered Bonatti to lug nearly eighty pounds of oxygen cylinders up to Compagnoni and Lacedelli, who were positioned in the highest camp. Bonatti couldn't do it alone, and he knew the only individual on the mountain who could help him was Amir Mehdi, a slight, sad-eyed high-altitude porter from Pakistan's Shimshal Valley. Mehdi agreed, and off they went, carrying oxygen to the two lead climbers, supposedly camped at a designated spot at 8,100 meters.

But when Bonatti and Mehdi arrived at the location later that evening, there was nothing and no one to be seen. They scoured the slopes around them, shouting in frustration. Finally, they heard one of the lead climbers calling from above, "Leave the oxygen and descend."

Mehdi was frantic by that point, pacing, kicking at the slope, and howling in pain. His toes were crammed inside Italian army boots two sizes too small. They were beginning to freeze. Bonatti felt it was too risky to attempt a night descent, so he stomped out a platform on which to bivouac until morning. *Bivouac*—a word that climbers have jokingly defined as "French for mistake."

The night sky dazzled with a million stars so bright the two men could see their reflections in the snow. As the paralyzing cold encircled them, they shivered, clinging together, sharing their warmth on the highest open bivouac in history at that time. But the starlight faded when the first gusts of a blizzard moved in. Driving snow plastered the climbers' clothing and coated their faces. The desperate night dragged on. At times, neither Bonatti nor Mehdi was sure if they were alive or dead.

Finally, shortly before dawn, Mehdi howled one last scream and stumbled off the platform, intent on reaching the tent more than 350 meters below. As Bonatti watched him reeling down the slope in the half light, appearing confused, clumsy, and out of control, he doubted that Mehdi would make it down alive.

He was wrong. Mehdi, his feet numb with frostbite and his face contorted in pain, eventually lurched into the camp, where Isakhan, another Hunza high-altitude porter, tended him. Bonatti arrived hours later.

At 6 p.m. on that same day, July 31, 1954, Compagnoni and Lacedelli summited, making the first ascent of K2. But their victory had come at a terrible price.

Mehdi was transported to a hospital in the city of Skardu and then to a military hospital in Rawalpindi, where doctors amputated all of his toes and a third of one foot. Eight months later, he returned to his home in Shimshal. He had lost the ability to climb and could no longer support his family. The Italian government notified him that he had been given an award, and over the years Compagnoni sent him various books and letters. Mehdi left them unopened. Defeated, suffering, and unheralded, he died in 1999.

The contrast between the two expeditions could not be more pronounced for the men who lived in the shadows of these great mountains. The ten Nepali climbers who topped out on K2 in 2021 became social media darlings. Their fame escalated as countless videos and victorious photographs—along with the spectacular video of them singing their national anthem—brought joy to a world mired in a pandemic slump.

Nearly seventy years earlier, Amir Mehdi had simply shuffled back to his barn, placed his ice axe in the corner, and announced he never wanted to see it again. He spent the remaining forty-five years of his life in pain and obscurity, supported by his family.

What had so fundamentally changed between 1954 and 2021? Was it that the ten Nepalis *reached* their summit, while Mehdi merely *enabled* the summit for others? Or that the Nepalis had control of their actions and could make their own decisions on the mountain while Mehdi was just following orders? Was the shift partly due to the enormous change in the skills and ambitions of local climbers? Did Western observers finally grow to accept and recognize, applaud and reward the accomplishments of climbers from Pakistan and Nepal? Was there an increasing awareness of the need to move beyond a colonialist view of mountaineering to one that was more inclusive, more equitable, and more just? And what part did social media have in this transformation?

This book is about climbers with names few have heard; climbers from remote villages; climbers who were quiet, trusted partners; climbers whose expectations rose with their growing experience. Ultimately, it is about climbers who are transforming mountaineering in the highest mountains on Earth through their abilities to forge new ground, to guide and mentor, to create successful businesses, and to realize their personal dreams.

To understand more fully their evolution from silently supporting sahibs to basking—sometimes wilting—in the glow of the spotlight, we will have to go back much further than 1954, all the way to the end of the nineteenth century. Some of these stories may be troubling, even shocking, to many twenty-first-century ears.

In a world that is more divisive than ever, there can be a dearth of compassion and patience for multiple attitudes and historical perspectives. Navigating the truth is a difficult and complex process and involves memories that are sometimes selective, often patchy, but always worth hearing. Sherpas and Hunzas, Astoris, Baltis and Magars: I have done my best to listen and learn from them, at times trying to find echoes of long-vanished voices between the lines of archival records and historical volumes, other times hearing tales directly from protagonists still living and working in the heights. This is their story.

CHAPTER ONE

Ten Rupees a Digit

I could not walk so fast as a horse. I no had wings. And when I was ill, they not let me ride. They looked me as a dog, thinking themselves very clean people.

—GHULAM RASSUL GALWAN, *Servant of Sahibs*

A bdul Bhatt stood tall, gazing out at the angry crowd of servants, cooks, and horsemen under his supervision. A wizened Kashmiri hunter, Bhatt squinted into the sun, summoning all of his authority to retain control of the situation. The men had just learned that, in addition to the serving and cooking and handling of ponies packed with food and equipment bound for Nanga Parbat—which they had been doing for the past eight days—they would now need to shoulder the loads themselves. The trails had become too steep and rocky for horses.

They were outraged, and Bhatt supported their anger. These proud men were not porters. They would not carry packs on their backs for foreign climbers. After quieting the men, Bhatt launched into an emphatic speech demonstrating his intent to support every Kashmiri man who refused to submit to the white man's authority. They were on strike.

The white man in question was Willy Merkl. The year was 1932, and thirty-two-year-old Merkl was the leader of a German expedition to Nanga

Parbat. The Himalayan peak's name translates as the "naked mountain," but would eventually become known as the "killer mountain," thanks to its grim climbing history.

Merkl fired the striking Kashmiris and began searching for replacements from the mountainous regions of what would eventually become northeast Pakistan. He found 120 Astori men, 40 Baltis and 30 Hunzas, none of whom were enthusiastic about the work being offered, and all of whom were terrified of setting foot on the mountain. The Astoris, who were from the Nanga Parbat region, were well aware that British mountaineer Albert Mummery and his Gurkha companions Raghubir Thapa and Goman Singh had disappeared on its flanks in 1895.

The motley group eventually made their way to Fairy Meadow, an aptly named bucolic grassland fringed with lofty pines and sprinkled with blue forget-me-nots. Above them towered the immense, ice-clad bulk of the north face of Nanga Parbat. The 8,125-meter massif forms the western corner of the Himalaya, the 1,500-mile range of mountains that includes ten of the world's fourteen 8,000-meter peaks, and countless others in the 6,000- and 7,000-meter range.

Willy Merkl was fair-skinned and bearded, handsome in a Bavarian kind of way. A mountaineer with considerable experience in the Alps, this was his first expedition to the Himalaya. His biggest problem was money. He had invited a couple of wealthy Americans to join the team to top up the coffers, but he had ignored the advice of British climbers who suggested he hire Bhotia and Sherpa porters from Darjeeling. He wanted cheaper options.

⸻

The British had been coming to the Himalaya for years, and while their focus had primarily been Everest, they had fine-tuned the practice of hiring local help from the Bengali town of Darjeeling. Sherpas from the Khumbu Valley in Nepal had been migrating to Darjeeling since the middle of the nineteenth century, escaping the impoverished Khumbu grind of herding yaks and of growing whatever grains could withstand the severe climate. The young men who left the Khumbu region for Darjeeling were typically dirt poor; they hadn't owned the land or the yaks, but had worked for others who did. They were usually indebted. These men were considered "small people," while their bosses were "big people." The flourishing town of Darjeeling was a hill station for wealthy British and Indian families who came up in the summer months to escape the sauna-like conditions of the lowlands. It vibrated with excitement: polo matches, afternoon teas, dinner parties, and fancy-dress balls. And increasingly, foreign adventurers heading to the hills. Darjeeling offered Khumbu Sherpas more lucrative work: driving rickshaws and portering paid better than the agricultural work at home. With these opportunities came the hope of escaping the "smallness" of poverty. A chance of liberation.

While Darjeeling was primarily a British outpost, two Norwegians were the first to alert foreigners to the value of Darjeeling climbers back in 1907. When Carl Wilhelm Rubenson and Ingvald Monrad-Aas came close to succeeding on Kabru, a satellite peak of 8,586-meter Kangchenjunga, they did so with Darjeeling Sherpas. "If they are properly taught the use of ice axe and rope," Rubenson wrote, "I believe that they will prove of more use out here than European guides, as they are guides and coolies in one."

The Norwegians weren't the only ones struck by the Darjeeling Sherpas. Scotsman Alexander Mitchell Kellas was traveling with Sherpas from Darjeeling in 1909 when he attempted several peaks in the Kangchenjunga region. Back again in 1911, Kellas, who looked more like an absentminded professor than a climber, set off on a climbing frenzy, making ten first ascents. Most were with two Sherpas named Sona and Tuny. Like the Norwegians, Kellas was impressed with their skills and their potential as serious alpinists.

By the 1930s, Sherpas living on the edge of Darjeeling in a shantytown called Toong Soong Busti learned that carrying loads for foreigners was considerably more lucrative than pulling rickshaws. They also soon realized there were gradations of "big" and "small" in porter work. If you were willing to go high on a mountain, your load would be smaller. The smaller your load, the "bigger" you were. Together with the glamorous mountaineering clothing and equipment, this lifestyle was a far cry from the suffocating indebtedness of life in Khumbu.

But it was several days' journey by train and on foot from Darjeeling to Nanga Parbat, so Merkl had rejected the idea of hiring Darjeeling Sherpas and chosen to rely on local, less expensive help. Hunzas had been assisting surveyors and adventurers exploring the Karakoram and Hindu Kush since the nineteenth century, and were accustomed to moving through mountainous terrain. As Britain and Russia had tried to outmaneuver each other politically, probing for weaknesses in those formidable mountain barriers, locals had become the essential, though unheralded, players in a period of history that eventually became known as the Great Game.

Trouble arose almost immediately during Merkl's expedition. He had whittled his budget by rationing calories: Western climbers were allocated 3,000 calories per day, local climbers only 1,800. Those 1,800 calories were devoid of meat, milk, cheese, fruit, or sugar. Eighteen hundred calories basically represented a starvation diet, considering the workload. Western climbers barely eked by; even on their 3,000-calorie diet, they lost twenty to fifty pounds during the course of an expedition.

Merkl had been warned by members of other foreign expeditions that local porters tended to be sullen, ill-tempered, and unreliable. He'd been told that, compared to Darjeeling Sherpas, they often appeared unreasonable, going on strike at every opportunity, stealing, and complaining. But there was a fundamental difference in their economic arrangements that inevitably influenced their attitudes. Darjeeling Sherpas worked for wages, however meager, that they could keep for themselves and their families. In contrast, Hunza porters often came as indebted labor to their local ruler—the Mir of Hunza. Most of their earnings went to the Mir. Even worse, they were forbidden from leaving an expedition unless released by the expedition leader. No wonder they seemed sullen, ill-tempered, and unreliable to their employers.

One of the Germans on Merkl's team, Fritz Wiessner, tried his hand at negotiating with the locals at Fairy Meadow when they refused to venture up the mountain. He offered them a bit of salt and cooking oil and promised to double their flour rations. But the porters soon realized there wasn't enough equipment to go around. They would need to share the tents and sleeping bags and stoves while on the mountain and, more importantly, divvy everything up at the end of the expedition. Much more valuable than their paltry wages, the equipment was what they prized. The haggling continued until Wiessner finally convinced a few Hunzas to climb higher.

After three months, seven camps, tent-destroying avalanches, fierce snowstorms, altitude sickness, trail-breaking through chest-deep snow, and terrifying falls, the team reached 7,000 meters on the Northeast Ridge of Nanga Parbat. By this time, most of the Hunzas were sick. Although they'd discovered a feasible route up the mountain, it was too late in the season to continue. Merkl and his team considered the expedition a failure, one that they laid squarely on the Hunzas. Elizabeth Knowlton, a wealthy American invited primarily as a scribe (and not allowed to climb higher than 6,100 meters), described the Hunzas as "capricious and temperamental, physically almost as sensitive to hardship as Europeans, no stronger than the sahibs in load-carrying, and much quicker to succumb to illness. Altogether, as mountain porters, they were . . . most unsatisfactory."

Her assessment seems ungenerous. The foreign climbers—big strong men from an affluent nation—were accustomed to a protein-rich diet and plenty of it. They were well-trained athletes outfitted with the best clothing and equipment to be found at the time. The much smaller Hunza porters were impoverished farmers and tribesmen. Although they were incredibly tough, it's not surprising they would become exhausted and fall ill on a daily allotment of just 1,800 calories, which consisted mostly of carbohydrates. Additionally, their equipment was substandard compared to the Westerners' gear: blankets instead of sleeping bags, less durable boots, and flimsy outerwear. No wonder the Hunzas felt the harsh conditions more acutely than the foreigners did. The Hunzas also likely had little understanding of—or commitment to—the Germans' obsession with this mountain.

Nevertheless, the locals provided Merkl with a useful scapegoat for the "failure" of the expedition. He would not make the same mistake twice. He would hire Sherpas on his next try, if only he could afford them.

When Adolf Hitler became chancellor in Germany in 1933, he appointed a sports commissioner to encourage physical prowess among the German people. One of the approved activities was mountaineering. Himalayan climbing offered the perfect setting for the Nazi obsession with "the triumph of the will." Merkl was duly rewarded with full sponsorship from the Nazi state for his second expedition to Nanga Parbat in 1934. But as any sponsored athlete knows, financial support includes an expectation of success. Merkl understood what was required. His first task was to recruit thirty-five Sherpa and Bhotia porters from Darjeeling. Rickshaw work in Darjeeling paid around fifteen rupees a month. Merkl's expedition offered more than double, so there was no shortage of interest among the Darjeeling porters.

One of those hired was Ang Tsering. Born in 1904 in Thame in the Khumbu region of Nepal, Ang Tsering was already experienced in the mountains, having been on Everest with the British in 1924, and Kangchenjunga in 1929, 1930, and 1931. His calm demeanor belied the dramas he had already undergone.

The man Merkl hired to lead the porters was Lewa Sherpa, a Darjeeling climber who had been the sirdar—leader of the porter team—on Kangchenjunga in 1930 and who had suffered terribly the following year on Kamet. Sent down alone from Camp 5, he sustained frostbite so severe he could barely move by the time he reached base camp. He left the mountain on a pony, weeping at the prospect of losing his feet.

English mountaineer and botanist Frank Smythe, leader of the Kamet expedition, described Lewa's pitiful departure:

> *The tears were streaming down his cheeks and he was sobbing bitterly, not, I believe, so much from the pain as from what he felt to be an undignified position and thoughts of the future. He was but a shadow of his former self, and we could not help but perceive in his moral breakdown and distress the essential difference between the European and the native. Had one of us been seriously frostbitten he would at least have tried to bear his misfortune with stoical calm and fortitude. But a native cannot control his feelings; he is a child.*

Maybe one of the European climbers would have tried to hide his emotions, but the European would have *chosen* to risk freezing his feet for a summit, unlike Lewa. And the European would have had more financial means to aid his recovery and less fear of being unable to support his family with a disability. Ultimately, Lewa lost his toes to Kamet. In his case, however, he was able to return to the mountains as a sirdar, a job that allowed him to spend most of his time at lower elevations, coordinating and directing the porter team.

Sherpas and Bhotias prided themselves on their ability to function at high altitude. While nobody in 1934 understood *why* they performed so well, medical studies would eventually reveal that centuries of living in hypoxic, high-altitude environments had created a genetic adaptation. Their bodies had greater oxygen uptake, delivering more oxygen to their muscles and creating a metabolic efficiency that people from lower elevations had to work much longer to achieve.

The Sherpas traveled by train to Calcutta (known as Kolkata today) and then on to Kashmir, where they joined six hundred local porters for the trek to base camp. Their first major hurdle was the 4,100-meter Burzil Pass between the towns of Srinagar and Gilgit. After wading through deep snow for sixteen hours with fifty-pound packs on their backs, many of the porters became snow-blind. Caused by overexposure to ultraviolet rays, the condition is excruciatingly painful. To make matters worse, as the foreigners schussed down the far side of the pass on their skis, the local porters had to stumble along wearing sandals made of cloth and straw. They reached the mountain after almost a month of travel, but the troubles only intensified.

Alfred Drexel, one of the German mountaineers, fell ill at around 5,800 meters on June 7 and quickly became delirious. None of the climbers fully understood that Drexel was suffering from altitude sickness. This lack of knowledge would inevitably lead to more tragedy.

Drexel managed to descend to Camp 2, where he waited for Sherpas to carry oxygen up from farther down the mountain. But nobody knew where the oxygen had been cached. Pasang Norbu, one of the strongest Darjeeling Sherpas (nicknamed "Pasang Picture" because of his work as a photographer's assistant), went on the hunt, up and down between camps like a yo-yo, while Drexel's condition worsened. He finally tracked down the oxygen in base camp that evening. Together with Sherpas Gaylay and Dakshi, he left base camp in the dark, climbed up through the icefall by the light of a kerosene lantern, and reached Camp 1 at 10:25 p.m. Merkl greeted them with tea and cigarettes to prepare for the next stage of their climb. The Sherpas ventured out again at midnight, intent on delivering the oxygen to Drexel. But when they arrived at Camp 2, he was already dead. They carried his body down to base camp, where the German climbers buried him, wrapped in a Nazi flag.

Eleven days later, Merkl started his summit bid. By now, they were seriously behind schedule. And Merkl was under enormous pressure to climb the mountain. The route he had chosen involved a long, undulating traverse at extremely high altitude, up and over the shoulder of a subpeak, down to a saddle, and then up again to Camp 7 at 7,185 meters. Too much time, too much altitude.

There were nineteen climbers high on the mountain, including Sherpas Nima Dorje, Ang Tsering, Kitar, Dakshi, Nima Norbu, Da Thundu, Pinzo Norbu, Nima Tashi, Gaylay, Pasang Kikuli, Thundu, and Norbu. Below them lay a series of camps, which could have offered some backup support, had they been fully stocked with provisions, sleeping bags, and support climbers. But they weren't. The camps were empty. Everyone and everything was high on Nanga Parbat, poised for the summit bid.

The following morning, Thundu and Norbu were so ill they needed to go down. In order to start the descent to a lower camp, however, they first had to climb 120 meters up and over a subpeak, and then traverse a steep ice wall. Together with Fritz Bechtold, one of the German climbers, they finally crawled into Camp 4.

The next day a storm moved in, dumping a load of snow on the mountain, cutting off the rest of the men who were now at Camp 8. Stranded in their tents at 7,480 meters, the summit climbers waited for the blizzard to end, clinging to hope. Pasang Picture tried to melt snow for tea, but the wind was so strong he could barely keep the primus stove lit. From time to time, he ventured out of the tent, crawling over to the sahibs' tent with a bit of precious liquid.

The storm continued throughout the night, and by morning it was obvious there would be no summit in these conditions. They needed to flee, hopefully all the way down to Camp 4. Although they had taken six days to climb from Camp 4 to Camp 8, they were now going to try to cover the same ground in one day. Once more, they first had to go up and over the subpeak. Possibly for that reason, Pasang Picture and Pinzo Norbu left their sleeping bags behind; lighter packs would mean faster traveling. Nima Dorje must have thought the extra weight was worth it, because he rolled up his sleeping bag and lashed it to the outside of his pack.

The wind was so strong that at one point it lifted Nima Dorje and tossed him into the air. Luckily, he was tied in to a rope of five men, so he hung there, suspended above the ridge while his teammates clung to the mountain. When an even more powerful gust grabbed him, his ropemates began skidding toward the edge of the bottomless Rupal Face. They threw themselves at Nima Dorje, grabbing his legs and pinning him down. They were able to save him, but not his sleeping bag, which was ripped from his pack and sailed off down the mountain. Now the Sherpas had no sleeping bags at all.

After dropping down off the exposed ridge, Erwin Schneider and Peter Aschenbrenner untied from the rope and removed their skis from their packs. The snow was much deeper here and the wind less strong. One can only imagine their sense of relief as they attached their bindings to their boots, knowing they could glide quickly and easily down the slope. The skis were their ticket to Camp 4. Before pushing off, Aschenbrenner indicated to Pasang Picture that the three Sherpas should follow their tracks down the mountain. But how? The Sherpas had no skis. By late afternoon, Schneider and Aschenbrenner were safely ensconced at Camp 4, while the Sherpas floundered, sinking up to their knees with each step.

Likewise intent on retreating, Merkl set out with German climbers Uli Wieland and Willo Welzenbach, as well as Sherpas Ang Tsering, Kitar, Dakshi, Gaylay, Da Thundu, Nima Tashi, Pasang Kikuli, and Nima Norbu.

Somewhere between Camps 8 and 7 they bogged down in the storm and were forced to bivouac in the open with only three sleeping bags among them. Nima Norbu died in the snow that night.

By morning, both Merkl and Wieland had frostbite in their hands, but more seriously, Dakshi, Gaylay, and Ang Tsering were too weak to move. The rest of the group left them there, likely intent on their own survival.

Since Kitar, Da Thundu, Nima Tashi, and Pasang Kikuli were moving faster than the Germans, they arrived at Camp 7 first, only to find there wasn't much to celebrate: just one standing tent packed solid with snow. No food, no fuel, no sleeping bags. Merkl and Welzenbach arrived about an hour later and told the Sherpas to keep descending since the Germans would need the tent. Wieland never made it; he died 30 meters from Camp 7.

Kitar, Da Thundu, Nima Tashi, and Pasang Kikuli started down toward Camp 6, but soon lost their way. High on Nanga Parbat, they were forced to spend the night in a snow cave—their eighth night above 6,700 meters and fourth night in the storm. The Darjeeling Sherpas had been without food for three days and had not sipped a drop of water for two. In the morning, miraculously, they were still alive.

Immediately before reaching the steep traverse below the subpeak, they spied someone struggling in the snow—it was Da Thundu's brother, Pinzo. With him were Pasang Picture and Nima Dorje, left behind when Schneider and Aschenbrenner had skied off to Camp 4. Now a group of seven, the Sherpas managed to creep across the airy traverse and reach the fixed ropes that would take them down the almost vertical icy face. This should have been a moment to celebrate—the fixed lines were a beacon of safety. But they had neither crampons to negotiate the ice nor descenders to attach themselves to the fixed lines. Instead, they held on as best they could with their frostbitten fingers. Nima Dorje's hands were so numb that he twisted his arm around the fixed line in an attempt to hang on. When he stopped, Da Thundu shook him, urging him to keep moving. There was no response. Nima Dorje had died with his arm curled around the line. Da Thundu climbed over him and almost immediately came upon Nima Tashi, also dead. He carried on toward the tent at Camp 5, and there discovered his brother Pinzo Norbu, lifeless in the snow.

The four severely frostbitten Sherpas who were still alive—Da Thundu, Pasang Picture, Pasang Kikuli, and Kitar—finally staggered into Camp 4 on July 10.

High above them, another drama was unfolding. Ang Tsering, Dakshi, and Gaylay, who had been left at their bivouac in the snow somewhere between Camps 8 and 7, were still alive.

"We should leave now," Gaylay said, as he shook the snow off his body.

"No, I can't see," Ang Tsering replied. "I'm snow-blind. I need one more day. We have to wait because I know the way."

"I can't move either," Dakshi chimed in. "I'm too weak. One more day of rest is all I need." Gaylay, who was on his first Himalayan expedition, didn't argue, but remained with his partners. It's impossible to know if he stayed because of loyalty or because he feared descending the mountain alone. They spent a second night in the open. The following morning Ang Tsering was still blind and Dakshi still ill. They continued waiting, spending a third night without shelter. By morning Dakshi was near death, so Gaylay and Ang Tsering started down without him.

The horrors continued to mount. At Camp 7 they found Wieland's body in the snow and Merkl and Welzenbach alive inside the tent. Welzenbach appeared close to death, but Ang Tsering suggested trying to move everyone down to Camp 4. Merkl refused, citing his exhaustion and his confidence that climbers would soon arrive from Camp 4 to rescue them.

Merkl and Welzenbach spent another night in the tent at Camp 7 while Gaylay and Ang Tsering slept outside on the snow, their fourth night out in the elements. Welzenbach was dead by morning. They remained one more day at Camp 7, waiting for a rescue; Merkl in the tent with his deceased partner, Gaylay and Ang Tsering out on the snow.

The next morning, Merkl, Gaylay, and Ang Tsering descended to the saddle and then started up from the low point toward Camp 6. Both Merkl and Ang Tsering had frostbitten feet and could barely walk. Stumbling and shuffling, they almost reached Camp 6, but not quite. The three exhausted men lay down in the snow for a night in the open—Gaylay and Ang Tsering's sixth. Hungry, thirsty, and hypoxic, they drifted into a delirious state, wrapped around each other for warmth. The snow sifted over them throughout the night. By morning they were merely three snowy mounds on the endless white expanse. They had been without food for seven days and without fluids for six.

They emerged from their snowy coffins with leaden legs, stiff from the cold, their empty stomachs aching.

"Gaylay, you should go down and get help," Ang Tsering urged. "Go to Camp 4. Send some help up for us."

"No, it's better if you go. You are stronger. You can move faster. I will stay with the sahib. You go."

Ang Tsering left alone for Camp 4—and survival.

During his descent he passed body after body, like a macabre parade of death, frozen in time. Down and down he stumbled on his frostbitten feet, clinging to the fixed lines, past Camp 5, into darkness. He lost his way at one point and slipped, skidding to a stop at the edge of a crevasse. He called out from the precarious position, and eventually climbers from Camp 4 heard his cries and came out to drag him down to the tent. He cradled a hot mug of tea in his stiff, frozen hands, sipping it slowly. Merkl and Gaylay were still alive, he told them; they needed help. Ang Tsering recalled that one foreign climber and two porters mounted a half-hearted rescue attempt for Merkl and Gaylay, but realistically, nobody had the strength to move up anymore.

Four years later, Paul Bauer, with the 1938 German expedition, found Gaylay's frozen body stretched out on the snow high on Nanga Parbat. Next to him was Merkl, in a seated position.

It was tempting for foreign climbers to see this heartbreaking image as evidence that Gaylay was so devoted to Merkl he gave his life to remain with him. The truth is that we don't know the full story, or Gaylay's reasoning for remaining behind. The possibility of loyalty certainly arises, or perhaps he was motivated by the Buddhist sense of compassion. But maybe it was simpler than that—given the depleted state they were all in, we don't know if Gaylay was thinking clearly at all. He could have remained out of sheer exhaustion. Maybe Ang Tsering truly was the strongest of the three, with the best chance of reaching Camp 4 and rousing a rescue party. Ang Tsering later confided to Tenzing Norgay, though, that he believed both he and Gaylay could have safely managed the descent.

━━━

While the truth about the decisions and actions on Nanga Parbat will never be known, photos reveal the final outcome of this tragic expedition with brutal clarity. In one, Schneider, Aschenbrenner, Fritz Bechtold, and Peter Müllritter are back at base camp. They are seated on the ground, arms around each other, comforting each other. What are they thinking? Are Schneider and Aschenbrenner recalling the moment they strapped on their skis and schussed away from Pinzo Norbu, Pasang Picture, and Nima Dorje? Are there feelings of regret that they couldn't rescue their ropemates? Guilt? Relief that they are still alive?

A second photo shows the four Sherpas who survived the harrowing fixed-line descent: Pasang Kikuli, Kitar, Pasang Picture, and Da Thundu. Their frostbitten hands and feet are wrapped in bandages. They are seated together in their woolen underwear. There are no embraces. They are not touching each other. They are not even looking at each other. They appear to be in shock and in pain. Da Thundu's head is bowed, and he looks utterly spent. The others gaze off into the distance: not at the camera or each other, seemingly at nothing at all. What are they thinking? About how they will feed their families without the use of fingers and toes? About their teammates frozen to the fixed lines? About the horrors of sleeping in the snow night after night?

Perhaps they are too exhausted to think.

Predictably, German public response to the expedition was fiercely critical of both its defeat and its disastrous end. There was plenty of blame to share among the survivors and their dead leader, Merkl. Ironically, the overwhelming magnitude of the tragedy only strengthened the connection between Nanga Parbat and Germany, guaranteeing renewed commitment by the government to claim its first ascent. Planning for the next attempt began almost immediately.

Back in Toong Soong Busti, where most Sherpas lived, reactions to the news of the loss of life were mixed. Tenzing Norgay explained, "There was mourning and grief in many homes in Toong Soong Busti, but there was also a certain deep pride in what our men had borne and accomplished."

The surviving Sherpas had to deal with their frostbitten bodies. Ang Tsering lost all his toes to amputation. When he arrived at the Victoria Hospital in Darjeeling, the nurses discovered maggots living in the holes where his digits had been. After six months in the hospital, he was released to a life of continuous pain. In later years, Sherpas were compensated for amputations due to frostbite—ten rupees per digit and twenty rupees for the index finger, thumb, or big toe. But not in 1934.

Despite their amputations, both Da Thundu and Pasang Picture returned to Nanga Parbat with a new German team. On June 15, 1937, sixteen men were together at Camp 4: nine Sherpas, including Pasang Picture, and seven foreigners. At 12:10 a.m., a catastrophic avalanche thundered down, completely burying the camp. There were no survivors. By chance, Da Thundu was in a lower camp at the time.

Decades later, Jonathan Neale, author of *Tigers of the Snow*, asked Da Thundu's widow, Lhamoo Iti, "What is the most important element in a climber's survival: strength, intelligence, or luck?"

"Luck," she replied.

On Nanga Parbat in 1937, it was luck that saved Da Thundu's life.

When he was asked to return to Nanga Parbat in 1938, he said no.

⁂

Ang Tsering married Nima Dorje's widow, Pasang Diki, and brought her son Dawa Temba into his home and heart. Over the next twenty-five years, he and Pasang had seven more children together. During much of the time, Pasang managed alone while Ang Tsering was away in the mountains. When Indian historian Nandini Purandare asked Sherpa wives in Darjeeling how stressed they had been, worrying about the safety of their husbands while on expeditions in the 1930s, she was taken aback by their response. "The women did not know how to react to such questions," she said. "They had been too busy to worry."

In 2001, Tashi Tenzing, grandson of Tenzing Norgay, was strolling along a road in Toong Soong Busti. He spied an old man shuffling out from the doorway of a modest home. His body was bent from years of carrying heavy loads, his joints creaky and sore from too many nights sleeping out on the snow, his face as lined as a topographical map and framed by a shock of silvery hair. It was Ang Tsering at ninety-three years of age. The same Ang Tsering who had survived expeditions to Everest, Kangchenjunga, Kamet, Nanga Parbat, and more, working for the British, the Indians, the Germans, and the Swiss. Ang Tsering, who had climbed high, carried heavy loads, and later led dozens of Sherpa porters in his role as sirdar. Ang Tsering, who had lost all his toes to frostbite. One of the first professional Sherpas, who after all the dangers and hardships and injuries, lived peacefully as an elder within the community that respected and cared for him. He died the following year, in 2002.

CHAPTER TWO

A Thin Black Wallet:
Tragedy on K2

The story should be about the existence of multiple stories and about bringing them to light. . . . It should involve shifting our focus from one-way-of-being to recognizing the multiple-ways-of-being.

—PASANG YANGJEE SHERPA, *Alpinist 51*

There isn't a high-altitude climber alive who isn't terrified of frostbite. For good reason. At temperatures well below freezing, a lost mitten or an ill-fitting boot almost guarantees some level of harm.

As climbers go higher, their oxygen uptake plummets, reducing the body's ability to produce heat. Combined with dehydration and cold temperatures, wind and exhaustion, the diminishing volume of plasma in the blood turns it to sludge, slowing its flow. The body's survival instinct sends signals to the blood vessels in the extremities to constrict, forcing more blood to the vital organs. This redistribution of blood might save a climber's life, but fingers or toes or an exposed cheek or nose can become collateral damage.

What happens next is truly chilling: ice crystals begin to form in the spaces surrounding cells. As water is lost from the cells, dehydration hastens their destruction; the blood vessels no longer function properly.

At first, the frostbitten area turns white, and there is pain or a tingling sensation. Later there is no feeling at all. With severe frostbite, the ends of digits become as hard as wood.

In an ideal situation, as soon as a climber notices the first signs of frostbite, they will immediately take shelter in a tent and, with their partner, warm the freezing appendage against a stomach or armpit. Rehydration and rest will help to reduce the damage. If stopping isn't possible, the next best strategy is for the frostbitten climber to keep moving to encourage as much blood circulation as possible. The worst-case scenario is to stop moving, without any shelter: the dreaded high-altitude open bivouac.

After thawing, the damaged areas blister and hemorrhage, bringing excruciating pain. If the frostbite is bad enough, the appendages die, turn black, and must be amputated.

This is what the surviving Sherpas, including Pasang Kikuli, were forced to endure after their desperate retreat off Nanga Parbat in 1934.

Born in 1911 in the remote Rolwaling Valley, Pasang Kikuli migrated to Darjeeling at a young age to begin his life as a porter. A small yet unexpectedly strong man, he had an expression that appeared perpetually sad, as if he had just heard devastating news. By the time he was eighteen, he was already in high demand: Kangchenjunga in 1929, 1930, and 1931, Everest in 1933, and, of course, Nanga Parbat in 1934.

Despite his debilitating amputations, Pasang Kikuli was back at work two years after Nanga Parbat with an expedition co-led by British explorer Bill Tilman and American mountaineer Charlie Houston to the mysterious, unclimbed Nanda Devi.

Everything about this expedition was arduous: the approach, the precipitous narrow paths clinging to the rocky cliffs high above the deep gorges, the swiftly moving streams, even the food. Several members of the team became sick with dysentery, and by the time they reached base camp, the highly experienced Kitar was gravely ill. Shortly after, he died. Tilman later wrote that Kitar "did not seem to us a very likable type of Sherpa." His comment seems callous, but it reflects the taciturn leadership style accepted by many of Tilman's Western partners at the time. Pasang Phutar, who was also on the Nanda Devi team, was critical of Tilman's leadership style, which he considered insensitive. He held Tilman responsible for Kitar's demise. Ang Tsering agreed, and never forgave Tilman. He later adopted Kitar's physically disabled but brilliant son, cared for him, and provided him with a proper education.

Pasang Kikuli fared better than Kitar on Nanda Devi. Tilman found him to be an exceptional worker and the "only one worth a place on a serious show." One of the Americans, Art Emmons, agreed that Pasang Kikuli was "by far the best porter, a fine personal servant, energetic, and hardworking."

When Bill Tilman and British climber and geologist Noel Odell reached the 7,816-meter summit of Nanda Devi on August 29, 1936, they set a record for the highest mountain climbed at the time. Following the ascent, Houston teamed up with Tilman to leave the Nanda Devi Sanctuary over Longstaff's Col, a high pass that no one had crossed before. Pasang Kikuli joined them. He had been Houston's personal Sherpa throughout the expedition, a practice that was typical for the time, but one that felt odd to Houston. Nevertheless, the two hit it off, and their partnership was strengthened during the difficult traverse of the col, during which they encountered everything from ice-encrusted rock walls to deep, avalanche-prone snow. Razor-backed moraines and swiftly flowing rivers made the journey out of the mountains equally harrowing.

Two years later, when the American Alpine Club asked Houston to lead the first American expedition to K2, he invited Pasang Kikuli to be his sirdar.

K2 is located in the Karakoram, the magnificent range of mountains that is home to four 8,000-meter peaks, over thirty 7,000-meter peaks, and countless more in the 6,000-meter range. But it's not only the heights that impress; their structure is also remarkable. Rapier-like spires emerge from four colossal glacier systems to slash the razor-blue Karakoram sky. The immense, remote region of what is now Northern Pakistan is sparsely populated, and until recently, its Balti residents were isolated from the outside world by perpetual political tension and difficult access.

This was the first seriously viable attempt on the second-highest mountain in the world, though explorers had been poking around the area for over fifty years. Back in 1886, Francis Younghusband crossed the difficult, 5,500-meter

Mustagh Pass, located west of K2. He did so thanks to a guide from the town of Askole named Wali, four Balti porters, several Ladakhi porters, and thirteen horses. Wali had been over the pass before, so he knew what to do when they reached the steepest bits: he joined turbans and waistbands and segments of rope from the horses to fashion a kind of safety line for the caravan. When the way became too icy, he cut steps with his pickaxe, opening the route down off the pass. "I freely confess that I myself could never have attempted the descent, and that I—an Englishman—was afraid to go first," Younghusband admitted. "Luckily my guides were better plucked than myself."

Italian Roberto Lerco explored the area on and around K2 in 1890, and Sir Martin Conway, accompanied by four Gurkhas, arrived in 1892. The year 1902 saw the first expedition openly aspiring to climb the mountain. It was led by Oscar Eckenstein, an anti-establishment climber whose father had immigrated to England from Germany. His partner was the climber/magician/poet/occultist Aleister Crowley. Their eclectic crew suffered from bouts of malaria—in addition to the threat of physical violence when Crowley confronted one of the team members with a revolver. Unsurprisingly, they failed to reach the summit of K2.

Seven years later an Italian expedition arrived, led by the Duke of the Abruzzi. On his team was Vittorio Sella, one of the most celebrated mountain photographers of all time. His mesmerizing images of the mountain captured its geometric perfection, its bony, jagged architecture. But climbing this Karakoram giant would prove to be a harshly punishing endeavor. Another member of the team, the scientist Filippo De Filippi, was appalled at the rations allotted to the porters—only about 900 grams of coarse meal each day. But he was amazed at their output, writing that he knew of "no other race capable of an equal amount of work in such a severe climate, upon nourishment so poor in quality and meagre in quantity."

Assisted by their five hundred porters, including four experienced alpine porters, the Italians reached well over 6,000 meters on the southeast spur of the mountain. The continuous rockfall so discouraged the porters that they wisely refused to carry loads any higher.

There were other exploratory trips to the region in 1929 and 1937, but between 1909 and Houston's expedition in 1938 no one made a serious attempt to climb the mountain. Where was everybody? The British were distracted with Everest, while the Germans had gravitated to Nanga Parbat and Kangchenjunga.

The Darjeeling Sherpas, including Pasang Kikuli, were everywhere, supporting foreign climbers on whatever mountains they chose. K2 waited in glorious solitude.

....

The relationship between Sherpas and Westerners at this time was based on a model that regarded sahibs as masters and Sherpas as servants. Robert Bates, one of the members of Houston's American team—a highly educated individual—wrote, "Though slight of build, [Sherpas] are strong, willing, and above all filled with enthusiasm for mountaineering. To them an attempt on a high mountain is a pilgrimage and the white climber almost a holy man." To modern ears, his statement sounds patronizing and elitist—which it was—but Bates was merely reflecting the attitude among white mountaineers of the day.

In the Kashmir city of Srinagar, Houston's team met up with their six Darjeeling Sherpas: Pasang Kikuli, Tse Tendrup, Pasang Kitar, Pemba Kitar, Phinsoo, and Sonam. Bates described the approach march as "Millionaires' Row in expeditioning." After smoothing the ground, setting up the tents and inflating the air mattresses, the Sherpas would lay out their personal sahib's sleeping bag, diary, and toilet kit, and then "take off his master's marching boots, if he would let him. Such luxury doesn't exist in civilized countries."

As sirdar, Pasang Kikuli was responsible for the Darjeeling Sherpas as well as the seventy-five local porters hired to carry loads to base camp. Within the first days of trudging up the Baltoro Glacier, the inadequacy of the porters' equipment became clear. They struggled up the ice in straw and goatskin moccasins, lugging unwieldy wooden devices that the Americans called "coolie crutches," which they used to cut steps in the ice and leaned on to help support their heavy loads. The Sherpas and Americans were better equipped with nailed leather boots, wool socks, and proper snow goggles, as well as insulating and windproof layers of clothing. It seemed that each subsequent expedition planned and budgeted more equitably for the high-altitude Sherpa staff. Yet the needs of the porters weren't taken seriously, even though they made these expeditions possible by carrying the loads to base camp. They suffered terribly.

The Sherpa team performed well on K2, ferrying supplies and building tent platforms on the relentlessly steep mountain. Pasang Kikuli, Phinsoo, and Tse Tendrup were the stars. Up and up they climbed on the Abruzzi

Ridge: Camp 3 on July 5, Camp 4 on July 13. Finally, only three Americans and three Sherpas remained on the highest reaches of K2. When the Americans decided the Sherpas had reached the limits of their climbing abilities and should descend, Pasang Kikuli begged to go higher. Houston relented. The wind roared down like a freight train, battering the men, tossing them about, ripping at their tents, dulling their senses, and eroding their willpower. But ironically, it wasn't the wind that defeated them; it was a miscalculation in the number of matches required to light the stoves at their highest camp. They ran out.

Even though the 1938 expedition ultimately failed to summit K2, the team of Americans led by Charlie Houston and of Sherpas led by Pasang Kikuli had laid the groundwork for Fritz Wiessner's attempt the following year.

There are many ways to characterize the 1939 K2 expedition, most of them negative: disjointed, uncommunicative, unbalanced, inexperienced, and tragic. German-born Fritz Wiessner had immigrated to the United States in 1929 and wasted little time establishing himself as one of the country's top climbers, particularly on rock. He was a strong leader—powerfully built and with an iron will. Some considered him *too* strong. Other American climbers often described his style as "Teutonic," an unfair reference to his ethnic origin. But most who had climbed with him noted his single-minded, authoritarian approach to both climbing and human relations.

Unfortunately for Wiessner, his first choices for team members didn't work out: one by one, the invited climbers dropped out until he was left with a distinctly inexperienced group. In fact, many within the American climbing community felt he should postpone the trip until he could build a stronger team.

What they didn't know, and Wiessner did, was that the strength of his team would come from Darjeeling. He had recruited nine Sherpas, five of whom had been with Houston the year before. Pasang Kikuli, Phinsoo, and Tse Tendrup had all climbed and carried loads high on the Abruzzi Ridge; Pemba Kitar and Kikuli's brother Sonam rounded out the group of returning Sherpas. Newcomers included Pasang Kitar, Tsering Norbu, Dawa Thondup, and finally, Pasang Dawa Lama. A photograph of the Sherpas taken in Srinagar portrays a group of proud and confident high-altitude climbers. If you consider the strength of the Sherpa team, the 1939 expedition was very strong indeed, a signal of the future, when the power—and later leadership—of Himalayan expeditions would come from Sherpas rather than from foreign climbers.

As in 1938, Pasang Kikuli was not only the expedition leader's personal Sherpa, he was also the sirdar, supervising the other Sherpas employed to work on the ridge and the 122 porters hired in Askole to carry loads to base camp.

Their journey took them through a spectacular landscape. Verdant apricot orchards gave way to fields of poppies. Milky rivers rushed from the glaciers. Boulders tumbled down into the narrow, winding canyons; and eventually the soaring rock towers of the Karakoram came into view. The villages became increasingly impoverished, and living conditions grew harsher the farther the team marched. The porters, who were paid pennies a day, were once again badly equipped. Some were barefoot, others clad in sandals made from worn-out tires; a few wore yak-skin shoes. Their clothing was patched and filthy, and when the night temperatures plummeted, they wrapped themselves in worn pieces of blanket. Wiessner's limited budget hadn't included snow goggles for everyone, so the porters improvised by carving slits into pieces of cardboard to protect their eyes from the burning ultraviolet rays. Those who could still see led those who were snow-blind.

After days of walking on glacial rubble and ice, they neared the confluence of the Baltoro, Vigne, Godwin-Austen, and West Gasherbrum Glaciers, where the porters declared a strike. Porter strikes were not unusual. They were often a bargaining strategy for better pay or better equipment—in this case, snow goggles. As such, they frequently took place at the most inconvenient spot imaginable from the Westerners' perspective.

Having resolved the strike with promises of extra pay, the expedition members finally rounded a bend and there it was—K2. A magnificent pyramid of rock and ice. After another day's march, they reached its base, where the porters collected their pay and fled back to their villages, likely relieved that they had survived. Now only the Americans and the Sherpas remained.

⸺

Perhaps because of the weakness of the American climbers on his team or because of his single-minded drive, Wiessner led the entire expedition from the front: breaking trail, choosing camps, chopping steps, and pushing out the route. With the support of the Sherpas, he equipped a series of camps with stoves, gasoline, food, sleeping bags, and mattresses. But the American climbers struggled, suffering from altitude sickness, frostbite, exhaustion, and low motivation. The only one who shared Wiessner's drive to reach the summit was Dudley Wolfe, a bulky man with a blue-blood pedigree. Theories abound about why Wolfe was chosen for the K2 team, but his wealth was likely a factor. Nevertheless, Wolfe lugged himself higher and higher in support of Wiessner and the ultimate goal.

As Wiessner, Wolfe, and the Sherpas climbed ever farther from the safety of base camp while the rest of the team retreated, two alarming gaps emerged: a physical gap and a communication gap. Without radios to share information, it was impossible to know what was happening to climbers higher on the mountain or what was expected of those at the lower camps. The Sherpas were tasked with relaying messages between camps in a language not their own.

The Sherpas, additionally, were unaccustomed to climbing on technical terrain without Westerners, a tradition that was designed for their safety since they weren't yet deemed to be sufficiently skilled for a mountain as steep and difficult as K2. But because the Americans, other than Wiessner and Wolfe, were either unable or uninterested in going high, the Sherpas were often forced to make climbing and route-finding decisions on their own. Although the Sherpas performed well on the mountain, both the supply chain and the communication system collapsed.

By July 14, Wiessner, Wolfe, Tse Tendrup, Pasang Kitar, and Pasang Dawa Lama were at Camp 8 at 7,700 meters. Because he was still suffering from his earlier frostbite, Pasang Kikuli was not with them. Wiessner chose Pasang Dawa Lama and Dudley Wolfe to establish one last camp at the upper end of the Shoulder—the last reasonably level bit of ground—for the summit push. When a gaping crevasse blocked the way, Wiessner and Pasang Dawa Lama managed the awkward crossing, but Wolfe couldn't do it. He retreated to Camp 8. Wiessner and Pasang Dawa Lama carried on to a final camp a mere 670 meters below the summit. They had one small tent, two sleeping bags and mats, a stove and fuel, and six days of food.

On July 19, Wiessner and Pasang Dawa Lama crept out of the tent and started up. Wiessner was in front as usual. He took one look at the icy Bottleneck and decided that the rock cliffs to the left looked safer. But they were also much slower, despite his remarkable rock-climbing skills. Loaded down with pitons, carabiners, food, and extra clothing, Wiessner led out. Pasang Dawa Lama followed, carrying two pairs of crampons and an extra rope. Neither had supplemental oxygen.

Leading every pitch, Wiessner inched his way up the ice-encrusted cliffs for nine interminable hours, tapping in pitons, clipping his carabiners, securing the hemp rope, and studying the rock to determine his next moves. Pasang Dawa Lama watched him, belayed him, and then followed. Blessed with temperatures above freezing, Wiessner frequently removed his mitts to perform the delicate moves.

At 6:30 p.m. they were at 8,383 meters, a mere 230 meters below the summit. A short traverse would take them to the summit snowfield—success seemed assured. But as the sun slipped to the horizon, and then dipped below it, the temperature plummeted. Wiessner tried to move up, but the rope came tight. Pasang Dawa Lama wasn't following.

"No, sahib," he said. "Tomorrow."

"What do you mean?" Wiessner called down. How could they stop now?

"It's too late; we must turn back." Pasang Dawa Lama was adamant.

Wiessner considered untying and continuing alone to the top—but what about Pasang Dawa Lama? There was no way, Wiessner thought, the Sherpa could manage the technical descent back to Camp 9 on his own. And if Pasang Dawa Lama stayed out all night with his substandard boots, he would definitely lose some toes, if not his life. Wiessner reluctantly accepted Pasang Dawa Lama's decision, and they started down. They had plenty of food. There was tomorrow.

While Wiessner didn't initially credit Pasang Dawa Lama for his actions that night, they probably saved not only his own life, but Wiessner's as well. The same could be said for Wiessner, since he descended with Pasang Dawa Lama rather than abandoning him.

The descent was tedious, rappel after rappel. At one point, a rope caught on the crampons attached to Pasang Dawa Lama's pack, and as he tried to untangle the mess, both pairs tumbled to oblivion. At last, they crawled into their tent at Camp 9 at 2:30 a.m.

Exhausted from their efforts, they slept in the following day. In fact, they slept most of the day, lounging in the high-altitude sunshine. On July 21, they headed out for a second go, this time up the Bottleneck rather than the rock band.

The snow was hard and glazed with ice. Perfect for crampons, but they had none. Time for plan B. They would descend to Camp 8, Wiessner decided, to pick up some crampons, and then climb back to their high camp and try again the following day. Since the weather was stable, this seemed like a minor setback to him.

Pasang Dawa Lama felt otherwise and asked for someone else to replace him as Wiessner's summit partner. Wiessner agreed. Down they went, Pasang Dawa Lama with his sleeping pad, sleeping bag, and clothing, Wiessner more lightly laden since he planned to return to Camp 9 the same day with a new partner from Camp 8. He wasn't sure who it would be.

But they found only Dudley Wolfe, alone, at Camp 8—clearly not a suitable summit partner. Wiessner decided to descend to Camp 7 for additional fuel and food and a partner. The three started down, Wiessner out front chopping steps. The hours slipped by, the air temperature cooled, and a mist moved in, obscuring the visibility.

The cause of the accident that happened next is unclear, but in a flash, all three climbers were sliding and tumbling down the slope. Wiessner managed to arrest the fall and hold them, but Wolfe lost his sleeping bag.

Badly shaken, they limped into Camp 7 well after dark, to another shock: There were no climbers, no sleeping bags, no air mattresses, and no crampons! The tent doors yawned wide, the tents were stuffed with snow, and bits of food lay scattered around the dilapidated camp. Stunned, they salvaged one of the tents, crawled in, and shivered under Pasang Dawa Lama's sleeping bag.

Desperate now, Wiessner developed plan C. He and Pasang Dawa Lama would carry on down to Camp 6, and Wolfe would remain at Camp 7 with Pasang Dawa Lama's sleeping bag. Why? It's not clear. Wolfe may have been exhausted. Perhaps he was a summit contender after all. Or Wiessner may have wanted to descend to Camp 6 and head back up to the highest camp as quickly as possible to avoid jeopardizing his own next summit bid. Hauling Wolfe along would slow them down.

At 11 a.m. on July 23, Wiessner and Pasang Dawa Lama crawled out of the tent at Camp 7 and started down to Camp 6. Another shock. The two Camp 6 tents were folded with only a bit of food and fuel. There were no sleeping bags and no air mattresses. Camp 5—the same. Camp 4—no sleeping bags. Camp 3—completely empty. Even Camp 2—no sleeping bags.

Exhausted, confused, and demoralized, the two wrapped themselves in a tent to stay warm overnight. The following day they staggered into base camp. Pasang Dawa Lama suffered from cracked ribs as a result of the fall a few days earlier, and there was blood in his urine from damaged kidneys.

Only now did Wiessner discover how disjointed the team had become. While he and Pasang Dawa Lama had been inching their way toward the summit of K2, two of the Americans had directed the Sherpas to strip the upper camps and had already left the expedition. Porters had arrived to start the trek back to Askole. The expedition appeared to be wrapping up.

Furious, Wiessner demanded an explanation. There was none. Rather, just a mess of miscommunication, in part due to language barriers and in part due to a misunderstanding of what had been happening high on the mountain. Fingers were pointed, accusations made, and excuses offered. But the fact remained that everyone except Dudley Wolfe was at base camp, and Wolfe was completely incapable of descending the mountain on his own.

The expedition shifted to rescue mode.

On July 25, Phinsoo, Dawa Thondup, Pasang Kitar, and American climber Jack Durrance started up. They reached Camp 2 the first day, Camp 4 the second. Dawa Thondup became ill, and Durrance was hit with altitude problems, so they prudently decided to descend. Before they left Camp 4, Durrance asked Phinsoo and Pasang Kitar to continue to Camp 7 but Pasang Kitar objected, saying that he and Phinsoo—both slightly built—couldn't lug Wolfe down the Abruzzi Ridge, should he need to be carried. Durrance saw his logic, so he and Dawa Thondup headed back to base camp, planning to ask Wiessner and Pasang Kikuli to head up to support the rescue mission. They discovered that Wiessner was worn out from his time high on the mountain. Ignoring his frostbitten toes, Pasang Kikuli agreed to go up, taking Tsering Norbu with him.

On July 28, Pasang Kikuli and Tsering Norbu left base camp to join Pasang Kitar and Phinsoo. In a herculean effort, the pair gained 1,500 meters in six hours, reaching Camp 4, which, to their surprise, was empty. Pasang Kitar and Phinsoo had obviously changed their minds and continued up, so Pasang Kikuli and Tsering Norbu did so as well. Another 580 meters, all the way to Camp 6. Their single day's ascent from 5,030 meters to 7,100 meters is almost inconceivable.

The men at base camp were watching through binoculars. On July 29 they could see three men ascend the steep couloir between Camps 6 and 7. Some time later, three figures descended the same couloir. But which three? What was going on?

Later, the story emerged: Tsering Norbu remained at Camp 6 to prepare tea for Wolfe and the others. Pasang Kikuli, Phinsoo, and Pasang Kitar reached Camp 7 at noon and found Wolfe lying in his sleeping bag, almost delirious. He had spent thirty-eight days above 6,700 meters without supplemental oxygen and had been without food or water for days. The inside of the tent was fouled with excrement. He begged them to return the following day, when he promised to descend with them after one more day of rest.

The three Sherpas returned to Camp 6. The next day a storm forced them to remain in the tent. On July 31 they headed up once more to rescue Wolfe. Once again, Tsering Norbu stayed back to brew tea. Tsering Norbu watched his teammates kick steps up the steep couloir above camp. He turned to the stove, melting snow, heating water, preparing for what would surely be a tired group arriving in a few hours. He waited. He brewed. He peered up the slope. No one appeared.

On August 1, he continued waiting, brewing more tea. Still no one appeared. On August 2, he fled to base camp.

A major storm swept the mountain on August 5, destroying any hopes of survival at Camp 7. Wolfe was lost, along with Pasang Kikuli, Phinsoo, and Pasang Kitar. Two days later, the remaining climbers and Sherpas joined the porters on their sad march to Askole.

⸺

Wiessner delayed his return to the United States and was still in Srinagar when Germany invaded Poland on September 1, 1939. In late October the American Alpine Club (AAC), official sponsor of the expedition, launched an investigation into the tragic events. This highly unusual undertaking was likely influenced by Wiessner's German origins. Wiessner fought back in his own defense by declaring, "After all, a Himalayan mountain is like war! You must expect a few casualties!"

Charlie Houston wasn't part of the inquiry, but he was certainly affected by the tragedy. In a private letter to his friend, the climber and photographer Bradford Washburn, his feelings were clear: "Wiessner is to blame for most if not all of the mishap, and I don't believe I can ever forgive him. I didn't know Wolfe, but I knew and dearly loved Pasang [Kikuli] and P[h]insoo, and what they so gallantly did, *alone*, I can't forget."

Before going to K2, Wiessner had confided to Houston, "If I can climb this mountain, I'll be set for life. Then I can come home, marry a rich girl, and retire." That plan didn't quite work out. But although he was forced to leave the AAC in disgrace, Wiessner was later reinstated and he continued climbing well into his later years.

Pasang Dawa Lama also took part in many more Himalayan expeditions, becoming one of the greatest Sherpa climbers of his generation. In 1954 he made the first ascent of Cho Oyu, the 8,188-meter peak that straddles the border of Nepal and Tibet. His Austrian partner Herbert Tichy admitted his motivation for the trip came not from the climbing establishment but from Pasang Dawa Lama, who had hatched the idea while the two were sitting around a campfire during an exploratory trip through Nepal the previous year.

Tichy later wrote about an incident at Cho Oyu's Camp 3, located at 6,900 meters and immediately below an icefall. He, Pasang Dawa Lama, and Adjiba Sherpa had arrived at the site midafternoon, after a long day of climbing. Fully intending to set up the tents and spend the night, Tichy recalled that "Pasang wouldn't hear of it. . . . He fixed his eyes on the ice-fall as though it had personally insulted him." Days later, the highly motivated Pasang hiked out to the village of Namche Bazaar to pick up extra supplies for the team. When he arrived at Marlung, a distance of thirty miles from Cho Oyu, he learned that a Swiss team was poised to make an attempt on the mountain. Furious, he marched nonstop to base camp and climbed all the way to Camp 3. Thirty miles and more than 3,000 meters of elevation gain in just two days. The next day he guided the two badly frostbitten Austrians, Tichy and Sepp Jöchler, to the top.

Pasang Dawa Lama, who had convinced Fritz Wiessner to retreat from high on K2 in 1939, now had his summit moment—as he would again in 1958 when he made the second ascent of Cho Oyu. He had graduated from high-altitude belayer to high-altitude climber to high-altitude guide. This was another important step in the transition from unskilled labor to highly skilled leadership on the highest mountains on Earth.

⁂

In 1993, British alpinist Roger Payne discovered some scraps of bone and clothing near K2 base camp. Two years later, American climber Scott Johnston was walking along the glacier above K2 base camp when he also noticed something unusual—a thin black wallet lying on the ice. "In the coin purse were some old British coins, some safety pins, and a couple of buttons," he said. A few steps away Johnston discovered a torso protruding from the ice—a spine, ribs, and neck. "There were remnants of a gray wool sweater over an Oxford cloth striped cotton shirt. There were leather pack straps but no pack." He believes the remains may have belonged to Phinsoo or Pasang Kikuli, the British coins hard-earned payment for their work on the mountain. "The torso was very small," he added.

Pasang Kikuli was twenty-eight years old when he disappeared on K2, leaving behind a young widow and two small children.

∙∙∙∙∙∙

High mountain tragedies are often shrouded in mystery. They are difficult to dissect because they lack objective witnesses; the altitude and exhaustion don't promote rational thought. Memory is selective. There is usually plenty of blame to pass around. But ultimately, nobody was ever held accountable for the first four victims of K2.

These early dramas are not merely narratives about heroic individuals proving themselves in the rarefied air of the high mountains of Asia, as they were portrayed in Western accounts of the era. Nor are they one-sided stories of loyalty and sacrifice. In the case of the foreign climbers, patriotic pride and colonialist attitudes may have clouded their decision-making, as did insufficient knowledge of the effects of high altitude. For the local workers, poverty and lack of jobs forced them to take orders that could compromise their safety. Triangulating the truth from numerous perspectives and memories is a difficult task.

Instead, as anthropologist Pasang Yangjee Sherpa suggests: "The story should be about the existence of multiple stories and about bringing them to light. . . . It should involve shifting our focus from one-way-of-being to recognizing the multiple-ways-of-being." Da Thundu, Ang Tsering, Dudley Wolfe, Fritz Wiessner, Willy Merkl, Peter Aschenbrenner, Lhamoo Iti, Pasang Diki, Pasang Kitar, Phinsoo, and Pasang Kikuli are all part of those multiple stories.

CHAPTER THREE

Darjeeling Tigers

We had as much time as we wanted to relish the marvels and grandeur of the Himalayan world.

—ANG THARKAY, *Sherpa: The Memoir of Ang Tharkay*

The first time Ang Tharkay set foot on Everest was in 1933. He was with a British expedition on the Tibetan side of the mountain. Young and inexperienced, he was low on the porter pecking order, even bullied by the veterans. They called him weak, sick, and useless.

It's true he was weak and sick, since he was suffering from bronchitis. But he certainly wasn't useless. Paid twelve annas (about thirty-three cents) per day, he broke trail through deep snow, cut steps on the icy bits, and used crampons and rope ladders—all complex and arduous tasks that were new to him. Ang Tharkay progressed up the mountain: Camp 2 at 6,000 meters, Camp 3 at 6,400 meters, Camp 5 at 7,830 meters. When frostbite set in he descended to Camp 4, but almost immediately turned around and carried loads all the way to Camp 6 at 8,350 meters. There, he received an anonymous package containing fifty packs of cigarettes and twelve boxes of matches, along with a letter that falsely claimed his wife was having an affair back in Darjeeling.

Ang Tharkay's first impressions of his British employers were not complimentary: "The expedition organizers barely treated us as humans," he said. "The latrines that had been built were reserved exclusively for the 'sahibs.'" Later, however, while he was suffering from frostbite at Camp 5, his opinion softened: "The sahibs were very good to us. They made bandages for us and gave us food."

Ang Tharkay was not alone on that historic high carry on Everest. With him were seven other Sherpas: Da Tsering, Nima Dorje, Ang Tsering, Kipa Lama, Pasang Kikuli, Tsering Tarke, and Rinzing. When a storm moved in as they were dumping their loads, British climber John Longland escorted them from Camp 5 down the North Ridge—then a completely unknown route—all the way to Camp 4, where they collapsed in exhaustion.

The 1933 expedition marked the beginning of a long and illustrious career in the mountains for Ang Tharkay, one of the first generation of elite climbing Sherpas. He would become the father of the modern Sherpa guides as we know them today.

While the Germans were throwing themselves at Nanga Parbat and the Americans at K2, the British continued to solidify their grip on Everest—a mountain that Nepalis knew as Sagarmatha and Sherpas knew as Chomolungma.

British interest went back as far as the creation of the Alpine Club in 1857, when British mountaineers began speculating about the possibility of climbing the earth's highest mountain. A survey party led by Captain Cecil Rawling caught a glimpse of it in 1904. "Towering up thousands of feet, a glittering pinnacle of snow, rose Everest," Rawling wrote. "It is difficult to give an idea of its stupendous height, its dazzling whiteness and overpowering size, for there is nothing in the world to compare it with." But within a decade, most of the world had become distracted by the greatest of all distractions, war.

In 1921, two years after the Treaty of Versailles formally ended World War I, the Mount Everest Committee (a joint project of the Royal Geographical Society and the Alpine Club) sent a new reconnaissance expedition to Everest. The team's tactics were shaped by the conflict that had dominated their lives so recently. Adapting a military style, the British led what could more accurately be described as mountaineering "assaults." And while the British assumed the role of generals, those in the trenches, including Ang Tharkay, were Sherpas.

The British team included a thirty-five-year-old schoolmaster, George Herbert Leigh Mallory. Lanky, graceful, and handsome in a sensual kind of way, Mallory would eventually become one of the most iconic of all Everest personalities. But not in 1921.

Straddling the border of Nepal and Tibet, Everest is now routinely climbed from both sides. But in 1921 the Kingdom of Nepal's borders were sealed shut, so the only option was to go through Tibet. The British climbers sailed first to Calcutta, then traveled by train to Darjeeling, and finally embarked on a six-week trek through the tropical forests of India's northeastern state of Sikkim and onto the barren Tibetan plateau. Their objective: find the base of Everest. With them were thirty-eight Sherpa climbers from Darjeeling. Although Mallory wrote extensively about the expedition's forays probing around the base of the mountain, he said almost nothing about the men from Darjeeling who had worked on the mountain with him.

The following year's Everest expedition was a serious attempt, and the team was proportionately bloated in size. The party departing from Darjeeling included thirteen Europeans, one Tibetan interpreter, five Gurkhas, and forty Sherpas, plus cooks and hundreds of porters. Once the group reached the mountain, the leaders' methods resembled the strategies of warfare, with "advances," "depots," "winning" and "losing" ground, "attacks," and "wins and losses." In the end, it was mostly about loss.

On June 7 Mallory led a party of seventeen men on four separate ropes up to the North Col. The slopes were heavily laden with snow from a recent storm, and the expected happened. Seven Darjeeling climbers—Lhakpa, Temba, Sange, Dorje, Pema, Pasang, and Norbu—were swept to their deaths in an avalanche.

Mallory privately expressed deep remorse to his wife, Ruth, yet his official report was less compassionate and somewhat inaccurate: "The porters had come to have a share in our enterprise, and these men died in an act of voluntary service freely rendered and faithfully performed." His teammate T. H. Somervell was more sympathetic: "Only Sherpas and Bhotias killed—why, oh why could not one of us Britishers have shared their fate?" In chilling contrast was Sir Francis Younghusband's response to the tragedy: "They have done so splendidly it is particularly bad luck. But thank goodness no European life was lost."

In compensation, the Mount Everest Committee paid 250 rupees to each of the families of the dead climbers. This amounted to one year's average salary per man and equaled £17.50 in British currency at that time (about US$50 today).

Despite the disastrous ending to the 1922 attempt, the Mount Everest Committee immediately applied to the Tibetan government for permission to return to the mountain in 1923. The expedition was delayed until 1924, and as before, Mallory was on the team. By this time, it was almost unimaginable that there could be a British team without him, for he had become a kind of superstar, an icon, Britain's one last hope during an age of fading imperial dreams. His importance to the team was also a harbinger of how future mountaineering narratives would tend to focus on individual Western heroes, relegating local climbers and porters to the background. Shortly before leaving England, Mallory declared, "This is going to be more like war than adventure. I don't expect to come back."

Once again, the Brits employed a Sherpa team from Darjeeling. They had made it to base camp, where Ondi, one of the strongest Sherpas, became ill with pneumonia. When his condition deteriorated, he was carried down to a lower altitude. Nobody expected him to survive. Four weeks later, however, to everyone's surprise, Ondi showed up back at base camp, carrying a heavy load on his back, keen to return to work on the mountain. Ang Tharkay later described him with fondness as "one of those rough characters, a sore trial to lovers of the quiet life, but a real thruster in time of storm and stress. Ondi is liable at any time to fall foul of the Darjeeling police. . . . On the very day on which he collapsed he had carried a load to Camp I without complaint."

Despite a strong team and the help of over two hundred Sherpas and porters, including three—Norbu Yeshe, Lhakpa Chedi, and Semchumbi—who reached Camp 6 at 8,140 meters, the mountain was not climbed. No Sherpas were lost in 1924, although two porters, Shamsher (a Gurkha) and Manbahadur (a cobbler), died in the early stages of the expedition. The much better known chapter of this saga is that George Mallory and Sandy Irvine disappeared into the mist, fulfilling Mallory's dire prediction and fueling speculation among climbers to this day about whether the two reached the summit.

Stunned but not beaten, the Mount Everest Committee applied for a permit for 1926. But the Tibetan authorities were having none of it. They were annoyed by a number of unflattering scenes Captain John Noel had included in his film about the expedition, *The Epic of Everest*, in which Tibetans were depicted eating lice and performing other acts perceived as disgusting. Even more outrageous was Noel bringing six holy lamas from Nepal to England and parading them onstage as "dancing lamas" at the London premiere of the film.

Shut down in Tibet as well as in Nepal, the Everest Committee turned its attention to a different mountain, Kangchenjunga, less than fifty miles from Darjeeling.

In response to the growing interest in the high mountains of Asia, a group of mountaineers formed the Himalayan Club in 1928. Although based in India, this was not a club for locals. Membership was by invitation only, and those invitations were limited to foreigners. The club assisted and advised members on all aspects of expedition logistics, providing some much-needed structure to the hiring process for Darjeeling porters and climbers.

During the next few years, most climbing activity focused on Kangchen-junga, and most teams hailed from Germany. Darjeeling Sherpas played a major role, hauling punishing loads, setting up camps, and climbing high on unknown terrain with substandard clothing and equipment. The most experienced Sherpas were called "Tigers"—a badge of honor that earned them an extra half rupee per day. Unfortunately, Tiger status didn't guarantee safety. On May 8, 1930, Chettan Sherpa, a Tiger with two Himalayan expeditions under his belt, was killed by an ice avalanche on Kangchenjunga.

Shortly after, the Sherpas went on strike. They were beginning to appreciate their value and exercise their negotiating muscle. The issue—surprisingly— wasn't the risk of death in the mountains; the Sherpas wanted to corner the market by excluding Bhotias from high-altitude work.

A German team heading to Kangchenjunga in 1931 managed to come to an agreement, but it's a shame they did. If they hadn't, four people might not have perished. Even before getting to the mountain, a porter named Babu Lall and the sirdar, Lobsang Sherpa, died of tropical fever. Several weeks later, Pasang Sherpa fell 550 meters from Camp 8, along with German mountaineer Hermann Schaller. Both were killed, and the climb was called off. One of the surviving members of that team was Ang Tharkay.

Ang Tharkay was born in 1907 in the village of Khunde, situated at around 3,840 meters in the Khumbu region of Nepal. The eldest in his family, Ang Tharkay lived with his parents and siblings in a two-room house built of rough stone. Describing his parents with clear-eyed candor in his memoir, he recalled that his father was a teetotaling heavy smoker, and that his mother—like most Sherpa women in his village—liked to get drunk from time to time. They subsisted on a diet of potatoes, turnips, and carrots that they eked out of their meager, barren strip of land.

"I crossed the high country of our isolated Himalayan region from every direction, and everywhere and always I saw the snow-covered high peaks," Ang Tharkay later said. "I gained a respect for them that verged on adoration for the gods that ruled over our little world. We were forbidden . . . to try to visit their sanctuaries. At that time, I never thought that my future career would force me to go against my childhood faith."

Ang Tharkay's job was shepherding the family's goats, but he found the excursions with his father over the high passes into Tibet, trading in wool and salt, much more exciting. It was on one of those passes—the 5,741-meter Nangpa La—where Ang Tharkay first experienced altitude sickness, though he had no idea what it was. A ferocious headache, vertigo, and temporary loss of sight gave him a taste of his future life as a climber when he would venture higher and higher into the thin air.

One day, a village friend returned from Darjeeling with thrilling tales of work with foreign expeditions to the highest mountains. Ang Tharkay became intrigued. The diminutive, knock-kneed young Tharkay soon headed off to Darjeeling in search of adventure. He landed a porter position on the 1931 German Kangchenjunga expedition and, two years later, climbed to 8,350 meters on Everest. In photos, his dazzling smile belies the hazards he faced.

Then, Ang Tharkay had a lucky break. Two, actually. He met and married his young bride, Ang Yangjin, and he met British explorer and climber, Eric Shipton. Known for his spartan approach to the mountains as well as for his hypnotic blue eyes, Shipton was looking for a handful of porters for an exploratory trip in 1934 to the still-unclimbed Nanda Devi, India's second-highest mountain. He chose Ang Tharkay among them. For six months they traveled with Bill Tilman, eventually discovering a barely perceptible passage that led through the vertical maze of the narrow Rishi Gorge into the flower-strewn Nanda Devi Sanctuary. Above them towered the magnificent mountain, "nearly crushing us with its glorious splendor," Ang Tharkay recalled.

Ang Tharkay absorbed all he could from Shipton: how to climb, how to set up high-altitude camps, and how to strategize and organize an expedition in Shipton's minimalist style. He even nurtured a friendship with Shipton and Tilman, as they shared food and tent space and solved problems together.

Their bond was an example of the mutually beneficial relationship that Sherpas were starting to enjoy with some Western climbers. Anthropologist Sherry Ortner has studied the behavioral patterns closely in her work. "The Sherpas had the notion of a *zhindak*, a patron or protector, who would help a lesser person to succeed.... Zhindaks do not directly bestow success—wealth, position and so on—but only facilitate achieving it, helping the hero to help himself," she observed. While there was a power imbalance between a zhindak and a Sherpa, from the Sherpa's perspective, the relationship was still reciprocal. If a Sherpa took good care of a sahib, the sahib would take good care of the Sherpa. The relationship demanded respect and dignity from both sides.

Yet as Tashi Sherpa, who wrote the foreword for the English edition of Ang Tharkay's memoir, pointed out: "You have to read between the lines. The equation is always there, in little snippets: the losses, the frostbite, the troubling issues that always existed in a very subtle avatar... but always got somewhat brushed away quietly in a mutual celebration of the relationship between the Sherpa and the sahib."

For his part, Shipton felt he fully understood Ang Tharkay's value as a companion: "He has been with me on all my subsequent journeys to the Himalayas, and to him I owe a large measure of their success and much of my enjoyment."

At the end of the Nanda Devi trip, Shipton asked Ang Tharkay if he would join him on another expedition. With no hesitation, Ang Tharkay said yes. Shipton was in charge of the 1935 Everest reconnaissance expedition, during which Ang Tharkay first teamed up with his young house tenant, Tenzing Norgay—who would, of course, go on to many high-altitude adventures of his own. They shared a tent on the expedition, and even shared a two-person sleeping bag at one point.

The following year, Ang Tharkay was back on Everest with ten porters under his supervision. One of them, Rinzing Bhotia, shone the brightest when he led a group of four British climbers and three Sherpas to the North Col at 7,022 meters. This may have been the first time a Sherpa took the lead on a mountain at this elevation, a sign of the future.

The 1936 Everest expedition failed to summit, and the British considered it a disappointing performance, but it was certainly a valuable experience for Rinzing Bhotia and Ang Tharkay.

Later that year, Ang Tharkay joined Shipton again on a return trip to the Nanda Devi region. With them was his young friend Sonam Tensing, known as Sen Tensing. They had no intention of climbing the mountain, since Tilman had recently done so, but they explored the area and climbed as many peaks as they could. One was 7,066-meter Dunagiri, a stunningly beautiful pyramid that forms part of the Nanda Devi Sanctuary wall. Ang Tharkay later remembered, "Mr. Shipton bet me that I would not reach the summit. I accepted the challenge." They were clearly on friendly terms on this, their third expedition together.

But more significant than Dunagiri was the overall atmosphere of the adventure. "This expedition made me very happy," Ang Tharkay said. "It was different from the others I had been on. . . . We only attempted the climbs that interested us. . . . We had as much time as we wanted to relish the marvels and grandeur of the Himalayan world."

After the climbing frenzy, Ang Tharkay and Sen Tensing joined Shipton and his lover, Pamela Freston, in Bombay where the two Sherpas first glimpsed the unimaginably luxurious lives of sahibs away from the mountains. Glimpsed, but only partially experienced, as Shipton's biographer Peter Steele explained: "The Sherpas slept on the floor outside the memsahib's hotel bedroom, and spent the morning going up and down in the lift." Although the Sherpas and Shipton shared everything while on expedition, that sense of equality and comradeship didn't appear to apply to life in the city. The adventure took an unfortunate turn after the Sherpas parted ways with Shipton. Traveling by train to Darjeeling, they were robbed in Calcutta of all their earnings. They returned home as penniless as when they had left.

In 1937 Ang Tharkay and Shipton embarked on an even greater adventure to the Karakoram where they explored a vast region from Srinagar all the way to the Shaksgam Valley. Upon reaching the Baltoro Glacier, Ang Tharkay was overwhelmed: "The view of the glacier and the giant peaks—the highest being K2—seemed unimaginably beautiful to me, more beautiful even than the view of Everest and the other peaks in the eastern Himalaya."

The following year he was back on his "home mountain"—Everest—this time with Tilman as leader. In addition to all his other duties, Ang Tharkay was now sufficiently experienced to help the British climbers determine the best route to the highest camp. This was yet another step in his career, one that he could not have imagined when he first crossed those high passes into Tibet with his father, suffering from his high-altitude headache.

While he had been on four Everest expeditions, and on each one he'd assumed increasing leadership responsibilities, Ang Tharkay was not yet done with the mountain. But a number of major events would intervene before he could return.

The first was World War II. Since there were almost no expeditions to the Greater Ranges between 1939 and 1945, Ang Tharkay, like all Darjeeling Sherpas, was forced to look elsewhere for work. He made do by arranging horses, porters, and cooks for smaller treks in the Darjeeling region.

The second event that altered Ang Tharkay's life, and affected all local climbers from South Asia, was the end of the British Raj in 1947. In its place emerged two independent states, India and Pakistan. Partition, the name of what became the greatest human migration in history, was a bloody affair forcing millions from their homes, leaving millions dead. Ongoing fighting between India and Pakistan closed the Baltoro region to climbing for years, and when it finally opened up, Sherpas from Darjeeling found they were no longer welcome in the Karakoram. Pakistani climbers were now the only option for expedition work there, both on the approach marches and at altitude.

The third event that created a major impact on expeditions in the Himalaya occurred when Tibet slammed shut its doors in 1950, effectively blocking access to the north side of Everest. At the same time, the Rana regime in Nepal collapsed. Although Nepal had a king, the position was ceremonial; for one hundred years the real power had been with the Rana families who ruled strictly and cruelly. With them out of power, Nepal opened its doors a crack, allowing access to mountains within its borders.

Among them was a mountain that would change the history of high-altitude climbing, and Ang Tharkay's life—Annapurna.

CHAPTER FOUR

Father of the Modern Sherpa Guide

Life as a Sherpa is not a joke.

—ANG THARKAY, *Sherpa: The Memoir of Ang Tharkay*

Ang Tharkay was smitten. "They made a strong impression on me, both because of their appearance and their honest pleasantness," he said of the French climbers who had hired him. "I had never met a team of mountaineers who were so kind, so athletic, and had such an impressive appearance. Although I was intimidated by their poise and their elegant clothing, I was maddened by being unable to understand their language."

To the annoyance of every other nation sending expeditions to the Himalaya, it was the French who secured the first permit from Nepal to tackle an 8,000-meter peak completely within its borders. Not only one—but two: 8,167-meter Dhaulagiri and 8,091-meter Annapurna, located near each other on either side of the Kali Gandaki River Gorge. No one had ever climbed either mountain. And what's more, nobody knew how to reach them.

The 1950 expedition was led by Maurice Herzog, an engineer from Lyon. With him were the leading alpinists of France, including Louis Lachenal,

Lionel Terray, and Gaston Rébuffat. Their sirdar was Ang Tharkay, whom they paid the going rate of seven rupees per day.

From the outset, Herzog demanded an oath of obedience from his team, forbidding them from publishing anything about the expedition for five years. He would have full control of the Annapurna narrative. It likely didn't occur to him to demand the same of Ang Tharkay, who, with a mysterious Western co-author named Basil Norton, later shared his own version of the adventure.

Ang Tharkay was clearly taken with the entire team, but Herzog made the strongest impression:

> We were particularly enraptured by his skin tone, a brown that was close to our own. His manners were refined and full of intelligence. His luminous eyes, his tousled black hair, the lovely form of his face that was perfect down to the very last detail, his beautifully sculpted nose, and his ever-smiling mouth made him a man whom we could not help but love from the very first meeting. As primitive as we Sherpas are, we are rarely wrong in our assessments of beauty and strength, and above all in our intuition about the qualities of the heart. Our leader immediately and spontaneously earned our admiration and loyalty.

Ang Tharkay's close observations weren't limited to Herzog. Lionel Terray, tall and thin and intimidating at first, reminded him of a Pathan Afghani mountain man. Louis Lachenal oozed experience and confidence, and Gaston Rébuffat was very, very tall. So tall that Ang Tharkay reported he had to crane his neck sideways in order to look up at him.

His team of Sherpas included Ang Dawa, Ang Tsering, Dawa Thondup, Sarki, Fou Tharkay, Aila, and Adjiba. In total, the Sherpas had survived thirty-one expeditions to the high mountains of Asia, a sharp contrast to the French team, from which only one member—their cinematographer, Marcel Ichac—could claim a single Himalayan adventure. The French had chosen their Sherpa team well.

The Sherpas seemed to have felt they had chosen their sahibs well, too. As they began their approach march, they reveled in the French cuisine. Ang Tharkay described the feasting: "During the evening, the sahibs began distributing rations such as we had never tasted before.... France must be a remarkable country to produce such remarkable dishes with such an exquisite taste." Not only did the French know how to cook, they didn't shy away from hard work. A veteran observer of expedition behavior, Ang Tharkay was amazed at the foreigners' willingness to participate in any task, no matter how menial.

While the French team lacked experience at altitude, Ang Tharkay could see that their climbing skills, honed on the steep walls of the French Alps, would be more than enough for the job. "I had never seen instruments or tools like the ones that they used, and we Sherpas stood in constant admiration of the bravery and skill with which they used their crampons, ice axes, and skis," he recounted. "In my entire life I had never seen more expert climbers."

Nevertheless, they struggled with the unknown and complicated terrain, wasting weeks going down one blind alley after another. It wasn't until May that they finally settled on a mountain—Annapurna—and a potential route—the North Face.

Despite an unrelenting season of snowstorms and high avalanche hazard, they had established Camp 4B at 7,160 meters by May 28. And despite the language barrier, the French and the Sherpas worked well together. As Ang Tharkay later acknowledged, Herzog "taught me the only French word that I know: *Bonjour*. I think that this is a way of greeting the people that one meets, and I have used it ever since."

On May 31, Herzog, Lachenal, Ang Tharkay, and Sarki started up the mountain on the final summit push. They passed their previous high point and began looking for a suitable site for Camp 5. On June 2, in a terrific windstorm that blinded them with snow, they set up the tents at around 7,500 meters. "The snow was so deep that we sank up to our waists," Ang Tharkay said. "With each step, we wondered apprehensively whether it would be our last, not only because of the risk of being buried but also because of the effort that our hearts and lungs were putting forth."

It was here that Herzog offered Ang Tharkay a chance at the summit.

"Tomorrow morning Lachenal Sahib and Bara Sahib go to the summit of Annapurna," Herzog announced.

"Yes, sir," replied Ang Tharkay.

"You are the sirdar and the most experienced of all the Sherpas. I should be very glad if you will come with us."

"Thank you, sir."

"We must have the victory together. Will you come?"

After a pause, Ang Tharkay replied. "Thank you, very much, Bara Sahib, but my feet are beginning to freeze. . . ."

"I see."

". . . and I prefer to go down to Camp IV."

"Of course, Ang-tharkey [sic], it's as you like. In that case, go down at once as it is late."

"Thank you, sir."

In his memoir, Ang Tharkay expanded on the stilted exchange:

> *I was wholeheartedly with him in this magnificent undertaking, and the idea of abandoning him at the moment of the supreme test seemed repulsive to me. But my feet were starting to cause me pain, and I was horrified at the thought of seeing them freeze. I looked directly into the determined face of my heroic leader. Alas! I was shirking my duty because I was not worthy of sharing that unequaled honor with him. . . . "Excuse me, Bara Sahib," I said to him pitifully. "But I am not worthy of this great task. I am profoundly grateful to you for the honor you have given me, and in all my life I will never forget this moment. . . . May God protect you, you and the valiant Lachenal Sahib!"*

Historians and mountaineers have long scrutinized and analyzed and speculated about Ang Tharkay's decision to descend with Sarki rather than to accept Herzog's offer of the first ascent of an 8,000-meter peak. Was Ang Tharkay not ambitious? Did he not understand the significance of the offer? Did he fear some mythical mountain goddess who might disapprove? Or was this a practical choice? For Ang Tharkay, frozen feet would mean losing the ability to work and support his family. The going compensation rate for amputations was still a mere ten rupees per digit. And in the case of death, compensation was only 1,000 rupees for a married man, 500 for a single man, and 500 for a female porter, married or single.

He knew plenty of families trying to survive without a principal wage earner. According to a list of Darjeeling climbers published by the *Himalayan Journal* in 1951, of the 175 names, "51 have died and 24 were killed in the mountains. Twenty-nine, still fit for mountaineering, are at present available in Darjeeling."

Ang Tharkay's decision turned out to be measured and wise. While he and Sarki descended to Camp 4, Herzog and Lachenal settled in for an uncomfortable night. The wind wouldn't let up, depositing spindrift onto their tent until it partially collapsed. On the morning of June 3, the wind had eased, but the air was bitterly cold. The climbers had eaten nothing the night before, merely sipped a little tea. Now, they didn't even bother with tea. By 6 a.m. they were moving.

The French had always intended to climb without supplemental oxygen, even though that would make them more susceptible to frostbite. And indeed, almost immediately Lachenal's feet began to feel the cold through his leather boots. Worried about frostbite, he stopped and removed his boots several times during the ascent, rubbing his feet and massaging his toes in an effort to restore some feeling. As his feet grew increasingly numb, he asked Herzog what he would do if he turned around. Herzog later recalled his thoughts at that moment: "Now we were nearing our goal. In an hour or two, perhaps, victory would be ours. Must we give up? Impossible! My whole being revolted against the idea. I had made up my mind, irrevocably. Today we were consecrating an ideal, and no sacrifice was too great. I heard myself say clearly: 'I should go on by myself.'" Lachenal responded simply, "Then I'll follow you."

Lachenal suspected he might lose his feet in the process. But he continued, because he was sure that if Herzog had climbed alone to the summit, he would not have returned. Lachenal's actions exemplified the values of a loyal mountaineering partner known as the "brotherhood of the rope."

At 2 p.m. on June 3, 1950, the two men stood on the summit of Annapurna. History was made.

After capturing the moment on film, they started down, and everything that could go wrong, did. Herzog stopped to retrieve something from his pack and removed his mitts to undo the straps, placing them on the snow beside him. Seconds later, a gust of wind snatched the mitts and blew them beyond reach. The implications were serious. He had no backups, though he did have an extra pair of socks in his pack, which he could have used to cover his rapidly freezing hands, had he thought of it. But combined with a prolonged period at altitude, the lack of oxygen, food, and fluids were all taking their toll on his judgment. Herzog carried on with bare hands.

Rébuffat and Terray waited at Camp 5, Ang Tharkay and Sarki at Camp 4. As the two summit climbers continued descending, they became separated. Herzog arrived first at Camp 5 and was greeted by Terray, who blanched at the sight of Herzog's hands—frozen solid as marble. Lachenal was nowhere to be seen. Terray eventually found him 100 meters below the camp, missing his ice axe, one crampon, his hat, and his gloves.

Lachenal begged Terray to help him descend all the way to Camp 2, where the expedition doctor could tend to his frozen feet. But a night descent was impossible, so Terray dragged and coaxed him back up to the tent at Camp 5. There, when Terray cut through the frozen leather that encased Lachenal's feet, they were white as alabaster. They were also far too swollen to force back into his boots. The only way to get him down the mountain, Terray realized, would be to give him his own boots, two sizes larger. But that would require stuffing his own feet into Lachenal's smaller, now partially destroyed footwear. Which he managed to do. Another act of loyalty to a teammate, this time not *by* Lachenal, but *for* Lachenal.

It stormed fiercely the following day, so the four French climbers only progressed as far as a crevasse where they sheltered from the snow and wind. With just one sleeping bag and no stove, the night was a desperate effort to survive. Snow-blind and frostbitten, exhausted and dehydrated, they stumbled into Camp 4 on June 5.

The rest of the descent unfolded as one increasingly grim ordeal, with the French climbers draped over their much smaller Sherpa companions, who strained to help them shuffle and slide down the mountain. "He [Terray] clung to my neck like my own son, although he was taller and broader than I was," Ang Tharkay said. By the time they reached base camp, neither Herzog nor Lachenal could walk. Expedition doctor Jacques Oudot began a series of agonizingly painful abdominal injections of novocaine, hoping to prevent further deterioration of their frostbitten digits. But he was soon forced to begin a daily round of amputations. "As we listened to [Herzog's] screams of pain, there was not a single one of us Sherpas who was not overwhelmed," Ang Tharkay said. "We all prayed for him."

During the next month, revolving teams of Sherpas and porters carried Herzog and Lachenal on stretchers through Nepal's lowland forests and jungles. Oudot continued his routine of cleansing, cutting, and bandaging the men's feet. The operating theater was usually a clearing in the forest, accompanied by dust, leeches, blood, pus, a nauseating stench, and ever-present flies. "I felt the eyes of the Sherpas and coolies upon me," Herzog wrote. "There was a new expression in their eyes, which I had not seen before. Was it pity, or grief, or a kindly indifference?" On the train journey to Delhi, Oudot continued amputating, one digit at a time. Lachenal eventually lost all his toes. Herzog all his toes and fingers.

Astonishingly, despite the physical and psychological terror of sacrificing so much for this mountain, Herzog remained ecstatic about the climb and everything it represented: "A new and splendid life has opened out before me." And indeed, Herzog's career blossomed, first as an industrialist, then as a politician. His book *Annapurna* became one of the most iconic works in mountaineering literature, published in more than forty languages and selling more than eleven million copies. His teammates fared less well: only two of the eight-person team—Jean Couzy and Lionel Terray—ever climbed in the Himalaya again. Although Lachenal eventually recovered enough to climb in the Alps, despite his amputations, he died in 1955 when he tumbled into a snow-covered crevasse while skiing in the Vallée Blanche near Chamonix.

As for Ang Tharkay and his Sherpa team, they returned to Darjeeling and continued working as high-altitude porters, leaving their families for months at a time to climb in the highest mountains on Earth.

Three years later, Ang Tharkay was invited to Paris for a screening of the film *Victoire sur l'Annapurna*, directed by Marcel Ichac. "Going to Europe on an airplane went beyond anything a Sherpa could aspire to," Ang Tharkay said. "Flying over the Alps reminded me of our gigantic Himalayan summits. . . . I felt an indefinable sense of exile when we neared this strange and marvelous country, where the masters of the world tend to live. I felt completely inferior to the white sahibs whom I had served for many years during their Himalayan expeditions." Ichac met Ang Tharkay at the airport. "Marcel Ichac insisted on carrying my suitcase, with these simple words that I will never forget: 'Ang Tharkay, in the Himalaya you were our porter, but today I will be yours.'"

Ang Tharkay's self-deprecating words sound odd to twenty-first-century ears, as does his devotion to Herzog. "I can only honor him by saying that we Sherpas believe that he deserved the homage that we, humble Himalayan natives, gave to him, one of the greatest alpinists whom we had ever served." But it's worth considering to what extent Ang Tharkay's words may have been filtered through or edited by his Western co-author.

Not everyone, it seems, shared Ang Tharkay's opinion. In 1988, Fou Tharkay, one of the last surviving Sherpas from the expedition, was invited to Paris. At a press conference, Herzog briefly greeted Fou Tharkay, whom he had not seen in forty-eight years. Shortly after, Bernard George, who was making a documentary about Annapurna, interviewed Fou Tharkay. George wanted his opinion of the influence Herzog and Sir Edmund Hillary—who also made history by taking part in a first ascent of an 8,000-meter peak, Everest—had on the people of Nepal. Hillary had accomplished far more as a philanthropist in the Himalaya than he had as a climber, working with local Sherpa communities to build schools and hospitals. Fou Tharkay was brutally honest in his response. "Hillary is a hero in Nepal, but Herzog, I don't think so. . . . I carried this man on my back until I could taste the blood in my mouth, and today he has only five minutes for me. It's too bad for him."

Although a "new and splendid life" did not open up for Ang Tharkay after the Annapurna summit as it did for Herzog, he became one of the most respected members of his Darjeeling community. To the outside world, Ang Tharkay remained almost completely unknown, save for the small group of foreigners active in the Himalaya at the time.

One of those who continued to appreciate him was Eric Shipton. When the British explorer returned to Darjeeling in 1951 to organize an Everest reconnaissance expedition from the newly opened Nepali side, he sought Ang Tharkay out. "I had not seen him since 1939," Shipton recalled, "when he was just a simple Sherpa porter. . . . Now he had graduated to a different sphere. I was somewhat apprehensive of what I would find; for success tends to spoil these simple people at least as readily as it does the sophisticated. He had cut off the handsome pigtail that he used to wear and his clothes were distressingly smart, but I was relieved to find the same shy reticence and the same quiet humour that I remembered so well . . . It was curious that, in spite of his constant contact with Europeans, he had learnt practically no English." Shipton should have greeted him in French; Ang Tharkay would likely have remembered what Herzog had taught him: "*Bonjour.*"

In 1954 Ang Tharkay became an instructor at the newly established Himalayan Institute of Mountaineering in Darjeeling. Besides teaching and mentoring the next generation of Darjeeling climbers, he continued working on expeditions: Cho Oyu, Dhaulagiri, Nun, Makalu, Kamet, and Everest. At age fifty-five, while on Captain Kohli's 1962 Indian Everest expedition, Ang Tharkay reached the South Col and thus became the oldest person to climb above 8,000 meters at the time. A kind of renaissance man, he set up his own trekking business; he worked as a road construction contractor in Sikkim; and he published a memoir. Even late in retirement, Ang Tharkay remained productive. Rather than stay in Darjeeling, he bought a piece of land south of Kathmandu near Daman, a place of hills and forests and lush green grass. There, he built a home and grew fruit and vegetables and raised animals, living out his golden years in the countryside. He didn't forget his former community: eventually he brought several homeless families from Darjeeling to live on the farm.

"My father was a simple and a very hardworking person, always with a smile on his face," his son Dawa Sherpa wrote. "Within our family, he did not talk much about the mountains and the expeditions he had gone on. . . . He was a very peaceful person, and I never heard him insult or criticize anyone." This man, with his mental toughness, his devotion to family, his generosity and humility, was also a pragmatist. "My father used to tell us, 'You must go to school to get an education for a better job and for a better life. Forget about going to the mountains as a Sherpa on expeditions. Life as a Sherpa is not a joke. It is real hard and you would not earn a good salary.' Today I feel I've been a very lucky person to have had such a father."

After a short illness, Ang Tharkay died in 1981 at the age of seventy-four. He was survived by his wife Ang Yangjin, one daughter and four sons. He hadn't sought fame, but had rather risked his life, year after year, for a few rupees and the promise of another job the following season. His name will forever be linked with those of Shipton and Tilman, for their many companionable, exploratory expeditions together. The apex of his career took place high on Annapurna, when he helped the French team make the first ascent, and then poured all his experience and devotion into caring for them on their descent. Yet despite his great contributions to the history of Himalayan climbing, because he was not a member, the *Alpine Journal* did not print an obituary following his death.

Nevertheless, Ang Tharkay set a standard that would eventually be met and surpassed, and his quiet mentorship of a young hopeful who had once lived in his house would produce the first Sherpa superstar—Tenzing Norgay.

CHAPTER FIVE

The First Superstar

I climbed Everest so that you wouldn't have to.

—TENZING NORGAY, *from* Touching my Father's Soul *by Jamling Tenzing Norgay, with Broughton Coburn*

Tenzing Norgay and Raymond Lambert were perched on a narrow rocky platform at nearly 8,400 meters on Everest's Southeast Ridge. It was May 27, 1952. They had a candle, a small tin, and a little food. No sleeping bags and no stove. By the meager warmth of the flickering flame, they melted snow for a few mouthfuls of water. They rubbed and pounded each other in an attempt to stay warm. "He was so big and fat that my hands hardly covered anything," Tenzing later told Tshultrim Chophel in a radio interview.

Lambert, a Swiss guide who had lost the tips of four fingers and all his toes to frostbite on Mont Blanc in 1937, was worried about Tenzing's feet. "For me it is all right, I have no toes. But you hang on to yours!" The flimsy tent shook and rattled all night, but they weren't sleeping. Sleep was far too risky.

The morning sky paled to a disappointing shade of gray, the surrounding peaks shrouded in mist. The two crawled out of the tent at 6 a.m. and took stock of their situation. "Lambert jerked his thumb at the ridge with a wink, and I nodded, smiling," Tenzing recounted. "We had gone too far to give up. We must make our try."

They fumbled with their crampons and oxygen bottles and began moving up the ridge. Hours passed. One foot in front of the other. Fighting with the faulty oxygen valves, they ultimately discarded the useless tanks. They took turns breaking trail, and when the ridge steepened, Lambert cut steps with his ice axe. Tenzing marveled at his partner: "Lambert was wonderfully good, because his short feet, with no toes, allowed him to stand on the tiniest places, just like a goat." Hours later, choking on wind-driven snow and crawling on all fours, they exchanged a few words from their limited shared vocabulary: *Ça va bien?*" said Lambert; "*Ça va bien,*" responded Tenzing. But it wasn't "bien" at all. They were still hours from the summit.

The South Summit was creeping into view when the two finally stopped. "We could have gone farther," Tenzing later said. "We could perhaps have gone to the top. But we could not have got down again. To go on would be to die. . . . We had given all we had, and it was not enough. We turned without speaking."

Even though they failed to reach the summit of Everest, Tenzing was grateful: "Well, it had been a great effort. And I had made a great friend."

Their friendship had a profound influence on Tenzing's life, but there were others as well who helped shape this remarkable man. Ang Tharkay welcomed him into his home when Tenzing was a penniless teenager. Eric Shipton gave him his first chance in the mountains on the 1935 Everest expedition. Tenzing's second wife, Ang Lhamu, supported him during his darkest moments when he became destitute and was suffering deep personal loss. It was on top of this multilayered foundation that Lambert's generosity of spirit gave Tenzing the confidence and trust that would eventually propel him to the top of the world's tallest mountain.

After the second Swiss attempt on Everest in the fall of 1952—also unsuccessful—Lambert could see their chances of a first ascent fading: the British had the only permit available for the following year. As the Swiss team prepared to leave the mountain, Lambert gave Tenzing his signature red scarf and pleaded with him to go with the British climbers, should they invite him. Tenzing protested, saying he was willing to wait until 1956 when the Swiss had another permit. But Lambert knew how invested Tenzing was in this mountain. After six expeditions to Everest, his friend—and his equal—deserved the summit.

Tenzing Norgay often said he was born in 1914 in Thame, in the Khumbu region of Nepal, but this was not the case. He was actually born in a tent at the edge of a lake in the sacred Kama Valley on the east side of Everest. Verdant, secluded, and surrounded by towering mountains, the 4,500-meter-high valley is in border country, a few miles inside Tibet.

Years later, as their Tibetan predecessors had done since the mid-1500s, Tenzing's mother, Dokmo Kinzom, and his father, Ghang La Mingma, bundled up their young son and his thirteen siblings, along with their paltry belongings and their yaks, and crossed the Nangpa La to the Khumbu Valley of Nepal. The land of Sherpas. The newcomers were impoverished, and their Sherpa neighbors considered them second-class citizens. They were known as Khambas. Tenzing was the eleventh of fourteen children, eight of whom died young. He and his family crowded into the second story of their stone house, which was warmed by the steam radiating up from the yaks that were equally crowded on the ground floor. Yak dung clung to the walls, drying in the sun in order to be burned as fuel in the coldest months. Tenzing remembered that they were "happy and contented because we did not know there was any other way to live."

Since Kinzom and Mingma expected Tenzing to become a lama, they sent him to a monastery to study. The dreary, repetitive routine of prayers and rote learning didn't appeal to the young boy, however, so he escaped and fled back to his parents. What Tenzing didn't realize was that this had been his one chance at an education. Extremely intelligent and ambitious, he regretted not being able to read for the rest of his life.

Having lost the opportunity to become a lama, Tenzing found that his family expected him to remain in Khumbu, tending yaks, farming, perhaps doing a bit of porter work over the high passes. But with his curiosity and natural charisma, he demanded more. He watched young Sherpas returning from Darjeeling, flush with cash, eyes flashing with excitement from the world of foreign climbing expeditions. Tenzing wanted some of that for himself.

When rumors circulated that the British would require porters for a pending British Everest expedition in 1933, Tenzing convinced his girlfriend, Dawa Phuti, to run off with him to Darjeeling. To the dismay of her wealthy father, who was hoping for a much better match, the two left with ten Khumbu friends for the land of opportunity. It was none other than Ang Tharkay who welcomed the young Tenzing into his home in Toong Soong Busti, the Sherpa shantytown perched above Darjeeling.

Although Tenzing was happy to have a roof over his head, his eyes were drawn to the glitzy world of Darjeeling below. Fine, high-ceilinged vacation homes built for the British and wealthy Indians rose amid the elaborate tiers of temples, the delicate scents of teahouses, and the imposing monolith of the Government House. And most importantly, there was the Planters Club, a social venue limited to the British. This was where porters were routinely hired for upcoming expeditions. Groups of Sherpas with tattered clothing and long braided hair would line up at the base of the shaded verandah, hoping that the foreigners lounging about on their comfy cane chairs, sipping Darjeeling tea, would choose them.

Tenzing's first foray to the Planters Club ended in rejection, so he headed back to herding cows. But not for long. Although he had no experience in the high mountains and therefore no credibility with the scrutinizing Westerners, Tenzing Norgay had pizazz. Perhaps his marriage to Dawa Phuti brought the extra twinkle to his eyes and the dazzling smile to his face. As Eric Shipton considered the rows of young Sherpas for his scaled-down 1935 Everest expedition, his eyes kept returning to Tenzing. "From a hundred applicants, we chose fifteen Sherpas to accompany the expedition from Darjeeling. Nearly all of them were old friends, including, of course, Angtarkay [*sic*], Pasang and Kusang; but there was one Tibetan lad of nineteen, a newcomer, chosen largely because of his attractive grin. His name was Tensing Norkay [*sic*]—or Tensing Bhotia as he was generally called," a reference to his Tibetan heritage. In addition to the smile, Tenzing undoubtedly had a good recommendation from his landlord and friend, Ang Tharkay.

Although the expedition failed to reach the summit of Everest, it was a dream fulfilled for Tenzing. He had been a lowly shepherd; now he was a high-altitude porter. His newfound status came with a bundle of perks: boots, parkas, a sleeping bag, snow goggles, and even an ice axe. His energy and enthusiasm propelled him all the way to the North Col, despite the spine-crushing loads. He was thrilled to find that he wasn't as severely affected by the increasing altitude as some of the other porters were—an observation that encouraged him even more. "When I am on Everest I can think of nothing else," he said. "I want only to go on, farther and farther. It is a dream, a need, a fever in the blood."

With Tenzing's stellar debut performance, he had no trouble getting more work: Everest in 1936, the Garhwal in 1937, the Nanda Devi area in 1938, back to elusive Everest the same year, and Tirich Mir in 1939.

Back in Darjeeling, Dawa Phuti gave birth to a son, Nima Dorje. They then welcomed a second child, a girl named Pem Pem. And soon another daughter, Nima. With the onset of the Second World War, expeditioning ground to a stop—as did employment for Darjeeling Sherpas. The enterprising Tenzing found work as a personal orderly to Major E. H. White, who was commanding a group of Scouts in the Chitral region in the far west of India.

But Tenzing's string of good luck was about to run out. His four-year-old son died of dysentery, and when he brought Dawa Phuti and the girls to Chitral to join him, Dawa Phuti's health declined. She died in 1944, leaving Tenzing with two young daughters to raise on his own. A much more somber Tenzing Norgay returned to Darjeeling in 1945.

There, Tenzing resumed his friendship with Darjeeling resident Ang Lhamu. Older than him by four years, Ang Lhamu already had considerable world experience, having lived in London as a nanny. Intelligent and practical, and unable to have children of her own, she happily assumed the role of stepmother for Tenzing's two girls. The couple made a striking image: tall and handsome Tenzing towered over Ang Lhamu, who more resembled a rock. And that's what she was for Tenzing during those lean postwar months. "I could never forget what she did for us all during those hard and bitter days," Tenzing said.

When the Canadian-born electrical engineer Earl Denman showed up in Darjeeling in the spring of 1947 with an audacious plan to climb Everest from the Tibetan side—alone—Tenzing knew it was hopeless. But he went anyway since he desperately needed the work. A month later, although having failed to climb the mountain, he returned to Darjeeling with 400 precious rupees and a woolen balaclava helmet that Denman gave him. One day, millions of people around the world would see this helmet in the photograph that would make Tenzing famous.

With barely time to change his clothes, he was off again, this time with a Swiss expedition to the Gangotri region of India. Tenzing found the Swiss climbers relaxed, less obsessed with protocol and hierarchy than the British, and generally more fun. The Gangotri trip was joyful, but the return to Darjeeling was decidedly not. While he was on the expedition the British Raj withdrew from India. With the country now split into India and Pakistan, ease of travel was a dim memory. He used all his earnings to get home to Darjeeling. Once again, thank goodness for Ang Lhamu for working multiple jobs to pay the bills.

Over the next couple of years, Tenzing took whatever work came his way. But a shift was occurring in neighboring Nepal that would have an enormous impact on his future. For foreign climbers, the opportunity of exploring Nepal's unclimbed mountains was like opening a giant box of chocolates, with one of the tastiest morsels being the possibility of approaching Everest from the south side.

Tilman and a small group of Americans, including Charlie Houston, trekked into Khumbu in 1950 to take a look. "I remember vividly walking with Bill through the autumn gold, reflecting on what we had seen, and what damage we and others like us might have set in train for this innocent, backward, beautiful country," Houston said. "We were all sad, knowing we were witnessing the end of something unique and wild, and the beginning of a period of great danger and immense change." Houston and Tilman took one glance at the south side of Everest and concluded it was impractical to climb, thanks to the Khumbu Icefall, a dangerous field of leaning seracs and hidden chasms that guard access to the upper part of the mountain.

Shipton and Ang Tharkay, on a separate exploratory reconnaisance a year later, came to a different conclusion. The race for Everest was on.

The Swiss snagged the first permit for the south side of Everest in 1952 because the British were busy on nearby Cho Oyu. Since Ang Tharkay was working with the British, the Swiss invited Tenzing to be their sirdar.

As a young boy, Tenzing had seen the hulking mass of Everest's north face from the Rongbuk Valley. And as a teenager, shepherding yaks in the high pastures of the Khumbu region, he had glimpsed the upper ridges of the mountain shimmering in the late afternoon sun. He knew it as Chomolungma, as Sagarmatha, and as Everest. But for Tenzing, it was his mother's name for the mountain that rang truest; Kinzom called it the "The Mountain So High No Bird Can Fly Over It."

After recruiting thirteen porters, Tenzing traveled with the expeditioners from Darjeeling to Everest through his home valley, where their procession stunned the villagers into silence. The clothing, the equipment, the pale Swiss faces—all so strange and foreign. And the Darjeeling Sherpas—so sharply dressed, so confident, such a swagger in their walk. They had left their villages as penniless teenagers and were now the picture of success.

Young Mingma Chering remembers standing in a crowd, staring at the exotic-looking foreigners. "It was fascinating," he said. "No one moved or spoke." He stared so long his neck cramped.

Most impressed of all was Kinzom, Tenzing's mother, who, now eighty years old, had trekked from Thame to Namche Bazaar for a tender reunion with her son. Quiet and reserved, but bursting with pride, she walked up to Tenzing. "*Ama la,*" he greeted her. "Here I am at last." They embraced.

The Swiss forged a route through the Icefall that had discouraged Tilman and Houston, and were soon up on the Western Cwm, the glacial cirque surrounded by the horseshoe of Everest, Lhotse, and Nuptse. Tenzing was thrilled because he was not only the sirdar, he was also Lambert's ropemate, officially "a full expedition member," as he recalled in his autobiography. Tenzing occasionally claimed theirs was an accidental pairing, but this is unlikely. After four expeditions to the mountain, he could certainly spy a good partner in Lambert. When the charismatic Lambert invited Tenzing to share a rope with him, Tenzing didn't hesitate. "It was . . . the greatest honour that had ever been paid me—and in my heart I swore I would prove myself worthy."

The pair did their best, but after two attempts at the mountain within one year, Lambert needed to return to Switzerland and Tenzing to Darjeeling. Despite Lambert's encouragement that he should join the upcoming British attempt, Tenzing felt defeated, demoralized, and exhausted. Almost twenty pounds underweight, feverish with malaria, and leaning heavily on the bottle, he went instead to a missionary hospital in Patna, and then back to his family to recover.

Soon after his return home, a letter arrived from Major Charles Wylie of the Himalayan Committee, inviting Tenzing to join the 1953 British Everest Expedition. Once more, he would be both a sirdar and a climber. He was torn. He badly wanted to climb the mountain with Lambert. But if he said no, Ang Tharkay would get the nod. As he mulled it over, Ang Lhamu lost patience. Their conversation must have left an indelible impression, since he later recalled every word from the exchange in his memoir:

> "*You are too weak,*" *she argued.* "*You will get ill again, or you will slip on the ice and fall and kill yourself.*"
>
> "*No, I will look out for myself,*" *I told her.* "*Just like I always have.*"
>
> "*You take too many risks.*"

"I am paid for climbing. They don't pay me for play. I must do what I am paid for."

"You are a daredevil," Ang Lhamu said. "You care nothing about me or the children, or what happens to us if you die."

"Of course I care, woman. But this is my work—my life. Don't you understand that?"...

"You will die."

"All right, I will die." By this time I was getting angry. "If I die I would rather do it on Everest than in your hut!"

We got angry, made up, then got angry again. But at last Ang Lhamu saw that I was determined, and said: "All right, you win."

Having won the argument, Tenzing began getting himself back into shape. No more cigarettes and no more alcohol. Darjeeling residents watched bemused as he raced up and down the nearby trails carrying a pack filled with stones.

It was finally time to leave. On March 1, 1953, dozens of friends and neighbors piled into Tenzing and Lhamu's house. Curious, supportive, and full of advice, they draped him in ceremonial kata scarves. The leave-taking, he remembered later, was bittersweet. Another risk-filled expedition—the outcome unknown. Nima gave her dad a treasure from her school supplies—a red and blue pencil for the summit.

Clad in a jaunty beret, military-style shorts, and puttees—strips of cloth wound around the leg from ankle to knee for protection and support—the thirty-nine-year-old Tenzing looked every bit a sirdar. His team was diverse, ranging from his seventeen-year-old nephew Nawang Gombu to the veteran forty-seven-year-old Dawa Thondup. His deputy leader was Dawa Tenzing, slightly older than Tenzing Norgay and a world apart in style. The quiet and restrained Dawa Tenzing retained his traditional clothing and braided hair. Despite their differences, Tenzing recognized Dawa Tenzing's strength—both in body and character—and knew he was the perfect partner.

One of Tenzing Norgay's misgivings about joining the British team was his concern that they would impose their class system in the mountains. This apprehension turned out to be justified. Upon arrival at the British Embassy in Kathmandu, the British retired to the embassy proper, and the Sherpas were relegated to the garage, a former stable with no toilet facilities.

It's hard to imagine what the British climbers were thinking, or if they were thinking at all, having tucked into their first gin and tonic and anticipating their comfy rooms. But the Sherpas *were* thinking, and they weren't happy. The following morning they relieved themselves on the road in front of the embassy, causing a proper British ruckus. The incident wasn't reported in the official British expedition accounts, but when Tenzing wrote his autobiography years later he included details:

> *Colonel Hunt [the leader] . . . refers to these various troubles hardly at all; and perhaps he is right, for his is an official account, he is writing as an Englishman for Englishmen, and certainly none of our difficulties were of any importance compared to the climbing of Everest. But each man must tell his story—as he lives his life—from his own point of view. And my story is not "official." I am not an Englishman, but a Sherpa. I must tell what I, not some one else, saw and experienced, or my book will have no honesty and no value.*

Tenzing was in an awkward position. He was a sirdar in charge of a team of Sherpas, but he was also a climber with a burning ambition to get to the top of a mountain. He needed to advocate for his Sherpa team but also get them to perform, because he knew no one would summit Everest without their concerted effort. "I felt like the middle of a sandwich pressed between two slabs of bread," he said.

This certainly wasn't the impression he made on Jan Morris, the *Times* journalist who had been assigned to the expedition. "I always remember with pleasure my first sight of this famous person, there in his own country, so keen and dashing and unspoilt. . . . He seemed the incarnation of healthy mountain living," Morris gushed.

Once on the mountain, the two most ambitious climbers, the two fittest climbers, the two *outsider* climbers, found each other quickly: Edmund Hillary and Tenzing Norgay. "An oddly assorted pair," Morris wrote, noting that Hillary, a tall New Zealander, "moved with an incongruous grace, rather like a giraffe," alongside the sharply dressed Tenzing, "a Himalayan fashion model." The giraffe and the model sprinted up and down the mountain, skipping camps, breaking speed records and most importantly, impressing their leader, John Hunt.

It was finally time for the summit teams to be announced. As the climbers huddled in the mess tent, "Tenzing sat there inscrutably, graceful and attentive, like a demi-god on parade before Zeus," Morris said. "For the rest, there was a distinct sense of excitement, and a sudden snapping of the tension when the two assault teams were named. First British climbers Charles Evans and Tom Bourdillon, then Hillary and Tenzing. I thought I saw the slightest flicker of satisfaction cross Tenzing's face, though in fact (we learned later) he considered a Sherpa should have been in both parties." When Evans and Bourdillon failed on their summit attempt, everything was up to Hillary and Tenzing.

The actual summit climb has been written about so many times and in every language imaginable that it's probably unnecessary to document each detail once again. But it would be disrespectful to ignore those final, historic hours.

⸻

May 29, 1953. Tenzing and Hillary left their tent at 6:30 a.m. Tenzing's feet were warmed by socks knitted by Ang Lhamu, and under his hood was Earl Denman's wool balaclava. Raymond Lambert's red scarf was wrapped around his neck and Nima's school pencil was tucked into a corner of his pack. Sluggish and slow, the two climbers plunge-stepped through deep, loose snow crusted with a film of ice. The slope felt unstable, as if it could slide at any moment.

"What do you think of it, Tenzing?" Hillary asked.

"Very bad, very dangerous."

"What do you think? Should we continue?"

"As you like."

They continued. At 9 a.m. they were already on the subsidiary peak, the South Summit, and there were no more questions between them. And yet, ultimately, there would be many questions, including what exactly happened between the South Summit and the Summit. Tenzing recalled that they climbed as equals, helping each other to the same extent. He was insulted by Hillary's later account of this final section of their climb. "I must say in all honesty that I do not think Hillary is quite fair in the story he later told, indicating that I had more trouble than he with breathing, and that without his help I might have suffocated."

There were other faux pas, including Hillary's suggestion that he'd hauled Tenzing up the final rock step on an extremely tight rope until the Sherpa flopped on the top like a "giant fish." More likely, they probably both resembled flopping fish at various points in the climb. It was an unfortunate comment that Hillary came to regret.

Today, what we see in these conflicting reports is complexity. Tenzing was emphasizing equality. Whether or not he intended it, Hillary seemed to be highlighting his position as a Westerner. Also clear is the value each of them placed on the details of their own performances on this iconic ascent. Neither wanted to look weak or inept.

The final moments lacked drama. The two men were short-roped together, and Tenzing held coils of rope in his hand as he followed Hillary. "We went on slowly, steadily. And then we were there. Hillary stepped on top first. And I stepped up after him." They shook hands. They embraced and thumped each other a few times. They spun round and round, taking in the immensity of the view: Lhotse, Nuptse, Makalu, Kangchenjunga, all the way to the Tibetan plateau. Hillary retrieved his camera from under his coat and Tenzing posed, one foot higher than the other, his ice axe held high with the flags of the United Nations, Britain, Nepal and India fluttering in the light breeze.

Neither Hillary nor Tenzing could have imagined what awaited them down below. They could not have foreseen how this climb would change their lives. How they would be forever in the limelight, examined and cross-examined, adored and vilified, envied and hated, celebrated and worshipped. On that mountaintop, they only had one job—to descend safely and rejoin their teammates.

When they arrived at base camp, everyone erupted with joy. Morris was particularly taken with the Sherpas' response to Tenzing. "As the greatest of their little race approached them," Morris wrote patronizingly, "they stepped out, one by one, to congratulate him. Tenzing received them like a modest prince. Some bent their bodies forward, their hands clasped as if in prayer. Some shook hands lightly and delicately, the fingers scarcely touching. One old veteran, his black twisted pigtail flowing behind him, bowed gravely to touch Tenzing's hand with his forehead."

The next morning, looking slightly older and thinner, Tenzing slipped out of base camp and wandered down to Thame to visit his mother.

News of the climb had already reached Britain, thanks to a coded message sent by Morris to the *Times* editors. Back in Darjeeling, Pem Pem, Tenzing's daughter, remembered a tall man named Natmal arriving at their door. "It was 2 June and Mummy and Nima and I were at home, she said. 'Mrs. Tenzing, I have good news for you. Tenzing has climbed Everest!'" Word spread quickly and their home was soon heaving with well-wishers. "I cannot say how happy I was," Ang Lhamu said. "In my joy I could think of nothing properly. I will tell you, I was afraid too much joy might bring me heart failure."

Only when Tenzing and the team arrived in Kathmandu did they begin to grasp the magnitude of what they had done. Dozens of journalists descended on them. Resentment arose almost immediately among the British climbers when the local media didn't seem interested in Hillary's presence on the summit—only Tenzing's. Nobody was prepared for this turn of events, particularly Tenzing; he couldn't even read the releases he was being pressured to sign. He was hounded into claiming he had summited first, then further harassed into saying he was Indian. Others insisted he declare Nepali nationality. Even though he had become a symbol of positive change for a postcolonial era, the joyous event was turning into a nightmare for him.

Shortly after, his entire family traveled to England to be fêted. None of the other Sherpas who had worked on the expedition were invited, and as they made their way back to Darjeeling they felt left out. Some blamed Tenzing for not including them in the limelight.

Tenzing and his family, meanwhile, were given an audience with the Queen, who asked Ang Lhamu how she had reacted to the news of Tenzing's success. "I bought him a present," Ang Lhamu said. Curious, the Queen asked what she had bought. Ang Lhamu giggled and blushed before whispering, "A tin of condensed milk." Their conversation drifted to Henry VIII. Ang Lhamu was curious about his appearance, so Queen Elizabeth II escorted her to a life-sized portrait. Ever more curious, Ang Lhamu asked about portraits of his six wives, all of which were located and admired.

After Everest, Tenzing became director of the Himalayan Mountaineering Institute, a position that provided a salary, benefits, and a pension. He traveled extensively, flying to European capitals for the many events that honored him. He moved into a spacious house with an expansive view of Kangchenjunga. He became a global superstar. But his post-Everest life was not without challenges.

He fell in love with a vivacious young porter—Daku—who worked at the Institute. She became pregnant, they married in 1961, and Daku moved into Tenzing Norgay's house, along with Ang Lhamu, Pem Pem, and Nima. Polygamy was not unheard of among Sherpas, but it was frowned upon in

Darjeeling. Tenzing's position in the community became compromised as neighbors sided with a saddened Ang Lhamu, who swallowed her pride for the sake of her husband's happiness.

Three years later, Ang Lhamu developed lung cancer and her health declined rapidly. She died at home. Tenzing and Daku had four children: Norbu, Jamling, Deki, and Dhamey. With his growing family, his spacious home, and extensive travels, Tenzing found his earnings were no longer keeping up with his expenses. To make matters worse, the Indian government forced him to retire from the Institute in 1976. Daku began spending more time in Kathmandu while the children were away at boarding school. Alone in his big house, Tenzing became increasingly isolated and depressed, turning to alcohol for companionship. His one constant friend was his daughter Pem Pem.

Tenzing wasn't the only Sherpa to struggle after a great success. His deputy leader on the 1953 expedition had been Dawa Tenzing. While he never achieved even a shadow of Tenzing Norgay's fame, he was considered one of the greatest Sherpa climbers of his time.

A fiercely private man who retained the traditional look—one long braid and his signature turquoise earring—Dawa Tenzing was known for his intelligence and sensitivity. He enjoyed a distinguished career, working as sirdar on several ascents of 8,000ers, yet his later life was also troubled.

When their son Mingma was killed in a climbing accident, Dawa's wife was mistakenly informed that both Mingma and Dawa had perished. Destroyed by grief, she threw herself into a river and drowned. Dawa spiraled into poverty and alcohol. Years later, while he was on a Buddhist pilgrimage to India with his second wife, their bus crashed into a deep ravine. Thirty-two people died, including another son and a daughter-in-law. Dawa Tenzing and his wife were seriously injured. He lost the use of his right arm and died in his sleep two years later.

Dawa Tenzing suffered his declining years as an isolated climbing Sherpa, while Tenzing Norgay languished under the spotlight. As James Ramsey Ullman, the co-author of Tenzing's memoir, wrote: "He is paying the price of fame, with no discount. As he himself puts it, he is an animal in a zoo, a fish in a bowl. And if the bowl exhibits him brightly it also holds him prisoner. . . . He is paying not only for fame but for being the man he is."

Tenzing was ambitious, but only to an extent; he just wanted to make the first ascent of Everest. In the end, the pressure was too great. When his son Jamling asked Tenzing's permission to join an Everest expedition, Tenzing said: "I climbed Everest so that you wouldn't have to. . . . You can't see the entire world from the top of Everest, Jamling. The view from there only reminds you how big the world is and how much more there is to see and learn." Jamling climbed it anyway.

Tenzing Norgay is admired for many reasons today, but perhaps his most enduring legacy is that he made the entire world aware of Sherpas. There are a number of superstar Sherpas today, but Tenzing was the first, and he will forever be the brightest. He became a symbol of hope and pride for millions of Nepalis, Indians, and Tibetans, and a source of admiration for people around the world.

On May 9, 1986, Pem Pem received a call from Tenzing's servant, urging her to come as quickly as possible. Tenzing was gravely ill. Pem Pem rushed over, only to discover that her father had died of a brain hemorrhage.

CHAPTER SIX

Forgotten Hero

The actors were all children of the West. We who watched it with concentrated souls were all from the East. Under the shadow of this grim mountain, East and West had not only met, but had been fused into one.

—MOHAMMAD ATA-ULLAH, *Citizen of Two Worlds*

Mohammad Ata-Ullah was minding his own business when he received an unexpected letter from American mountaineer Charlie Houston. A medical doctor, Ata-Ullah had survived a long and dangerous stint at the Khyber Pass while working with the British Army Medical Service. His next challenge had been surviving the bloodbath of Partition in 1947. Overnight, he was no longer Indian. By the time Houston contacted him, he'd become a Pakistani colonel, and had been recommended for Houston's 1953 K2 expedition.

Houston's failure to summit in 1938 had not diminished his dream of making the first ascent of this magnificent mountain. The Second World War and Partition had prevented any activity in the Karakoram for years. But thanks to some help from the American ambassador to Pakistan, Houston had secured a K2 permit, and he was anxious to get started. Since India and Pakistan were not on friendly terms, employing Darjeeling Sherpas was out of the question. Hence the letter to Ata-Ullah, inviting him to be the liaison officer, to facilitate logistics for the team, and to ensure they didn't stray into areas outside the permit.

Ata-Ullah's response was honest and endearing:

> *Although the spirit is willing, almost anxious to join you, my age and physique would not permit me to do much. Of technical mountaineering, I have no experience or knowledge whatsoever. Having made quite clear that it will be entirely under false pretenses, I accept your gracious invitation to become a member of your party. Yours sincerely, M. Ata-Ullah.*

The Pakistani colonel went to work immediately: practicing knots with a piece of rope; clambering up and down the steep, crumbling dirt walls of the drainage ditch behind his house; even borrowing an ice axe to practice cutting steps in those walls. There was only one niggling problem in Ata-Ullah's mind—his weight. He enjoyed his meals and rarely missed one. His slightly bulging stomach hadn't been an issue before, but he sensed it wouldn't be an asset on K2.

After a lengthy search, he finally found someone to lend him what he thought was a bathroom scale. He was horrified when a super-sized professional scale arrived in the back of a truck. With the help of his family, he moved it into the dining room—the only room in the house big enough to accommodate it. There, he monitored the results of his weight-loss program several times a day.

Leading a group of Balti porters who would carry loads to base camp, as well as ten Hunzas who would work on the mountain itself, Ata-Ullah coordinated the march from Skardu to K2: wake up at 3:30 a.m. for breakfast, strike camp, pack and distribute the loads, and be on the trail by first light. The atmosphere was friendly and democratic at first. Everyone—including the Americans—did their share of work around camp as well as carry loads. "The Americans were all for equality; they would pitch their own tents, fetch their own water, wash their own dishes, be the first ones up in the mornings and the last ones to go to bed after seeing that everything was in order," Ata-Ullah wrote in his memoir.

But gradually their behavior changed: "It is difficult to recollect when, and by what stages, they slipped from this high resolve. But before long, the Hunzas had taken charge of the Americans and relegated them to the role of indolent Grand Moghuls. Now the sahibs had a mug of hot tea thrust into their tents first thing in the morning by a wide-awake Hunza."

After eight days of trekking, they arrived in Askole. Ata-Ullah's newly svelte figure had become even slimmer, his blistered feet had healed and hardened, and his aching muscles were supple and strong. Having committed to this grand adventure, he now wanted to do more than spend a month or two at base camp. He wanted to climb.

Before long, he was coordinating the movement of supplies, climbing as far as Camp 2, while Houston and the Americans moved higher up the Abruzzi Ridge. When the Americans reached Camp 8 at 7,770 meters, they needed only three more days of decent weather to attain the summit. "Those three days never came," Ata-Ullah recalled. "Instead, news poured in over the radio of rains and floods affecting the subcontinent all the way to the Arabian Sea a thousand miles away. Our own special reports predicted grim weather day after day, with sickening regularity. I hated having to repeat all this to Houston." Imprisoned in base camp and stuck in Camp 8, the two arms of the team, separated by 2,750 meters of rock and ice, waited for something to change—anything at all that would allow movement.

On August 7, Ata-Ullah heard Houston's anxious voice on the radio.

"This is Camp 8. Are you there, Colonel?"

"Yes, Charlie. Is anything wrong?"

"I don't know. Art is not well. You are a doctor, and I want your advice."

Art Gilkey's leg was throbbing so hard he had fainted when he tried to stand. It was likely thrombophlebitis—a blood clot. His only chance for survival was to get down off the mountain for medical treatment; the clot could easily move to his lungs. Meanwhile, others in Camp 8 were suffering from frostbite in their feet. Trapped, with the storm raging on, their situation worsened by the hour.

Charlie and Ata continued their twice daily radio calls, trying to conjure up a solution.

"Hello, Base Camp. Hello, Base Camp. This is Camp VIII. How do you hear me?"

"I hear you very well, Charlie. How is Art? How are you standing up in this storm?"

"We are very good, Ata. . . . Art seems a little better today, but I don't see any prospect of his being able to climb for a long time. . . . What have you to suggest for therapy, Ata?"

"Charlie, that isn't my field," responded Ata, an eye specialist. "I can't suggest anything to do for him but what you're already doing. But I strongly suggest that I come up to help you. After all, you have two or three frostbite cases besides Art, and I can share your burden. Over."

"Ata, you can't possibly get up here in this weather," Charlie said, his eyes tearing up in gratitude at Ata's offer.

"I could try."

When Gilkey's chest pains indicated that the embolism had moved to his lungs, the situation turned desperate. They were high on a relentlessly steep mountain, with difficult, complex terrain below them, a storm in progress, and a completely debilitated climber who would need to be lowered.

The drama that followed will go down in the history of mountaineering as the ultimate brotherhood of the rope, the ultimate ice-axe belay, and the ultimate feeling of helplessness for those waiting below. Houston and his team wrapped Gilkey up in his sleeping bag, sedated him with morphine, and began the arduous and dangerous job of lowering him down K2.

They abandoned their first attempt when the avalanche hazard proved too high. On their second attempt, George Bell's innocent stumble on frostbitten feet led to one after the other of the roped-up climbers being pulled off the slope—seven men in all. But the one at the top—Pete Schoening—had jammed his ice axe behind a rock and wrapped the rope around the axe and his waist. When he saw the others falling, he threw himself onto the ice axe. The rope stretched as thin as piano wire, but it held. After collecting themselves and setting up a bivouac for the night, the injured and dazed climbers traversed over to retrieve Gilkey, who had been secured to the slope on an independent line. He had disappeared.

Down in base camp, Ata-Ullah and his Hunza partners waited for news. "We were witnessing an epic of endurance and devotion, and no stage could have been worthier in its loftiness and grandeur," Ata-Ullah later wrote. "The actors were all children of the West. We who watched it with concentrated souls were all from the East. Under the shadow of this grim mountain, East and West had not only met, but had been fused into one."

They paced. They prayed. They shouted into the radio, trying to make contact with the Americans. Fifty long hours later, they finally heard from the team.

Near the end of their desperate retreat, the Americans were greeted by a group of Hunzas who had climbed up to Camp 2 to meet them. The Hunzas embraced the exhausted climbers, praying and sobbing. They removed their packs and fed them rice and parathas and tea. "It was," said Bob Craig, "the deepest experience I've ever had with a human being."

Ata-Ullah felt they needed to erect some kind of memorial to Art Gilkey. Not far from base camp, and slightly above the point where the Godwin-Austen and Savoia Glaciers meet, they discovered a small ridge. Here, they built a 10-foot-high cairn that would eventually serve as a memorial for not only Gilkey, but also so many others who would lose their lives on K2.

Leadership of the expedition shifted from Houston to Ata-Ullah, since they were now on a rescue mission. Their departure from K2 was a sorry sight, with local climbers and porters—including Zafar Ali, Taki, and others whose names were unrecorded—assisting and carrying the injured and frostbitten Americans out of the mountains. George Bell, who was in the worst condition, was completely unable to walk. He was carried on a makeshift litter on the glacier by four porters, and eventually, when the trail became too steep and narrow, on the back of a porter named Mohammed Hussein. "At this point the biggest and strongest of the Satpuras took off his shoes, knelt down beside the litter, and with a gentle smile invited me to climb aboard," Bell said. "Sprawled on his back with my arms draped over his shoulders and clasped across his chest, I could peer over his shoulder and see exactly what went on. . . . In time I came to feel almost as secure on his strong back as I had on my own two feet during the march in. . . . Each time he put me down after a hard carry, he would turn around with a sympathetic boyish grin and inquire, '*Tik sahib?*' (Everything okay sahib?) It was impossible not to say yes."

Eleven days of carries over boulder fields, along narrow muddy ledges, and beneath the perilous rock walls looming above the foaming waters of the Braldu—by men who would never become famous, would never become rich. "We entered the mountains as strangers, but we left as brothers," Houston recalled.

One year later, 1954, Ata-Ullah received another letter, this one from Ardito Desio of Italy. K2 had still not been climbed, and Desio aimed to change that. He needed someone to hire and manage thirteen Hunza climbers and a multitude of Balti porters. Once again, Ata-Ullah agreed.

Desio and his team of eleven climbers had thirteen tons of gear that needed transporting to base camp, for this would be an all-out assault on the mountain. As an authoritarian and inflexible leader of a military-style climbing campaign, Desio felt the job required a firm hand. He would lead from below, issuing orders from base camp to the climbers above him.

In spite of the language barrier, Ata-Ullah was captivated by his new Italian friends: "The exuberant eagerness of young Walter Bonatti, the agile rhythm of Lino Lacedelli, the strong solid quietness of Mario Puchoz, the mercurial quickness of Sergio Viotto, the courteous charm of Ubaldo Rey, the sober optimism of Achille Compagnoni, the artistic talent of Mario Fantin, the sincere helpfulness of Pino Gallotti." But he soon observed problems. There weren't enough snow goggles to go around, and the porters suffered with watery, bloodshot, swollen, and painful eyes. Screaming in anger and fear, many porters dropped their loads and fled for home.

When they finally arrived at K2, Desio announced a plan for the Hunzas that was different than the American team's approach. Believing that local climbers weren't yet sufficiently skilled to climb difficult terrain at high altitudes, Houston had only allowed the Hunzas to carry loads as far as Camp 2. To ask them to go beyond that point, he reasoned, would be an unacceptable risk and responsibility. Desio thought differently, and he expected the Hunzas to go much higher.

And so in late July 1954, Amir Mehdi, from the Shimshal Valley of Northern Pakistan, was with the Italians at 7,740 meters, poised for a summit bid. Mehdi had performed well on the mountain, as he had on previous expeditions. In fact, he and Haji Baig had helped carry the famous Austrian mountaineer Hermann Buhl down to Nanga Parbat base camp after Buhl's lonely first ascent the year before. When Bonatti was tasked with delivering oxygen bottles to Lacedelli and Compagnoni's last camp, at a predetermined spot at 8,100 meters, he knew if anyone could physically manage the heavy loads with him, it would be Mehdi. "This man was remarkable, and had always been the best of all the Hunzas," Bonatti recalled. "In my opinion he was the only porter we had who could stand comparison with the best Nepalese Sherpas." His challenge was to convince Mehdi.

Bonatti began the discussion by promising a financial reward if the expedition succeeded. Mehdi listened but didn't respond. Then Bonatti added the enticement he suspected would sway Mehdi, but which he had no intention of honoring: a vague suggestion that he would be able to climb all the way to the summit with the Italians. Bonatti admitted "this was a subtle but necessary deception that, however, did have a grain of truth in it."

Although he didn't even have high-altitude mountain boots, Mehdi accepted the proposal.

Their dramatic story has already been told, but the truth about the motivations, the devious tactics, and the boundless ambitions that led to the first ascent of K2—and the tragic consequences for Amir Mehdi—took years to fully emerge. While Desio had demanded the diaries of all the climbers following the expedition and had shaped the original narrative in his trip report, he couldn't bury the truth completely. As time proved, his version of events was skewed, inaccurate, and incomplete.

Lacedelli and Compagnoni returned as heroes to Italy. Bonatti returned too, disappointed he hadn't summited and bitter at the lack of credit given to Mehdi and him for their selfless contribution to the success. When Compagnoni accused Bonatti of siphoning oxygen from his bottles, Bonatti successfully sued for libel. Lacedelli later tried to explain why he and Compagnoni had chosen a different site for their Camp 9—a site that was out of sight and out of reach for Bonatti and Mehdi. Had Bonatti and Mehdi found their tent in its originally planned location, Lacedelli confessed, there was a good chance Bonatti would have replaced Compagnoni on the final summit climb. The idea of such an outcome had been unacceptable to Compagnoni, so he had placed Camp 9 in a hidden position. It was an outrageous strategy, calculated and callous, especially since both summit climbers must have understood the risk for Bonatti and Mehdi, who would thus be forced to spend a night out with no protection from the elements.

When the triumphant expedition arrived in Karachi, suspicious Pakistani journalists accused Compagnoni of forcing Mehdi to wait below the summit rather than allow him to share in the glory of the moment—and noted that this delay caused Mehdi's severe frostbite. In response, the Italian ambassador to Pakistan held an inquiry. There were a lot of people in attendance with an equal number of slightly different stories: Bonatti, Compagnoni, Lacedelli, Ata-Ullah, and more. Amir Mehdi was not invited. His evidence, which was finally requested ten years later, was dismissed as confusing and unreliable by Bonatti, his lawyers, and the tribunal. What's even more shameful is that his role in the climb was barely mentioned in Bonatti's, Desio's, and Compagnoni's accounts. Even Ata-Ullah's memoir skims lightly over Mehdi's role, saying only that he suffered more than anyone on the mountain.

Nevertheless, the first ascent of K2 became a marketing phenomenon in both Italy and Pakistan: there were K2 stamps, K2 chocolates, K2 cigarettes, a K2 hotel, K2 spumante, and K2 baby food. A film about the expedition proved wildly successful, playing to sold-out houses throughout Italy. Desio, Compagnoni, and Lacedelli were hailed as heroes. Ata-Ullah thrived as well, and lived a richly productive life. He was decorated by the Pakistani government for his subsequent role in reorganizing the nation's health care system. Bonatti's life became defined by his bitter dispute with his three fellow Italians. Eventually, he left mountaineering in the Greater Ranges to pursue a career in journalism and to concentrate on hard climbs in the Alps. But at least he was physically intact.

Amir Mehdi, as we have seen, did not fare as well. When he finally returned home and placed his ice axe in the barn, he told his family he never wanted to see it again. "It reminded him of his suffering and how he was left out in the cold to die," said his son, Sultan Ali, in an interview with Shahzeb Jillani. It took Mehdi years to learn how to walk on his stumps.

In 1994, the Italians brought Mehdi and Sultan Ali to Islamabad to mark the fortieth anniversary of the first ascent. Compagnoni and Lacedelli were there as well. Sultan Ali recalled that no words were exchanged between his father and the Italians, even through translation. This would have been an appropriate time for someone to apologize to Mehdi. But he didn't ask for an apology, and none was offered.

"My father wanted to be the first Pakistani to put his country's flag on top of K2," said his son. "But in 1954 he was let down by the people he was trying to help." In the years since his death in 1999, Mehdi has occasionally been hailed as an "unsung hero," the man who was "betrayed," a "martyr of K2." But during his lifetime, Amir Mehdi was simply treated as collateral damage.

CHAPTER SEVEN

Not Allah, Little Karim

When I went to the mountains the way became clear for me.

—LITTLE KARIM

Twenty-three years would pass before the next ascent of K2. Tension over the region of Kashmir, where the Karakoram giants are located, had only increased since Partition. Since the area was increasingly considered too strategic and sensitive for foreign eyes, Pakistan closed the mountains to climbing from 1961 to 1974. Locals returned to herding their goats.

But before the doors slammed completely shut, a few expeditions slipped into the area, sometimes bringing challenging interactions. Qader Saeed, the Pakistani liaison officer on the 1957 Austrian Broad Peak expedition, had his hands full when the four-member team effectively split into two competing factions. Saeed became so fed up with team member Kurt Diemberger's behavior he advised the Pakistani government to ban him from the country.

In sharp contrast, American Nick Clinch led two expeditions to the Karakoram—first ascents of Gasherbrum I in 1958 and Masherbrum in 1960—and in both cases, relations between locals and foreigners remained cordial, by all accounts. On 7,821-meter Masherbrum, Pakistani Army captain Jawed

Akhter Khan joined Clinch for the second rope team's summit—the first time a Pakistani climber stood on the summit of a major peak in the Karakoram. Willi Unsoeld, who was on the first summit rope team, reported the climb in the *American Alpine Journal*, expressing his admiration for the Pakistani climbers. Unsoeld's article was the first to refer to local climbers as High-Altitude Porters—or HAPS—which at the time, was an expression of respect, but which eventually became a bone of contention for those who preferred to be called climbers rather than porters. Unsoeld saved some of his highest praise for Mohammed Hussein, whom he called "the strongest of the lot"—the same man who had carried George Bell from K2 in 1953 when Bell could no longer walk on his frostbitten feet.

After a fourteen-year hiatus from foreign expeditions, the floodgates opened in 1975. Nobody was prepared, particularly Pakistan's Ministry of Tourism, which approved nineteen separate expeditions to the Karakoram for a single year. The tourism officials making their decisions in their comfortable city offices didn't anticipate the impact of so many visitors on the remote and impoverished valleys of the Baltoro. They expected a tourism boom. What actually happened was quite different: food shortages, fuel shortages, labor shortages, and rampant inflation. The ramifications for the residents lingered long after the foreigners departed, because although the porters returned to their villages flush with cash, their fields were untilled and there was nowhere to spend their hard-earned money.

One of the first groups to arrive in the newly opened region that year was an American K2 expedition. The friction between the foreigners and their Balti porters was rivaled only by the tension within the team itself.

The problems started on the walk in. As many as six hundred young porters hoisted loads onto their backs, held in place by narrow ropes woven from animal hair. Clad in tattered cotton and homespun wool clothing and walking barefoot in cheap plastic shoes, they provided a stark contrast to their well-dressed employers. They traveled in groups of thirty to forty, advancing up the trail in waves. When they swept into a village, the pastoral silence erupted into chaos. There were arguments about payment, complaints about equipment, disappointments about performance, and ultimately strikes, which caused delays and wreaked havoc on the expedition budget.

The Americans felt that since they were paying well above the standard rate, the porters should be grateful. Instead, they demanded more. Not only more pay, but better clothing, more food, and more respect. Round and round the arguments circled: from English to Urdu; from Urdu to Balti; back to Urdu, and finally to English again.

Dianne Roberts, the only woman on the team, had a different perspective: "Team members talking about how we're getting ripped off. What shit! . . . So we're paying them high wages. So what? We'll still leave this country with far more than we've given the people here. . . . We invade their land, their culture, and expect everything to run the way it goes in America. Christ, we need some humility—both towards the people and the mountain. What arrogant, cold bastards we can be."

The conflict was actually even more complicated. The American climbers came to Pakistan with their previous experiences in Nepal as their benchmark. They had hired hundreds of porters in Khumbu to carry their food and equipment, and the Nepali porters were used to living in a region where every single thing was transported on their backs. There were no roads, but there were teahouses and villages where they had access to food and companionship along the way. The trek to K2 base camp was something else altogether. There were no teahouses or villages, not even a well-defined trail—just rock and ice and storms. The porters who may have appeared difficult were likely simply cold and scared. The youngest of them had been barely six years old, if that, when the last expedition had traveled through the area, so their experience was limited. And now there were eighteen more expeditions scheduled for the season. They understood there would be no shortage of work.

When altitude sickness dogged the HAPs on the mountain, the American team felt the Pakistanis had misrepresented their high-altitude experience. One of those "disappointing" men was Akbar Ali from the town of Arandu in the Basha Valley. Ali wanted to climb K2, not only carry loads for the Americans. But instead, he became ill. Although badly dehydrated and suffering from the altitude, his main complaint was his stomach. After being sent from Camp 2 to base camp to recover, he rested a bit and then vomited up around twenty-five parasitic roundworms, each of them at least ten inches in length.

Relieved that the mystery of his discomfort had been solved, Akbar Ali thought his problems were over. With a bit more rest, he reasoned, he could get back on the mountain. But his condition worsened when part of his intestine perforated. As its contents leaked into his abdominal cavity, he lapsed into shock. The medical team hooked him up to an intravenous bottle as he fought for his life, his temperature hovering above 105°F for days. He eventually stabilized but remained terribly fragile and weak.

When his blood pressure dropped dangerously once more, the team requested a military helicopter rescue. But where could a helicopter land? According to the Ministry of Defense, Ali would need to be carried from base camp all the way down to Concordia, where the Baltoro and Godwin-Austen Glaciers meet. Twelve porters bundled him into a sled and hauled him down the glacier as far as they could. When the traveling steepened, they supported him on either side as he shuffled along. When they reached the loose, bouldery moraine, the walking became too difficult for Ali, so Mohammed Hussein—the same man who had carried George Bell in 1953—hoisted him onto his back and carried him over the treacherous terrain. At fifty years old, Hussein was still carrying people off K2.

Akbar Ali survived, and surprisingly, so did the defeated American team. While the individual climbers left K2 in 1975 as sworn enemies, they mended their differences and returned to the mountain in 1978. They had learned some valuable lessons from that 1975 expedition: lessons about abandoning outdated colonial approaches to expeditioning and lessons about human respect. They learned that providing safety equipment for all the porters—not only the HAPS—was a basic requirement. And they came to understand that even small gestures of gratitude and respect could go a long way toward cooperation and performance.

Before the Americans returned, Pakistani mountaineer Ashraf Aman joined a 1977 expedition from Japan. On August 9, 1977, Aman claimed the title that Amir Mehdi had longed for—the first Pakistani to climb the country's highest mountain.

Born in 1938 in Aliabad, Hunza, Ashraf Aman was probably destined to climb. Growing up at an elevation of 2,206 meters and surrounded by wildness, he was totally comfortable in mountain environments. As a boy, he walked forty miles from Aliabad to Gilgit to attend school. He stayed in a hostel during the school week and trekked back to Aliabad for the weekends.

By the time he was invited to join the Japanese team, he had already been to Nanga Parbat with the Germans in 1962 and had climbed and guided in the Himalaya, the Karakoram, and the Hindu Kush. There is a photo of him, tall and slender and serious, on the summit of K2, reciting his country's national anthem and raising Pakistan's flag high above his head. The image electrified the Pakistani public and earned Aman a Presidential Award. Later, when he reflected on his moment atop that pinnacle of ice and rock and snow, he recalled hearing everything on earth murmuring prayers: "Mountains are my soul. . . . Mountains give the true bliss of a pilgrim."

Aman's K2 ascent was not without problems, though. When one of his Japanese teammates collapsed while descending the Bottleneck, Aman half carried him down to Camp 4. Since the tent was too small for both of them, he continued on alone to the next camp. When he finally reached base camp, he realized his toes had frozen. "My feet had been burned," he said in an interview with Pakistani journalist Yasal Munim. But Aman wasn't surprised. "I knew that this would happen," he had confided to his friends. He didn't have proper high-altitude climbing boots. "Despite all of this, I didn't feel any pain during the summit. There is a different kind of energy when you are up on mountains. Nothing else matters."

Ashraf Aman wasn't counting on his K2 success to assure his future. He knew the value of an education and subsequently earned an electrical engineering degree. After his adventure, he enjoyed a distinguished career as a climber, an expedition leader, an engineer, and the owner of a successful travel company. He could see that something was missing in Pakistan. In comparison to Sherpas from Nepal, Pakistani high-altitude porters weren't getting the training they needed to operate safely and successfully on technical terrain. So, he started teaching young Pakistani boys and girls who showed an interest in climbing. One of his students—Muhammad Ali Sadpara—would go on to become one of Pakistan's most famous climbers, and the inspiration for this book.

While Ashraf Aman remains virtually unknown outside his country, another Pakistani who helped at the training camp soon rocketed into international prominence.

Nazir Sabir is still instantly recognizable today, as there is only one person on this entire planet who looks like him. His bushy eyebrows are outdone only by his wild halo of black curls. When he smiles, Nazir's broad face splits in two and his dark eyes sparkle with humor. He was the first Pakistani climber to understand fame, to embrace it, and to use it for good.

Born near Gilgit in the Hunza Valley in 1955, Nazir grew up exploring the hills around his home. "I was one of the luckiest people to have been born right in the lap of the Karakoram. . . . I spent my childhood under the shadow of Rakaposhi, Ultar and all those big mountains," he told Pakistani journalist Sonya Rehman. "Mountains were always very holy places for me, very spiritual places that I understood much later in life. But even as a child I used to think a lot about what would be beyond these mountains—a hidden world, a mysterious world that was hidden by those four walls around my village." Legend has it that Nazir was inspired to climb because he believed he would be able to see America from the tops of the mountains.

In 1976 he made a remarkable first ascent of 6,660-meter Payu Peak. The ascent was significant, not only because it was a first ascent in Pakistan by Pakistani climbers, but also because Allen Steck, the only American on the team, had been invited in a support role to mentor the Pakistani climbers, rather than as a star climber. The following year, Nazir—along with Ashraf Aman—was asked to join the Japanese on K2. While Ashraf's rope team tagged the top, Nazir's rope team was forced to abandon their summit bid, surely a bitter pill for the ambitious young man.

His disappointment paled in comparison to his grief three years later when his older brother, Inayat Shah, was buried under an ice avalanche while attempting to climb Diran, a 7,266-meter peak in the Nagar Valley. But Nazir wasn't dissuaded from joining an expedition from Japan's Waseda University to K2 in 1981—this time as their liaison officer as well as a climber. The goal was the difficult and unclimbed West Ridge.

While leading the last four pitches to Camp 5 at 8,050 meters, Nazir faced a devastating reality—his fingers and toes were starting to freeze. When he informed his ropemate Eiho Ohtani that he would have to go down, Eiho refused to allow him to give up. Instead, he radioed down to their leader, Teruo Matsuura, and asked him to send his own larger-sized boots up to Camp 2. Eiho correctly reasoned that Teruo wouldn't need the boots in base camp. Nazir descended to Camp 2 to try them on. They fit, so he climbed back up the mountain in Teruo's footwear. "I went all the way to Camp 4 next day and joined my team," he said.

At 5 a.m. on August 6, 1981, the rope team of Eiho Ohtani, Nazir Sabir, and Matsushi Yamashita started up toward the summit. All three used supplemental oxygen for the first five hours, until they reached the ridge and realized that carrying the heavy oxygen equipment on this challenging terrain was too cumbersome. They dumped it.

By 6 p.m. they had reached only 8,400 meters, so they began digging a snow cave. Three hours later they crawled in, spooning to stay warm. They had nothing more than a candle to warm themselves: no food, no fuel, no water, and no sleeping bags. Nazir described the candle as "the last source of heat and light on earth." Some time during the night, he accidentally kicked the wall of the cave, collapsing it onto his teammates. But they survived, and by 6 a.m. they were climbing again, moving at a snail's pace.

Nazir's radio crackled to life; Teruo was calling from base camp. Concerned about their slow pace, the expedition leader directed them to turn back. Nazir couldn't believe what he was hearing. "For the next forty-five minutes there was a dramatic war of emotions, of confusions within confusions, between the higher heavens of K2 and base camp," he said. "I said 'Forget about what the leader said. I'm not going down because I missed K2 from so near last time.' . . . I said that in Pakistan we don't listen to a leader sitting far below."

Leaving Matsushi behind, Eiho and Nazir reached the summit at 11:30 a.m. Out of respect, Eiho tried to persuade Nazir to go first, but he declined, so the two made the last steps to the top arm in arm. "Ohtani wept as he called base camp," Nazir recalled. "I prayed for my four friends from 1977 and for all those who gave their lives in pursuit of their dream mountains." Three days later, they were back in base camp.

A documentary film of the climb, *Fifty-Day Struggle*, was shown throughout Japan, and Nazir became a household name both in that country and in his own. As his reputation spread within the mountaineering community, he became a go-to climbing partner for ambitious, elite alpinists. Just one year after climbing K2, he joined Italian Reinhold Messner on rapid-fire ascents of Gasherbrum II and Broad Peak, both done within one week and in alpine-style—each climber carrying his food and equipment without fixed lines or camps. Nazir also made several attempts on Nanga Parbat, including a winter attempt of the unclimbed Mummery Rib, and he led an all-Pakistani team to Everest in 1997. While that team didn't succeed, three years later, on May 17, 2000, Nazir stood atop the highest mountain on Earth, becoming the first Pakistani to do so. "In a way I was paranoid," he said. "But as soon as I took the last step . . . I held on to the summit as if it was running away from me. . . . I remembered my family, my sisters, parents. . . . It also felt like the whole of Pakistan was pushing me up the last bit of Everest."

In a lighter moment, he reflected that he had climbed all his 8,000ers in borrowed boots.

Nazir Sabir's global fame—rare for Pakistani climbers—has as much to do with his personality as his résumé. Fiery, confident, and gregarious, he is a natural leader, with stints as president of the Alpine Club of Pakistan and

Advisor on Education and Tourism for the government of Pakistan. He was even elected to the Gilgit Baltistan Legislative Assembly in 1994, becoming the first commoner to win that position by rallying mountaineers to support him. Once in power, he did all he could to fight corruption, building schools and roads, including a thirty-three-mile jeep road to the remote community of Shimshal. Until then, visitors had to walk three days on a perilous, cliff-hanging trail. The road, sometimes referred to as "the world's most dangerous," runs through a wild and rugged landscape, a nail-biting, three-hour experience.

Successful in business as well, today he runs an adventure travel company and hires Shimshali climbers as guides whenever possible. He travels the world as a lecturer, film festival jury member, and all-around mountain statesman. He has been honored in Pakistan many times as well as by alpine organizations around the world.

Fiercely loyal to his country and famously outspoken, Nazir was outraged by the terrorist attack on the night of June 22, 2013, when militants stormed Nanga Parbat base camp and started killing climbers from around the world. One of the victims was Ali Hussain, an experienced mountaineer and expedition worker from the Charakusa Valley. "Some fifteen ugly ghosts disguised as so-called humans came to the Base Camp under this face and brutally murdered eleven innocent lives many of whom I personally knew and some were close friends," Nazir railed on his Facebook page. "It is the greatest tragedy in the history of mountaineering and in the history of Pakistan. They have not only killed 11 unarmed and innocent people but have actually killed us all, the peace-loving people across Pakistan and specially the simple mountain communities across the northern mountain belt. . . . The people of Pakistan mourn this unfortunate tragedy. . . . We will stand together against this barbarism and terror and fail their agenda of aiming to isolate Pakistan from the world community and we will bring peace to our beautiful world together with our friends across the globe and yes we will fight to the end."

As he approaches his seventh decade of life, Nazir Sabir continues with that fight every day: promoting the mountains of Pakistan as the greatest underappreciated adventure playground on Earth; working to conserve wildlife in the Hunza Valley; raising his voice against the environmental and human disaster of the military conflict on the Siachen Glacier; and much more.

It's hard to imagine a greater physical contrast to Nazir Sabir than Moham-mad Karim. Standing 5'2" tall, with a beatific smile, Karim was known as "Little Karim." Born in the remote village of Hushe in 1954, he had no oppor-tunity to attend school, but from the age of six he had lots of time to roam the hills as he helped his parents shepherd the family's animals. "Even back then, I knew that I wanted to become a great guide and high-altitude porter," he told Pakistani journalist Obaid Ur Rehman Abbasi.

Hushe was a quiet place during his childhood years, but when Pakistan re-opened its doors to foreign climbing expeditions, people started to arrive. Little Karim remembered the day he spied a group of climbers while he was playing with friends on the Gondogoro La, high above the Hushe Valley. "A group of mountaineers descended the glacier. I had never seen anyone coming down our way from that side and, excitedly, ran up to them to warmly greet them," he said to Pakistani writer Shabbir Mir. "They gave me a whole handful of candy and biscuits, maybe because I looked like a five-year-old boy. That was my first encounter with this unique breed of sportspersons called mountaineers."

His first attempt at landing a job as a porter didn't go well. Sixteen years old at the time, the diminutive teenager looked more like ten—a mere child—seemingly incapable of carrying a load. He was about to start the long, disappointing trek from Skardu back to Hushe when a Swiss team, des-perately short on porters, hired him. Once given a chance, he exceeded all expectations, carrying heavy, climbing high, and always with good humor. His high-pitched laughter lifted the spirits of the Swiss.

When he tried to secure work with British mountaineer Chris Bonington, Chris reportedly dismissed him as too small to be of any use. According to a profile published forty years later, Little Karim "snuck his head between the big man's [Chris's] legs, hoisted the two metre-tall Brit on his shoulders and ran the length of an open ground. The assembled porters broke into fits of laughter, but [Chris] was impressed by the audition. Karim was granted his wish; he would be part of the expedition to K2."

Despite failing to climb K2, the expedition was a turning point for Little Karim. "The climb with the British was like a good luck sign; soon after, all doors to my success were opened," he said.

It was while working on a French expedition to K2 in 1979 that he became known as Little Karim. Since Karim was a common name in Pakistan, there happened to be three of them on the mountain. Every time someone called for "Karim," three people responded. The leader of the expedition finally resolved the issue by naming them Big, Medium, and Little, based on their relative size. The name stuck with Little Karim.

While on the Japanese K2 expedition with Nazir Sabir in 1981, he made a superhuman effort to carry loads of food and oxygen from 7,100 meters to 8,100 meters, where the summit climbers were stranded. The following day, they summited. Nazir later said that Allah had brought them supplies, but Little Karim clarified: "Not Allah, Little Karim."

In 1985, he not only carried loads for a French team on Gasherbrum II, but further endeared himself when he lugged Jean-Marc Boivin's fifty-five-pound hang glider to the top of the mountain so Jean-Marc could fly off the summit. French documentary filmmaker Laurent Chevallier captured his character in a film titled *Little Karim*. The portrait of Little Karim on Gasherbrum II was wildly successful, winning awards around the world. In the French village of Autrans, where he was a guest of a mountain film festival, attendees warmed to his smiling face and his humility, as well as his gratefulness to be with people who loved the mountains.

Despite all the smiles, Little Karim became outspoken about the changes happening in mountaineering. On a recent trip to Everest, he left in disgust. "I saw 2,500 people going in a line using oxygen at 5,000 meters and I was very put off," he said. "So, seeing the situation and crowds, I said goodbye." In contrast, he expressed special pride in local Hushe mountaineers: "I am very happy with Ali Durrani, who has scaled 8,000-meter peaks multiple times and has not used oxygen once. This is the real way to climb. Using oxygen is the same as roaming the market in some city."

Little Karim is best known today for carrying above his weight, but he should also be known for his rescue efforts: a German climber at 7,300 meters on Broad Peak, an Austrian woman at Broad Peak's Camp 3, a Spanish mountaineer at 8,300 meters on K2, a body recovery of a French man on Gasherbrum II, and on and on. "Summiting is easy for us, but these responsibilities are greater," he maintained.

After a lifetime of mountaineering, Little Karim slowed down in his sixties. "Since the last decade or so I had to quit mountains due to bad health," he explained, adding with an impish grin, "but I went against medical advice and summited a few more peaks."

Canadian alpinist Ian Welsted was on his way back from climbing K6 West with Raphael Slawinski when they stopped in Hushe. "Meeting Little Karim of Hushe was magical," he said. "Karim's tales of unrecognized high-altitude exploits put me in my place."

Ian was stunned by Little Karim's stories and the scope of his experience. "It was surreal sitting with a 60-year-old Balti and hearing his record of ascents, which put him near the top of the list of world mountaineers," he said. "In journals, Karim's ascents are usually listed only as 'accompanied by a high-altitude porter,' the euphemism for paid Asian climbers. I left our conversation feeling like the wool had been pulled from my eyes."

But what equally impressed Ian was Little Karim's lack of bitterness that he wasn't as famous or as rich as he might have been. He seemed content. "My father is a social worker by default," said his son Hanif. "He is a simple man. He does not need anything in life. Everyone wants to make a name for themselves but that is not the case of my father. He worked honestly and divided the money for his children, his community and only then himself." Hanif wasn't exaggerating. In 2008, a Spanish NGO built a hotel for Little Karim, intending it to be a source of income for him in his advancing age. Instead, he donated the building to the community, which used the revenue to improve the health and education facilities in the region. "He thinks and cares for his people more than he does for his family," Hanif said. "Many people have asked him why and how he is living in such poor conditions. This makes my father laugh. He says a real human being is one who uses what he has to help those in need."

Little Karim's greatest disappointment was his lack of education. "I once traveled to Canada to make a movie," he said. "A man left me in a hotel room and I could not figure out how to open the door for nine hours. . . . This was due to a lack of education. I had to count the rooms and remember mine after I put a string on the doorknob. That day I decided that without education, death is better. Then I made up my mind to give back to Hushe and invest in the children of Hushe." And so he did. Revenue from his hotel provided scholarships for over three hundred students. When Rolex gave him an expensive watch, he sold it and gave the money to schools.

"Since someone invested in me and gave me an opportunity, I had to do the same," he said. "I made a promise."

When Little Karim died in an Islamabad hospital in the last days of winter in 2022, all of Pakistan mourned for him. Climbers from around the world wrote moving reflections of their time spent with this modest, cheerful, and generous soul. When the Pakistani Army arranged for his body to be returned to Hushe, the village elders, climbers, porters, laborers, and shepherds lined the road, waiting. As the procession made its way to Little Karim's final resting place, the majestic Karakoram sentinels stood silently by.

CHAPTER EIGHT

Turning Points

I suppose our distant country holds little of interest for your public except for what of the strange can be written about it, and so you get a strange picture of us. We are neither primitive nor bizarre.

—RINCHEN LHAMO, *We Tibetans*

Pertemba Sherpa was cleaning the kitchen in a work camp at the Lukla airport in 1966 when he heard the familiar sound of an approaching helicopter. He wandered over to admire the machine when, out of the corner of his eye, he noticed a ruddy-skinned man sporting a jaunty straw hat approaching him. The man seemed curious.

"What's your name, son?"

"Pertemba Sherpa, sir."

In a clipped British accent, the Westerner asked Pertemba about himself and his family, while observing him closely. Athletic and strong, Pertemba looked far too fit to be cleaning a camp kitchen, but he didn't seem to mind.

The foreigner introduced himself as Colonel Jimmy Roberts and soon made a most attractive offer. "I'm looking for a strong young man to help me with my business. Would you be interested?"

Yes, indeed.

"If you ever come to Kathmandu, I will have a job for you, Pertemba."

Two weeks later, Pertemba was in Kathmandu, ready to start work. "I didn't think about anything—money, future prospects, a good life—when I accepted [the] offer. He did not explain what that job was, and I didn't ask," he later told Nepali reporter Kapil Bisht.

⁕⁕⁕⁕⁕⁕⁕

Born in 1948 in the village of Khumjung in the Khumbu region of Nepal, Pertemba was sent as a young boy to live with relatives in order to study, first at a monastery, and then at a school Edmund Hillary had opened. Since Pertemba wasn't a brilliant student, he failed to get a scholarship to continue his education past the fifth grade. Instead, he wandered off to Lukla in search of work. When Jimmy Roberts discovered him and hired him, Pertemba's future changed dramatically. He was soon employed on trekking and climbing expeditions. Over time, he evolved into an equal climbing partner to some of the world's top mountaineers during a great period of Himalayan exploration.

Naturally skilled and incredibly fit, Pertemba excelled in the mountains. He was a member of the Sherpa team on a joint British-Nepali military expedition to Annapurna in 1970, on an international expedition to the Southwest Face of Everest in 1971 led by Jimmy Roberts, and on Chris Bonington's 1972 Everest attempt, also on the Southwest Face. These were massive affairs, with complex logistics and difficult climbing. There were hundreds of loads of equipment that needed to be ferried up to multiple camps under the constant threat of rockfall, icefall, and avalanches.

By the time Chris returned to Everest's Southwest Face in 1975, Pertemba was his sirdar. At twenty-seven years of age, he was young for the position, but he had earned Chris's respect as someone who could not only oversee the Sherpa team, but who could climb and lead.

By the 1970s, foreign climbers had improved their equipment and technical standards so dramatically that the nature of expeditions in the Himalaya had changed. The most ambitious ones were increasingly attempting unclimbed and outrageously difficult lines instead of repeating standard routes. Their expectations of locally hired climbers rose proportionately.

In addition to mountaineering expeditions, Nepal was discovering a different kind of traveler—the trekker. The man who created, nurtured, and perfected this mode of travel was none other than Colonel Jimmy Roberts.

Partly balding, with a perpetually quizzical look on his face, Jimmy was born in India in 1916. A career soldier, he was appointed military attaché at the British Embassy in Kathmandu and quickly became involved with the expeditions passing through the capital. He had amassed a notable list of exploratory expeditions by the 1960s, spanning several decades of famous explorers all the way back to Tilman. Jimmy himself was not particularly successful at extreme altitude, but his attitude may have had something to do with his performance. "The boredom, the sheer and utter misery of war and the few moments of truth which make it sometimes seem worthwhile compare very closely with high-altitude climbing," he said.

What he did enjoy, however, was exploring. After the high-altitude "misery" part of an expedition was done, he took the time to wander through adjacent valleys and climb smaller nearby peaks. In doing so, he grew extremely knowledgeable about the remote corners of Nepal, which led him in 1964 to become the architect of the first trekking and mountaineering company in Nepal. He called it Mountain Travel Nepal.

His target market consisted of well-heeled travelers who had an appetite for adventure, but a desire to have someone else look after the logistics. He hired the most experienced Sherpa and Gurkha climbers in the country, and as a result, his services were in high demand. His former military training had honed his organizational skills, he knew the country, he had all the best Sherpas working for him, and he was keen to be part of the grand adventures. "The years from 1950 to 1965 were the golden age of climbing and exploration in Nepal," he recalled.

<hr />

The British, Yugoslavians, Japanese, French—all had ambitious projects requiring Sherpas on their teams, yet there was a subtle difference from earlier days. Sherpas, increasingly, were no longer considered merely hired hands, but companions in adventure.

One illuminating example is the first American ascent of Everest in 1963, led by Norman Dyhrenfurth. Sixteen Sherpas reached camps above 8,230 meters on two separate routes. One of them attained the summit—the barrel-chested and famously strong Nawang Gombu, Tenzing Norgay's nephew. Nawang and Jim Whittaker paused below the summit at 11:30 a.m. on May 1.

Jim gestured for Nawang to step up first.

"No, you go first," said Nawang.

"Come, let's go together," Jim replied, and they walked side by side up the last few meters to the summit. Nawang would touch the top again on May 20, 1965, becoming the first person to climb Everest twice.

‑‑‑‑‑‑

The man Jimmy Roberts relied on most at Mountain Travel Nepal was Pertemba Sherpa. But Pertemba wasn't Jimmy's only employee on the famous Southwest Face of Everest expedition in 1975. The entire high-altitude Sherpa team was from his company, including respected climbers Ang Phu and Ang Phurba. As expedition leader Chris Bonington recalled, "Jimmy Roberts' Mountain Travel Sherpas looked like mountain guides—they barely condescended to use the clothing which we had issued, preferring the approach march gear they considered more elegant. Some of them, Pertemba particularly, reminded me of French guides, with smart peaked cap and well-cut breeches."

Local climbers and guides no longer referred to their foreign employers as sahibs but rather by their names. The courtesy was sometimes, but not always, reciprocated. As essential as the Sherpas were on these climbs, foreign attitudes toward them still had a long way to go. Chris was committed to being fair and kind, but his tone might sound condescending, at least to culturally sensitive ears. "They are no different from any other employees on a daily wage, though—in common with any ordinary factory-worker in Britain—they need more than just money to command their enthusiasm as well as obedience," he said. "They need to feel that the job is worth doing; they need to develop friendship with their employers and to feel that their efforts are fully recognized."

The confidence and stylishness of the smartly dressed Sherpas didn't diminish the seriousness of their undertaking. Charlie Clarke, the expedition doctor, recalled leaving the village of Khumde en route to the mountain:

> *We saw a touching, solemn scene of a Sherpa parting with his family; the sacrificial fire of juniper, his wife and three children standing round—the silent prayer that he would return to them. A soldier leaving for the wars, pointless wars, wars he is fighting for someone else. How happy I shall be if we return safe with as many as we left Khumde.*

Chris relied heavily on both Pertemba and Ang Phu throughout the climb. "I consulted Pertemba at each step, occasionally irritating my lead climbers by accepting Pertemba's advice on what he felt the Sherpas could do, or even on route selection, in preference to their own," he later wrote. Chris promised them both a trip to England if they were successful, plus a shot at the summit for at least one of them. Ultimately, Pertemba got to choose which Sherpa would be on which summit rope team. He chose the second team for himself and assigned Ang Phu the third.

The first summit team consisted of Doug Scott and Dougal Haston. They topped out on the Southwest Face on September 24. Down at Camp 6, the second team waited: Martin Boysen, Mick Burke, Peter Boardman, and Pertemba Sherpa. Two days later, they crept out of their tents at 4:30 a.m. The night was still. A thin high haze skimmed the western horizon, and a billowing mass of cloud surged up into the Western Cwm below them. If they wanted to get to the top and back down to their camp without bivouacking, they would have to move quickly. The fixed lines were in place, so each man climbed alone, at his own pace, sucking on bottled oxygen and immersed in private thoughts. When Martin's oxygen set malfunctioned, he turned back. Now there were three.

The fixed lines ended at a gully snaking up to the South Summit. The storm was approaching more swiftly now. The wind had picked up and was swirling snow and ice crystals around the climbers. Mick had fallen behind, but Peter and Pertemba carried on. When they reached the top at 1:10 p.m., Pertemba attached his Nepali flag to a summit tripod erected by the Chinese earlier that year. Peter pulled a small tape recorder out of his pack to capture the moment. "Would you like to say a word to the viewers, Pertemba?" His response was too muffled by his oxygen mask for Peter to understand it, but Pertemba later recalled urging his summit partner to put the recorder away because he was concerned about the weather. Peter persisted, asking if he was tired. Pertemba answered firmly, "No." After celebrating with some chocolate and a piece of mint cake, they headed down.

A few hundred meters below the summit, they came across Mick, resting in the snow. "Mick, are you okay?" Peter asked.

"Yeah, good, just a little slow. I'm fine."

"You should come down with us. It's still a way to the summit, and it's getting late."

"No, I'm good. I'll tag the top and meet you at the South Summit. Can you wait for me there? I really do feel good, now I've had this bit of rest. I won't be long."

Reluctantly, they continued down without him. They waited for a time at the South Summit, huddling by a rock to avoid the bone-chilling wind. But the storm was worsening by the minute. Finally, as the light faded to dusk, they headed down.

Stumbling in the dark, they searched for the entrance to the gully that would take them down to the fixed lines. Eventually, they both reached the top of the lines. Rappelling for 350 meters in a howling blizzard, they were repeatedly dusted with avalanches sifting down from the upper slopes. At the end of the fixed lines, they still had to navigate a tricky traverse, tiptoeing across runnels of ice and snow interspersed with rock fins, feeling their way back to their camp in the dark. At 7:30 p.m. they finally staggered into Camp 6 and collapsed.

Mick Burke was not seen again, and there was no third summit attempt. The expedition was over. Shattered by Burke's death, Pertemba stopped climbing for four years.

While Sherpas had summited Everest before, Pertemba's ascent of the Southwest Face signaled one of the turning points in the relationship between local and foreign climbers. Sherpas were now expecting commensurate rewards in return for performing on extreme and completely unknown terrain with their foreign companions. Not only higher wages, state-of-the-art clothing and equipment, but opportunities to summit as well.

* * *

Four years later, when a powerful Yugoslavian expedition arrived to attempt the unclimbed Direct West Ridge of Everest, another Sherpa was included on the second summit team. Pertemba's Southwest Face partner, Ang Phu, joined Stane Belak Šrauf of Slovenia and Stipe Božić of Croatia on the summit on May 15, 1979, making Ang Phu the first Sherpa to climb Everest by two completely different routes. He died during his descent after an open-air bivouac at 8,300 meters.

When the news reached his village, Khumjung, there was an explosion of grief. Ang Phu's cousin stormed into base camp to confront the Yugoslavian team, struggling to understand what had happened, accusing them of incompetence, and destroying part of the camp.

Pertemba was co-leading an American expedition on the first ascent of Gaurishankar in the Rolwaling Valley when he learned of Ang Phu's death. "For years after he passed away, I could not bear to look at his mother," he later said. "We try to do something for the children of those who are lost to the mountains, but it's never enough."

Pertemba went on to survive two more Everest summits, including one with Chris Bonington in 1985. The climb was a fitting last act for the two climbers who, for a few outstanding years, had orbited around each other, enabling each to achieve remarkable results in the mountains they both loved.

When Pertemba retired from climbing high mountains, he launched a trekking agency and traveled widely. He became a highly respected member of the Nepali mountaineering community, volunteering his experience and time with the Himalayan Trust, the Kathmandu Environmental Education Project, the Himalayan Rescue Association, and the Nepal Mountaineering Association. When Bisht asked Pertemba what he considered his greatest achievement, he answered, "social work."

"I'm not going to take anything with me when I die," Pertemba said. "I love the mountains, animals and people. I have a bond with them. I want to improve the place where I was born, its flora and fauna. I want to save it. I can't sit and watch and do nothing. That is what I feel pride in, building a society, helping people." A mentor to many of the next generation of Nepali climbers, he is an example of someone who performed on the mountain when it was his turn to do so, and then stepped aside from that role when his expertise was more valuable elsewhere. He is now known as an "elder" in the community that means so much to him.

CHAPTER NINE

Tower of Babel

It is a very cruel thing to be forced to stand, facing a choice of death or destitution, while all around you money swirls in the cold wind but none of it sticks to you.

—JEMIMA DIKI SHERPA, *"Two Thoughts," Alpinist 47*

O ne by one, climbers emerged from their tents at Camp 4. They crouched low to attach their crampons, and then hoisted their packs. Weeks of storms had worn them down, but a brief weather window had revived their spirits. As their headlamps slashed the darkness in the early morning hours of August 1, 2008, each climber had one thought in mind—the summit of K2.

Ten teams. Thirty climbers. Almost as many languages. This was an unprecedented number of people on K2.

A series of high-profile suicide bomb explosions the year before had crippled Pakistan's tourism industry. In the aftermath, the Alpine Club of Pakistan successfully lobbied the Ministry of Tourism to slash fees for their 8,000-meter peaks and to remove the cap on the number of expeditions to the Karakoram. Hence the crowds.

The teams were operating independently, but everyone knew that with only one brief weather window there would be crowding high on the mountain. They would need to work together. The key to success would be fixed lines to assure the climbers' safety on both their ascent and descent. On this point, most agreed. What they hadn't quite worked out was how those lines were going to be installed. Who would do what, in what order?

The lead climbers approached the Bottleneck section—notoriously dangerous because of a threatening serac—a column of glacial ice—poised overhead. It looked like a perfect summit day. But the perfect day soon began to unravel. Mistakes, miscommunications, unrealistic expectations, and differing levels of expertise and fitness were all factors. And finally, the serac. Thirty-six hours later, eleven people were dead. Fingers were pointed, people were blamed, heroes were made, and everyone clung to their own version of the truth.

There were three Shimshali climbers high on K2 that day—Shaheen Baig, Mehrban Karim, and Jehan Baig—along with several Nepali climbers, including Chhiring Dorje Sherpa, Pemba Gyalje Sherpa, Jumik Bhote, and Pasang Lama. The rest were foreigners, including the Korean leader of the Flying Jump team, Kim Jae-soo; Basque alpinist Alberto Zerain; the Dutch leader of the Norit team, Wilco van Rooijen; Irish mountaineer Gerard McDonnell; Italian Marco Confortola; Serbian Dren Mandič; and a married couple from Norway Cecilie Skog and Rolf Bae. Their lives would intersect dramatically on K2.

From the beginning, there was confusion. There were no official guides on K2 that day. There were, however, plenty of high-altitude workers assisting some, but not all, of the teams. Fixing ropes was one of their most important jobs. Since the early 2000s, expeditions had come to rely on extensive fixed ropes on K2, and members all expected to use them, regardless of who fixed them and who paid for the work. Sherpas known as the Icefall Doctors had solved this problem on Everest by charging everyone on the mountain a fee to use the infrastructure they'd installed through the infamous Khumbu Icefall. Even though fixed ropes had become equally important on K2, there was no formal agreement among the climbers on August 1 about how the work would be accomplished.

When the much-anticipated weather window arrived, Shaheen Baig took control. Nazir Sabir called him the "safest climber around . . . one of the best in Pakistan." Shaheen was from the village of Shimshal, which was perched at 3,100 meters at the end of a terrifying jeep track. He knew K2 from bottom to top and had already summited it in 2004 without supplemental oxygen. This time, Shaheen was officially working for a Serbian team, but he quickly became the go-to man and voice of authority for all the teams. He negotiated labor disputes and came up with the overall multi-team plan to lace the upper part of the mountain with fixed ropes.

In addition to being Shimshal's leading mountaineer—and that's saying a lot for a community teeming with climbers—Shaheen was a climbing instructor. Two of his students, Mehrban Karim and Jehan Baig, were also on K2 that morning. The young pair had been scrambling around in the mountains since they were boys, shepherding their animals to the upper pastures. But they knew their future wasn't farming: it was climbing. Shaheen was proof of that. "Karim and Jehan became my little brothers," he later told American writers Amanda Padoan and Peter Zuckerman. "I set technical routes on the White Horn and made them climb the ice, over and over."

Both were soon launched on their careers. Jehan had earned respect and gratitude when he rescued a Japanese mountaineer on Gasherbrum II, and he was now working for a Singaporean team on K2. Mehrban had reached the summit of Nanga Parbat in 2005 with a French client, Hugues Jean-Louis Marie d'Aubarède, who was so pleased with Mehrban's performance he hired him for K2. The pair made attempts together in 2006 and 2007, without success. But Hugues wasn't giving up, and Mehrban was the man to help him.

Mehrban's wife, Parveen, wasn't so sure, for his client was already sixty years of age. "I asked him to stay in Shimshal," she said. "Then I begged." His father felt the same and implored Mehrban to remain at home, to consider a career in carpentry. But Mehrban calmed their nerves and convinced them the 2008 season would be both lucrative and successful.

On K2, Shaheen suggested a schedule: the first team of rope-fixers would leave camp at midnight on the first summit day and fix lines through the Bottleneck, finishing by dawn. The next group would leave one hour later, arriving at the Bottleneck with an unbroken line of ropes ahead of them. In six hours, everyone should be at the summit. Two p.m. would be the turnaround time for all climbers, allowing enough daylight hours to descend the fixed lines to Camp 4. The second wave of climbers, waiting at Camp 3, would then move into position in Camp 4 and try to summit on the second good weather day. Every radio would be set to the same frequency, ensuring smooth communication. All agreed.

But events rarely go as planned on a mountain. What no one had fully considered was the language issue. Reaching an understanding at base camp in a quiet tent with people of different languages and cultures was just barely possible. But the group climbing from Camp 4 on summit day would have to communicate with each other over crackling radios in half a dozen languages—a virtual Tower of Babel despite everyone's best intentions.

The second setback—and this was more serious—took place at Camp 2. Climbers had started heading up the mountain on July 28 in anticipation of the good weather. K2 is known as a treacherously steep mountain to *climb*. But it's an equally steep and dangerous mountain on which to *camp*. Particularly lower on the mountain, where camping spots are perched in precarious positions, tucked under small outcroppings to avoid the constant rockfall. The minuscule campsites are prone to crowding and sanitation issues.

When Shaheen and Chhiring Dorje Sherpa reached Camp 2, the place was already crammed.

<hr />

Chhiring Dorje Sherpa was one of two Nepalis climbing K2 as independent team members that week, a significant change from previous generations of Nepali climbers who had generally climbed the most difficult Himalayan routes under the leadership and employ of foreigners. Chhiring would climb independently on that August day, as well as accept all financial responsibility for his personal goal.

Born in 1974 on the floor of his family's one-room house in the village of Beding, high in the isolated Rolwaling Valley, Chhiring had overcome unbelievable odds. Two younger sisters and a younger brother had died as children, his mother had died giving birth to a stillborn baby, and his father had finally collapsed from the ongoing trauma. Chhiring was left to care for his four remaining siblings. He was twelve. He sold the livestock and began bartering his labor for food, but he needed to earn more. Two years later he walked to Kathmandu in search of work.

His uncle, Sonam Tshering Sherpa, found him a job hauling loads to Island Peak. After one month, Chhiring had earned more money than he had seen in his life—$90. The following year his uncle showed him how to strap on a pair of crampons and use an ice axe: he began carrying loads of more than sixty-five pounds up to the South Col of Everest, earning $450. For perspective, $450 was more than the average Nepali earned in a year at the time, and Chhiring had made it in one month.

The powerfully built Chhiring continued doing high-altitude work, fixing lines, breaking trail, hauling loads, and becoming wealthy in the process. He summited Everest and other 8,000ers multiple times. He founded a company, Rolwaling Excursion, and invited young Rolwaling men to join him. He married Dawa Phuti from Namche Bazaar, started a family, and moved into a sparkling new townhouse in Kathmandu with all the modern conveniences.

His business ambitions fulfilled, Chhiring turned his attention back to climbing. One important objective remained for him—K2 without supplemental oxygen. Dawa Phuti discouraged him, convinced that at thirty-four he was too old, too fat, and too comfortable to consider such an outrageous fantasy. She failed to dissuade him.

Now he and Shaheen Baig were at Camp 2, where thirty people were stuffed into overlapping tents, with no room to move freely and everyone feeling the altitude. Before long the streams of vomit and feces and urine that flowed freely through the camp were impossible to avoid. Inevitably some became ill, including Shaheen.

His condition rapidly deteriorated. His lungs started gurgling, and he began spewing up blood, a sign of high-altitude pulmonary edema (HAPE). Everyone realized that the most experienced man on the mountain, and the brains behind the rope-fixing strategy, would not be there to supervise it.

HAPE only passes when the patient descends to a lower altitude, but Shaheen felt that he had too much responsibility to go down. He delayed, hoping he would improve. His condition worsened instead, until he realized he had waited too long. He could no longer move on his own, but he understood the risks involved in requesting a rescue.

He called Nadir Ali Shah, the base camp cook for the Serbian team, explained what had happened, and asked to be left on the mountain. He accepted his mistake and would deal with the consequences.

Nadir ignored his request. Though he was not a climber, he scurried around base camp looking for someone to accompany him to Camp 2. Nobody stepped up. So, he scrounged some equipment and left base camp around midnight, alone. He radioed Shaheen to let him know he was coming. No response.

When Nadir reached Camp 1, he called again. Still nothing. At noon the following day he arrived at an abandoned Camp 2. Everyone, it seemed, had headed up the mountain. But where was Shaheen? Had he miraculously revived? Nadir finally found him curled up on the snow in the fetal position. The base camp cook injected Shaheen with dexamethasone and gave him oral antibiotics with a bit of water. Shaheen swallowed, vomited, and passed out.

Nadir now had a true emergency on his hands. When Shaheen regained consciousness, Nadir dragged him over to the fixed lines and clipped him in. Pushing, pulling, lowering, manipulating Shaheen's rappel device, and offering direction and encouragement, he slowly managed to inch them both down. Drifting in and out of consciousness, Shaheen begged to be left on the mountain. Nadir persisted.

They eventually reached base camp, where Shaheen's condition improved marginally. Realizing the expedition was over for him, he set off on the long trek down the Baltoro Glacier. Devastated with his performance, he was even more terrified of what might happen up high.

The weather window changed—shortened by a day—and the climbers on the mountain adjusted their plan. All except a handful of them now crowded into Camp 4, all planning to summit on the same day.

••••••

Pemba Gyalje Sherpa tried to offer some leadership to the group, though he later explained to American author Freddie Wilkinson that he had no professional responsibilities to any team and had no ownership of the rope-fixing plan. The quiet, fiercely devout Buddhist merely wanted an O2-free ascent of the mountain.

Pemba was the second Nepali on K2 that day who was climbing strictly for himself. Born at 3,000 meters in the village of Pangkhoma, roughly thirty miles south of Everest in eastern Nepal, Pemba grew up surrounded by mountains. He helped out on his family's farm and began climbing at the age of sixteen. He was soon working on expeditions, summitting on a regular basis. He had trained in Nepal, Europe, and North America, and he was one of the most respected guides and sirdars in Nepal. He would need all that experience on K2.

"We need flexibility," he urged the other climbers. "With eight members of the trailbreaking party, the leaders should be changed every fifty meters, to keep men fresh, always." If the fixing teams were unable to keep the lifeline moving up the mountain quickly and efficiently, climbers would catch up to them, and bunch up on the lines directly under the deadly serac that threatened the Bottleneck.

Pemba was so worried about the situation he couldn't sleep. At 10:30 p.m. on July 31, he was already up, wandering around Camp 4, waking people, insisting they start fixing lines. When Pemba realized there weren't enough rope-fixers, he convinced Chhiring to join them. Basque mountaineer Alberto Zerain offered to help as well. He wanted to get up—and down—the mountain as fast as he could. Now there were three independent climbers working on the rope-fixing team, each of them climbing without supplemental oxygen. Pemba and Chhiring shook their heads at the irony of the situation; they would normally get paid handsomely for this work on Everest. Here they were doing it for free.

The Pakistanis and the other Nepalis who were being paid for their work were struggling to communicate with each other. More seriously, they clearly disliked each other. Muhammad Hussein, who had fixed ropes through the Bottleneck in 2004 and who was working for the Serbian team, was upset. "It was unjust," he said. "K2 is our mountain, and Shaheen is our brother, the greatest climber in the region. He taught us to show respect to Buddhists and other foreigners, but the Sherpas didn't respect me."

Resentment, communication problems, and lack of leadership all contributed to the confusion that followed. Rope-fixing began only thirty minutes from Camp 4, something not ordinarily done on this relatively moderate stretch of terrain. But the Korean team had requested fixed ropes in this area, so that's what was done. Unfortunately, the Koreans had also fixed lines between Camps 3 and 4, which meant they were running out of rope. And the most difficult and exposed terrain still lay ahead. With 400 meters of line already in place, the rope-fixers had only 200 meters left for the entire Bottleneck. They would need more. So, Chhiring descended in the darkness to retrieve some rope from below. He was joined by Jumik Bhote.

⸻

Jumik Bhote was first brought to Kathmandu by his older brother, Pemba Bhote, in order to get an education. Their family was from Hungong, in the upper Arun Valley, where the schools had permanently closed after the Maoists took control of the village. The rise of the Maoist movement in Nepal was fueled by incidents that had taken place much earlier. One in particular was the massacre of most of the royal family in 2001 by the drug-addled playboy, Crown Prince Dipendra. Following the bloodbath, his uncle Gyanendra became king, but he quickly proved unfit for the job. Maoist rebels seized the day. The extravagant and much-reviled royal family lost their grip on power, and the rebels began invading the more remote areas of the country—places such as the upper Arun Valley. They destroyed schools, killed officials and teachers, and forced young boys to join them as child soldiers. Beatings, assassinations, torture, and sexual crimes became the norm.

The Maoists had promised a better, fairer life for impoverished Nepalis, but their actions belied their intentions. They killed over 17,000 people and forced more than 150,000 to flee their homes in what morphed into a civil war. Unemployment soared to around 50 percent as the unrest resulted in the collapse of tourism. For Pemba, who had been making his living driving a taxi in Kathmandu, and many others, the cycle of poverty continued.

When their entire family moved into their Kathmandu apartment, Jumik joined Pemba in the search for work. He began portering with various trekking companies and landed a job on an Everest expedition in 2006. He summited. A year later he summited again. The Korean leader of that team, Kim Jae-soo, invited him to climb Lhotse, the world's fourth-highest mountain, in the spring of 2008 and to be sirdar on their K2 expedition later that summer.

Jumik said goodbye to his pregnant partner, Dawa Sangmu, hired his little brother Tsering and two more Hungong climbers, Pasang Bhote and Pasang Lama, and left for K2. Jumik's meteoric career could have benefited from a bit more training and experience, considering the level of responsibility he would face on that immense and hazardous peak.

⸻

High on the mountain, the climbers continued up. A glimmer of gold touched the surrounding peaks and washed over them, warming them slightly. Looking back from the front of the fixing team, Pemba Gyalje could see a column of at least twenty people stretched out along the lifeline between Camp 4 and the Bottleneck. They were catching up.

All too soon the climbers were in the Bottleneck, calling up to the fixers. "Keep moving. We have no place to stand. What's the problem?"

Serbian climber Dren Mandič was moving faster than Norwegian Cecilie Skog, so he tried to overtake her in the steepest part of the Bottleneck. To do so, he had to unclip from the fixed line, pass her, and then reclip. In the process, he somehow lost his balance, then his footing. He grabbed Cecile, and they both toppled over. She was clipped in. He was not. At first, he skidded face down and still had a chance of self-arresting with his ice axe. Then one of his crampons struck a rock. He flipped over, sped headfirst down the Bottle-neck, and his helmet slammed into a rocky outcropping. He flew into the air and cartwheeled onto a snowdrift, where he stopped, lifeless. Stunned, the oxygen-deprived, brain-fogged climbers could only stare.

⸺

Twenty-five-year-old Pasang Lama was high above, leading up past the top of the Bottleneck, fixing lines across the traverse toward the summit. He punched through the deep drifted snow with each step, breathing fast and shallow through his oxygen emitter, marveling at his position on the upper slopes of K2 that day, fixing lines for these people from all over the world.

When he wasn't working as a porter, Pasang lived in a one-room apartment in Kathmandu with his parents, siblings, and cousins, trying to eke out a living to support his extended family of civil war refugees. Despite the down-turn in tourism in Nepal, there were still a few climbing expeditions that braved the unrest, providing Pasang earnings of around $3 a day hauling loads to base camps.

But he had no intention of continuing as a low-level porter, and he was soon working high on the mountains, fixing lines, setting up camps, and car-rying supplies. He summited Everest in 2006 and took a two-week climbing course at the newly created Khumbu Climbing Center (KCC) in Phortse. The KCC, founded by the Alex Lowe Charitable Foundation, offers climb-ing skills, mountain safety, rescue, and wilderness first-aid training to Nepali climbers. With the help of local instructors, like Panuru Sherpa, the KCC's training program gave Pasang the skills he needed for the opportunities about to appear.

When he met Korean climber Go Mi-sun on Lhotse, she encouraged him to join her on K2. At first, he hesitated. Four of his cousins were planning to work for the Korean team: Tsering Bhote, Pasang Bhote, Ngawang Bhote, and Jumik Bhote. Most of them were leaving families behind, and Pasang understood the implications if anything were to go wrong. But ultimately, he couldn't say no. The money was too good.

⸺

The hours passed. The slope had eased now for Pasang, and fixed lines were no longer necessary. He greeted Alberto, who was racing down the mountain, having already summited. When Pasang reached the top of K2, he switched off his oxygen and stood there, completely alone. It was 5:30 p.m. The sun, which he felt sure had only recently risen, was now slipping below the horizon. Turning slowly, he absorbed the panorama that spread beneath his feet, watching K2 cast its long shadow on the deepening hues of the Karakoram range. Pemba arrived soon after, and then Chhiring. Of the first four climbers on top, three had not used supplemental oxygen.

Shortly after, Jumik and his client Jae-soo arrived. They shared a cigarette. Mehrban arrived next with his client Hugues. Both were suffering from hypoxia.

Down at the bottom of the Bottleneck, a futile operation was playing out. The Serbian team felt that Dren's body needed to be recovered, even though they could see he was dead. Jehan had already been to the top of the Bottleneck, having carried an extra load of oxygen for Hugues. He rappelled down toward the recovery team and started helping them drag Dren's body toward Camp 4. But the others noticed that something was wrong with Jehan. He was stumbling. He seemed confused. He was probably starting to feel the effects of altitude but didn't realize it. Nobody else did either until Jehan slipped and started sliding, still holding on to Dren's lifeless body. He let go, then flipped over and, gaining speed, slid over a cliff and disappeared.

Now there were two people dead.

⸻

Above them, more climbers tagged the summit, starting their descent desperately late in the day. Shaheen's suggested turnaround time of 2 p.m. had passed almost six hours earlier. When Jae-soo's oxygen ran out, he pointed toward Pasang's cylinder. Pasang understood the gesture and gave him his.

As darkness fell, the descending climbers became confused, lost. The terrain wasn't steep, but it was featureless. Pasang tried to keep the frightened group moving together in the right direction by devising a makeshift rope system. He tied one end of the extra rope he had carried to the summit to his ice axe. The other end was with Jumik, who descended first, paying the rope out, showing the others the way. One by one, they held on to the handline. Chhiring descended beside them, ensuring that they held tight and kept moving. Once they all reached Jumik, Pasang sped past them, uncoiling the rope as he descended, leap-frogging the process. Their progress was slow but safe, and it would eventually get them to the fixed lines.

On the last length of handline, Pasang left his ice axe planted in the snow to keep the line intact. He knew he wouldn't need the axe in the Bottleneck because it was laced with ropes. He could easily rappel to the moderate slopes leading back to Camp 4.

Suddenly, a horrific crack boomed above them, and a chunk of ice broke off the leaning serac. The block hit Jumik, flipping him over and ripping off his mitts and one of his boots, then crushed the skull of one of the Koreans. Wrapped up in the stretched-taut line, the seriously injured Jumik and the Koreans were trapped.

Another crack. This one much louder. A second massive piece of ice calved off and plowed directly into Rolf Bae. It ripped him from the fixed lines, tore the ropes from the slope, and buried everything under tons of ice. His wife, Cecilie, was above him, frozen in terror.

Another climber, Lars Nessa, who saw what had happened, descended to her, took a 50-meter coil of emergency rope from his pack, and set up a short rappel. They rappelled and then down-climbed the rest of the Bottleneck, returning safely to Camp 4.

High above them, other summit climbers continued down, completely oblivious to what had happened. Pasang found the beginning of the fixed lines and, relieved, since he no longer had his ice axe, started rappelling. Luckily, he was paying attention when the rope ended abruptly in a frayed mess. What on earth?

Confused, he searched around and found another line attached to an ice screw. Everything seemed different than what he remembered from the way up, but he did what was needed, threaded his descender, and started down the line, straight into the mouth of the Bottleneck. But only for 50 meters.

Pasang scanned the slope with his headlamp, completely bewildered. He was standing on a small ice shelf in near-vertical terrain. He was clearly in the Bottleneck, but where were the fixed lines? He tentatively placed one cramponed foot below the shelf and quickly stepped back. The Bottleneck was pure ice, hard as glass. He would never be able to descend it without his axe.

A light slashed above him—Pemba rappelling the 50-meter length of rope. Chhiring arrived next. Crowded together on the small shelf, they tried to figure out what was going on. Were they all hypoxic? Had they not fixed lines here just a few hours ago?

Pemba made the first move. "I'm going to look for the ropes," he said, and started down-climbing the steep ice, carefully but confidently. Chhiring yelled to him when he was out of sight, but Pemba didn't respond. He was on his way to the safety of Camp 4.

Now there were two of them standing on the little ice shelf, one with an ice axe and the other without. Pasang understood the implication of the situation and gave Chhiring permission to leave. "You can go, too."

Chhiring later recalled the look on Pasang's face—blank resignation and wide, unfocused eyes. He took a moment before replying. "If we die," he said, "we die together." He clipped his safety tether to Pasang's harness and plunged his axe as far as he could into the ice. Then he stepped off the shelf.

It's important to acknowledge the magnitude of his decision. They were both essentially soloing down the steep, icy Bottleneck, in the dark—no fixed lines to save them in the case of a fall. Except with each step downward, with each smash of their crampons, with each plunge of Chhiring's axe, their risk was 100 percent greater than if they had actually been soloing, because they were tethered together.

Methodically they descended, and their system worked for a time. Then they were falling, tumbling, and skidding, picking themselves up, starting over. They kicked and plunged, a meter at a time. When they heard a soft slab avalanche cut loose above them, they threw themselves down and waited for the hit, but the debris only glanced off Chhiring's helmet. They stood up and continued. At midnight they reached Camp 4, their descent another example of the brotherhood of the rope.

Early the following morning, Pasang Bhote and Tsering Bhote, who had come up from Camp 3 the day before, were preparing to climb up into the Bottleneck.

"What's happening?" Pemba asked, when he noticed them getting ready.

"We're going up the Bottleneck," Pasang replied.

"The Bottleneck? What? It's too dangerous up there."

"Only two Koreans came down last night after you. Two Koreans and one of the Dutch. Three members of our team are missing with Jumik, and Mr. Kim [Kim Jae-soo] told us to go help them."

"Don't go under the serac," Pemba insisted. Pasang and Tsering didn't reply. "It's too dangerous up there," Pemba said one more time.

"We have to try. We have a job to do. . . . Keep your radio on."

The situation was grim. Many climbers—Dutch, Korean, Italian, Irish, French, Pakistani, and Nepali—were still missing.

Pasang and Tsering found someone lying on the slopes at the bottom of the Bottleneck. Although he appeared to be alive, he wasn't Korean so their job was not done. They radioed Pemba to come and help the unconscious man. From the description of his clothing, Pemba deduced it was the Italian, Marco Confortola. When Pemba and Dutch climber Cas van de Gevel reached the climber, they attached an oxygen mask to his face and turned the tank up to high.

Marco stirred, and then, in a panic tried to push it off, yelling that his ascent was meant to be completely oxygen-free. Pemba shook his head and held the mask in place long enough to calm him down, and then began helping him to Camp 4.

But not before an avalanche broke high above them, bringing two bodies catapulting down with it: Pasang and Jumik.

Pasang had been moving up faster than Tsering and was 300 meters above him when he reached the Koreans and Jumik, tangled up in the fixed lines and almost unconscious. Pasang managed to revive his cousin and two of the Korean climbers, and he had started lowering them down the mountain when another huge section of the serac cut loose. It scoured the Bottleneck, sweeping the Koreans, Jumik, and Pasang off the slope. Tsering saw the avalanche roaring toward him. He dashed sideways, ducked under a protruding rock, and prayed. The avalanche hit the rock and split, spilling down on either side of him, taking his cousins with it to the bottom.

⁑

Now there were eleven dead: Kim Hyo-gyeong, Park Kyeong-hyo, Hwang Dong-jin, Jumik Bhote, Pasang Bhote, Jehan Baig, Mehrban Karim, Hugues d'Aubarède, Gerard McDonnell, Dren Mandič, and Rolf Bae.

While all those lives were being snuffed out on K2, Jumik's wife, Dawa Sangmu, gave birth to a son. She named him Jen Jen.

⁑

Shaheen Baig was still on his way to Shimshal, strapped to a mule, slowly recovering from his close call on K2. As they clip-clopped down the trail,

Shaheen heard the sound of rotor blades. Aware that helicopters are often a sign of something gone wrong, he began to speculate: perhaps a foreigner with too much money had a frostbitten finger. But when the second and third flight thrummed overhead, his heart sank. Something terrible must have happened.

When he reached Askole, Shaheen ferreted out the news; it was much worse than he could have imagined. Among the eleven dead were two Shimshalis.

"I took it like a knife in the gut," Shaheen later said. He had trained Mehrban Karim and Jehan Baig; he had mentored them. They were his friends. He felt as if he had abandoned them. "I loved Karim and Jehan like brothers. I led them to K2. I was the only man who should face their families."

Desperate to beat the news to Shimshal, he hitched a ride to Skardu and found a truck headed for the Hunza region. He piled in, praying that Shimshal's lone satellite phone wasn't working. But he was too late. By the time Shaheen arrived, the entire village was in mourning.

As the survivors of K2 trickled into Islamabad, Pakistan's Ministry of Tourism hosted a reception for them. Nazir Sabir was there, since his company had organized the Dutch team's logistics. Emotions were running high. Wilco van Roojan approached Nazir, waving his bandaged, frostbitten hands in his face: "You need to train your high-altitude porters." Wilco felt the Pakistanis had failed him, even accusing Shaheen of feigning his illness. He later changed his opinion, but in that moment his words were cruel. "Pakistani high-altitude porters are not the right kind of climbers for K2," he said. "They are just too lazy to do the work."

Nazir wasn't taking it. "Some of our high-altitude porters aren't as trained as Sherpas, but we are not ashamed of them," he said. "They are not expected to do everything, and you cannot blame them for every problem."

Military helicopter pilots were accusing the Europeans of expecting—and accepting—rescues from base camp, even though they hadn't paid the mandatory insurance fee. The heated discussions deteriorated into an all-out yelling match, even shoving and punching. Nazir left in disgust.

Shaheen wasn't there, but he later heard what was said and, to this day, remains bitter about how the Pakistani climbers were disrespected.

In the aftermath, it was easy to forget that there were many heroic moments on K2 in 2008. Chhiring Dorje undoubtedly saved Pasang Lama's life. Pemba Gyalje and Cas van de Gevel did the same for Marco Confortola. Pasang Bhote and Tsering Bhote knew they were risking their lives when they climbed up into the Bottleneck in an effort to bring down the last of their team. Gerard McDonnell refused to leave the Koreans and Jumik Bhote in their tangled mess. Mehrban Karim and Jehan Baig did their best for their foreign employers. Nadir Al Shah saved Shaheen Baig's life. And there were likely more acts of heroism we know nothing about.

·······

Among the living, the ripple effects of the disaster continued.

Pasang Bhote's widow, Lahmu, met Kim Jae-soo in the lobby of the Hotel Annapurna. He had insurance papers for her to sign, as well as an envelope filled with Pasang's earnings and a collection from the members of the Korean team totaling $5,000. He couldn't stay long, he told her, because he was on his way to climb Manaslu.

Pasang Lama became ostracized by the Bhote family, who blamed him for not protecting his cousins. Wracked with guilt, he descended into the bottle for relief. When he finally emerged, months later, he headed to Manaslu. Climbing was what he knew.

Shaheen was so crushed by his grief that he left mountaineering altogether, working for years as an oil prospector in the Taliban-occupied North-West Frontier Province. He eventually returned to his previous profession, but with a bitter taste.

Chhiring continued climbing, with a goal of summiting all fourteen 8,000ers. He later moved to the United States with the help of an American client and was able to educate his two daughters and live a comfortable life.

National Geographic Adventure focused their attention on Pemba, labeling him a "savior" and putting his face on the cover of their magazine. They didn't mention the other Nepali and Pakistani climbers. Pemba later wrote a book about the climb, *The Summit*, with Irish mountaineer Pat Falvey. A documentary film of the same name described the devastating K2 season based on that story. Pemba stopped climbing above 8,000 meters after his K2 experience. Instead, he began guiding lower summits as well as instructing for the Nepal National Mountain Guide Association, an organization dedicated to educating Sherpa climbers.

In retrospect, Pemba thinks he understands why he was singled out for his heroism: "The mainstream media focused on the rescues of August second and third," he said. "Those rescues involved Western lives." The media also focused on the *successful* rescues rather than those that weren't. Although the knowledge of that imbalance doesn't diminish the value of all those heroic efforts, successful or not, the disparities remain.

Far from the spotlight, Nazir paid a visit to Shimshal. As president of the Alpine Club of Pakistan, he wanted to offer his respects to the families of those who had died on K2. He asked Mehrban's father, Shadi, how he was doing. "I've been cut in half," Shadi said, weeping. "I hide my grief in front of my grandchildren, but they see it. They feel it." Jehan's sons were suffering as well. Asam had become withdrawn, and Zehan lashed out at foreigners, accusing them of "killing our fathers."

Nazir tried to compose himself and offer some kind of comfort to the Shimshalis drowning in grief. He talked with them. He prayed with them. But eventually, he did the only thing left—he wept with them. The village of Shimshal has never fully recovered from the tragedies of August 1 and 2, 2008.

The history of the 2008 season on K2 isn't permanent or unchangeable. No history is. There are as many truths as there were actors in the drama. Usually the dominant party—the "winner"—writes the "official" story of events such as this. While some of the climbers have been fêted and rewarded for their efforts, others' accounts have gradually faded into the mist. It's by reading between the lines, searching for those quieter voices, that we learn the more nuanced aspects of what happened and why.

CHAPTER TEN

Days of Joy and Sorrow

My family says I am old now and cannot reach summits, but even as old as a lion gets, he does not lose his footing.

—HAJI ROSI

      •

J uly 18, 2021. Broad Peak was crawling with climbers: Russians, Koreans, Pakistanis, Belgians, Canadians, and more. After summiting with Korean team leader Kim Hong-bin, Muhammad Hussain, known as "Little Hussain," was on his way down with five other Pakistani climbers. It was almost midnight, dangerously late in the day to be so high on a mountain.

The descent was going smoothly until Little Hussain heard a woman calling for help. Russian climber Anastasia Runova had fallen and was trapped about 30 meters below the summit ridge on the Chinese side of the mountain.

"I went down . . . and saw that the terrain was a bit sketchy," Little Hussain said. "I fixed a rope and approached the woman and communicated with her. She was scared and wanted to be rescued." Together with his fellow Pakistani climbers, he helped her back up to the ridge, and by 8 p.m. Anastasia was starting down the normal descent route with the assistance of three other foreign climbers. An Explorersweb account of the incident later dismissed

Little Hussain's efforts: "Reportedly, a porter helped Anastasia back up and they began to descend."

But the crisis on the summit of Broad Peak had only begun. "The unfortunate thing that happened next was that Kim mistakenly rappelled down to where the woman had been stranded and ended up getting himself into the same predicament," Little Hussain explained. "I held my head, dejected."

He tried to pull Kim Hong-bin back up to the ridge, but he was too heavy and Little Hussain was running out of energy. At midnight Little Hussain called down to Hong-bin that he needed extra help. He radioed Camp 3, which was at 7,000 meters. Two Russians—Anton Pugovkin and Vitaly Lazo—responded to the call.

They dressed, rounded up some first-aid equipment, and started back up the mountain. Anton came across the descending Anastasia and, after injecting her with the anti-inflammatory drug dexamethasone, helped her down to Camp 3. Vitaly continued up to Little Hussain, where he discovered a chaotic scene: "After saving the girl, [Little Hussain] cried, because he was so tired that he could not save Kim. He had no strength left. Hussain asked people to help, but all the 'hero-climbers' were exhausted and passed by." They could see Hong-bin, who had been standing most of the night, alone, stranded, waiting for a rescue.

"Kim, can you hear me?" Vitaly called down. A faint voice drifted upward in response. Vitaly immediately began setting up a rope rescue system.

Little Hussain was both impressed and relieved: "He was exceptional and set up such a sophisticated rope system. He descended to Hong-bin and gave him some water and tied him to some ropes and gave him instructions. . . . We would pull him three to four feet before he would go back down. The Russian would go back again to guide him."

Then Hong-bin's jumar jammed, and somehow detached from the rescue rope. To the shock of both Little Hussain and Vitaly, the Korean climber disappeared down the Chinese side of Broad Peak.

Little Hussain had been a close friend of Kim Hong-bin's, who, because of frostbite, had been climbing without fingers since 1991. Little Hussain had climbed with him on Gasherbrum I and had wanted to be with him on Broad Peak, Hong-bin's final 8,000er. "It was not meant to be," Little Hussain said. "That day was filled with joy and sorrow. I had saved the Russian woman, which made me happy, but was unable to save Kim. I was very sad. Saving the Russian lady was suicidal for me because it was dangerous and risky but I had to. . . . My reward will be in the next life, since saving one life in Islam has a lot of meaning."

Anastasia Runova was not the first climber that Little Hussain had rescued from a dangerous situation, nor would she be the last. He has executed six high-altitude rescues and seven body recoveries to date. Little Hussain should be a celebrated hero both in Pakistan and abroad, but as he explains, "I am not educated and cannot promote myself. There is no secure future for me. My children are studying but they struggle to get enrolled into good schools and that saddens me." His story is repeated over and over in the high mountain villages of Pakistan's Balti region, but few outside the area have heard such tales. Rescues and body recoveries are a necessary part of high-altitude work for these men. They pursue this work to earn money for their children's education, and their success is based on longevity. "God willing, I can continue climbing another ten years," Little Hussain says.

Thanks to the recent explosion of interest in climbing in the Karakoram, he will have no problem finding work. Since guiding 8,000-meter peaks has become commercially viable, the area has been awash in international clients. Almost all those clients require high-altitude assistance. While many of the guiding agencies come from Nepal, it's Pakistan's northern mountain villages that now provide many of the high-altitude staff. Men like Little Hussain.

Little Hussain is from the village of Machulu in the Hushe Valley. An idyllic place, with terraced fields defined by neat rows of tall, stately poplars, houses creep high up the hillsides until only the undulating summer pastures remain. Looming over the grazing grounds are gray, cathedral-like rocky minarets and spires, topped with a dusting of snow.

Slim and carefully groomed, Little Hussain started working in the mountains in 1998 as an assistant cook. He quickly advanced to carrying loads for a Korean women's climbing team on Gasherbrum II. When one of the high-altitude porters became ill, Little Hussain kept going up, all the way to the summit. "Given that no one else was employed in my family, I had to summit GII, where I raised the flag of my country," he said. "I prostrated there and thanked God and asked Him to give me more opportunities."

God obliged. But Little Hussain's ambitions aren't limited to climbing. "The dream is to set up a proper school," he said. "I, along with Muhammad Ali Machulu and Ali Raza Sadpara, are the most experienced climbers [in Pakistan today]. We can pass on our knowledge to the next generation."

Unfortunately, Little Hussain's dream will likely remain that—a dream—since official government support seems muted at best. Pakistan's federal budget tells the story: it spends 8 percent on educational needs; only 1 percent on health needs; but a whopping 25 percent on its military. There is little commitment from the highest levels of government to Pakistani climbers; this set of priorities means no proper training facilities, inadequate life insurance, and no pensions when they become too old to climb. Fellow high-altitude climber and school planner Muhammad Ali Machulu has pointed out that most of the money earned on Pakistan's mountains goes to Nepali guides and outfitting companies. Muhammad Ali would know: he has been working in the mountains for thirty years.

"I got into this field because my household was not good financially and I was the elder son," he explained. "What should I do now, I thought to myself? I have no education, but my father fed me well and I turned out to be healthy." He took that good health to some on-the-job training on 8,034-meter Gasherbrum II. An angular piece of geometric perfection, the summit pyramid is guarded by walls of towering ice, fields of tumbling seracs, and labyrinths of gaping crevasses. One long, bony spine of rock leads upward. Muhammad Ali summited on his first try and has repeated it four more times. Like Little Hussain, he is scarcely known outside the tight community of Pakistani climbers. "I am illiterate," he says, a simple but profound explanation of a limitation that holds many gifted local climbers captive.

Like many Pakistanis, Muhammad Ali fixes ropes and hauls loads for foreigners who are "collecting" the fourteen 8,000-meter peaks. He would like to climb all fourteen as well—the goal hangs in the rarefied air like a one-way ticket to financial freedom, since climbing all fourteen is attractive to sponsors. But it's unlikely to happen, because without an education Ali can't promote himself to prospective sponsors. He will never climb the fourteen 8,000ers without sponsors.

The literacy hurdles aren't the only challenge for modern Pakistani climbers. In many remote villages, reliable drinking water and secure food are lacking. Almost half of the kids in some of these communities do not attend school and the literacy rate is less than 60 percent. Children must leave their villages for a complete education. Boarding schools cost money—money their parents often earn at extremely high risk. "People our age are dead," Muhammad Ali points out the stark reality. "Our mountain companions have a short life span, because they work risking their lives." The mortality rate of Muhammad Ali's generation is truly shocking.

But still, he continues climbing, trying to balance the financial pressure with the risks, the rewards, and his family's concerns. "We do not tell the whole truth to our families," he admits.

⸺

If you continue up the valley past Machulu, you reach the village of Hushe, where climbing legend Little Karim was born. There is nothing after Hushe except rock, ice, and snow. Hushe's 780 inhabitants have a life expectancy of only fifty-three years. Most people dwell in rock and mud houses along the main street or in a labyrinth of alleyways nestled between the rushing waters of the Hushe River and the arid slopes of its steep banks. Hushe residents live off their wheat fields and vegetable patches, their livestock, and most importantly, their mountains. Gateway to some of the most dramatic mountains in the Karakoram—Laila Peak, K6, K7, Murtaza Peak, and the big one, 7,821-meter Masherbrum—Hushe is home to more climbers per capita than any other village in Pakistan.

There are dozens of Hushe climbers whose résumés would make them celebrated heroes in Western countries. Men such as Hassan Jan, who has worked in the mountains since the age of seventeen, and as a high-altitude climber since the age of twenty-eight. Apart from all his summits, he has done plenty of high-altitude rescues and climbed with many of the world's most famous alpinists. Today, at almost fifty years old, he is pragmatic about his future. "My plan of summiting the five 8,000-meter peaks in Pakistan is complete," he said. "It was my dream to summit all fourteen of the 8,000ers, but now the time is finished to do this task." Instead, he continues with high-altitude work and runs a modest training program in Hushe.

Helping him is Taqi Hushe. Born in 1976, Taqi ignored his father's advice to go to school and instead began work as a porter. He regrets his decision. As he advanced through the ranks of kitchen help to porter to high-altitude climber, he racked up summits for twelve years before beginning to question his future. "I thought, 'Till what age will I work as a high porter?'" He turned to his neighbor, Little Karim, for advice. Unlike most in Hushe, Little Karim had traveled widely and had a worldly view. He said, "Allah gave all these mountains to us as a gift. The mountains are like gold for us." He advised Taqi to start a mountaineering school.

Easier said than done. Having invested his own savings, and after overcoming endless red tape and daunting organizational hurdles, Taqi created the Hushe Welfare Mountaineering and Climbing School. "Together with a few others, we started by giving the aspiring climbers training which we had learned by ourselves in the mountains," Taqi explained. He bought used ropes, tents, sleeping bags, and climbing equipment and took a team of young climbers to Broad Peak in 2013. There, he met renowned Italian alpinist Simone Moro, who encouraged him and offered to sponsor the school and an expedition to K2. In 2021, Taqi led an independent Pakistani team to the summit of K2.

Taqi's goal is to train young climbers and elevate the profile of Pakistani mountaineers. But literacy still proves to be a barrier. "I can't express my words and vision in front of influential people," he said. He dreams of replacing the old equipment left over from foreign expeditions with new, state-of-the-art gear for his teams. "Climbing is not tough," he blithely stated. "The only difficulty is resources."

One Hushe climber who benefited from Taqi's school is Ali Durrani; he led all-Pakistani teams on Broad Peak and K2. Ali doesn't use supplemental oxygen on his climbs and even enjoyed a cigarette on the summit of K2 in 2021. But he lacks technical ice-climbing skills, or as he calls it, "blue ice training." Ali is ambitious, but he's also practical, which is why most of his climbing is in support of foreign teams. "We are poor people, 90 percent of our people are impoverished," he explained in an interview in 2021. "And due to COVID we did not earn in 2020."

But it's not only COVID-19 that has interrupted the earning potential of Pakistani climbers. The terror attacks of September 11, 2001, sent a chill around the world, particularly in the Pashtun tribal areas along the border between Pakistan and Afghanistan. This region had strong connections to the Taliban fighters who retreated from Afghanistan to regroup for future wars. As a result, the numbers of climbers and trekkers coming to the Karakoram dropped significantly after 9/11.

Equally catastrophic was the 2013 massacre of eleven climbers in the Diamir Valley on the west side of Nanga Parbat. The terrorists were never prosecuted, tourism in Pakistan collapsed, and climbing expeditions dwindled to a trickle for a time. The Gilgit Baltistan police department subsequently created a special unit designed to accompany and protect foreign expeditions in Pakistan, but the economic impact on peace-loving and welcoming communities far from the terrorist tensions was devastating.

One reliable source of employment is the ongoing war with India. Many young men who grew up in Pakistan's high mountain villages are now working with the army near the Siachen Glacier, where they live six months at a time in a state of perpetual readiness to defend. Living in rudimentary plastic igloos at 5,400 meters, they guard the border with India in a stand-off that has lasted decades, learning many mountain skills in the process.

Hushe mountaineer Yousuf Ali, who is now in his early fifties, spent his younger years fighting along the disputed Line of Control between India and Pakistan. The life-altering experience prepared him for the high-altitude work he's done ever since. He has climbed many Pakistani giants and has carried loads on so many expeditions to Gasherbrum II that he can't keep them all straight in his mind. "Even though I summited K2, the Kargil War was much more difficult," he said. Probably an understatement. American alpinist Steve Swenson recalled seeing the results of that war when he was in northern Pakistan in 1999. "I watched busloads of bloody, bandaged Pakistani soldiers fresh from the battlefield," he wrote. "I had never seen such a vivid display of the horrors of war. Witnessing these wounded young men, many of whom looked like they were teenagers, overwhelmed me."

And yet, Yousuf remains a patriot. "I want to serve my country as long as I can," he said. "Dying is not a problem as long as it's for a cause. I want to do something big in life." Many would argue he already has.

Like Yousuf, Haji Rosi continues to climb well into his fifties, not only because he *loves* to climb, but because he *needs* to climb; he has seven children. Working on expeditions since 1988, he now refers to himself as an "*old high porter.*" He explained, "My family says I am old now and cannot reach summits, but even as old as a lion gets, he does not lose his footing."

Many Pakistani climbers are optimistic about their future, confident their line of work is gaining more respect, more pay, and more support to counteract the risks. Fazal Ali from Shimshal does not share that optimism. Maybe because Shimshal has seen more than its share of tragedy in the mountains, going back to Amir Mehdi's 1954 experience on K2.

Fazal is a highly accomplished climber whose résumé includes three K2 summits, one without supplemental oxygen. He is also a patriot. "To raise the flag of Pakistan on these mighty peaks is a major factor," he said. But pride for his country isn't enough. Fazal has climbed with famous foreigners for years—alpinists such as Gerlinde Kaltenbrunner, Edurne Pasaban, and Ralf

Dujmovits—and he believes that, with the right financial support, Pakistanis could equal their accomplishments.

He pointed out that the best Pakistani climbers, like Rajab Shah, might receive the Presidential Award for their climbs, but are rarely compensated with more tangible rewards. Presidential Awards don't pay the bills. Instead of awards, Fazal Ali lobbies for life and injury insurance for professional high-altitude climbers.

"Our people are strong and fit," he said. "I have worked with strong foreigners, and no one is more capable than our Pakistani climbers." But when he's not on expedition, Fazal does not return to a personal fitness coach, a climbing gym, a training program, and a sponsor contract. Fazal returns to Shimshal. "I maintain my fitness by working in the fields," he explained.

Shimshal climber Shaheen Baig is also skeptical about the future. A survivor of many high-altitude expeditions, including the 2008 K2 disaster, he is now committed to training the next generation of Pakistanis—both boys and girls—together with Qudrat Ali. Their Shimshal Mountaineering School is noteworthy for its focus on empowering upcoming alpinists by teaching them the basics and helping them understand the balance between their skills and their ambitions.

Both men grew up in Shimshal before the jeep road was built. Qudrat used to walk for days to his high school in Gilgit—a distance of roughly 125 miles. On the way home, he would pick up bits of work as a porter from Passu to Shimshal.

Shaheen and Qudrat insist that the focus of their mountaineering school is safety, instilling the mindset needed to excel in the profession. "This includes knowing when to turn back," Qudrat told Pakistani writer Kamran Ali. As usual, the problem is money. The building that houses the mountaineering training school was funded by Simone Moro and other Italian sponsors, but the training is self-financed by Shaheen and Qudrat.

Simone became involved because he was impressed with the gender equity. "So open-minded, girls and boys were treated as equal," he observed. The school taught, led, and sponsored eight Shimshali girls—Dur Begum, Farzana Faisal, Shakila Numa, Takht Bika, Hafiza Bano, Mera Jabeen, Hamida Bibi, and Gohar Nigar—on the first winter ascent of 6,050-meter Manglik Sar. Qudrat also summited a 6,000-meter peak with his daughter, Sohana, and plans to climb an 8,000-meter peak with her. But Shaheen isn't encouraging his children to follow in his footsteps. He said their diet and soft lifestyle are vastly different from the much harder life he had, creating an enhanced risk factor for them, particularly if they want to climb as a profession.

Most Pakistani climbers are clear-sighted about the evolving high-altitude scene in Pakistan. "I used to hear about foreign climbers early on, about them opening routes along with Pakistani high porters who would accompany them, but this has now changed," said Shimshal climber Abdul Joshi. "Since the profession became commercial, things are different. . . . Pakistanis and Nepalis do the work, but recognition is given to those who have paid money. Practically these foreigners are not climbers at all because they cannot do anything on their own." There was a note of bitterness in his comments.

The tiny Balti village of Sadpara radiates layer upon layer of color: the lush green of poplar forests, the tawny gold of ripening grain fields, the towering sandy-hued peaks that encircle the valley. Each autumn the valley explodes in brilliance as thousands of leaves shimmer in the low-angle sunlight that filters in over the ridgelines, now frosted a startling white. At 2,600 meters, Sadpara is an ideal training ground for climbers. In fact, almost twenty climbers currently working in Pakistan's highest mountains are originally from that region.

One of the first climbers to make a name for himself was Hassan Asad Sadpara, the first Pakistani to climb six 8,000ers, including one outside his country—Everest. And he did all except Everest without supplemental oxygen. Before he died of cancer in 2016, he achieved the dream of many Pakistani climbers—an education for his children.

His brother Sadiq, first learned to move on steep ground by carrying loads of wood on his back across the slippery slopes above the village. Sadiq's introduction to climbing took place in 1999, when he summited Gasherbrum I on his first attempt. For the next twenty-two years, Sadiq worked as a high-altitude climber, with teams from Poland, France, Italy, and elsewhere. He has climbed all of Pakistan's 8,000ers, including Gasherbrum II a whopping six times. But he still needs to supplement his income with a small shop selling used mountaineering gear, as well as growing and selling potatoes, and herding his livestock.

It's important to acknowledge the financial challenges that Pakistani climbers face. Their performances are staggering, especially when you consider the lack of formal training and the absence of good equipment. Everything is secondhand and worn: jackets, boots, mitts, crampons. "I buy secondhand stuff on discount," Ali Musa Sadpara explained. "One pair of shoes costs me 2-300,000 pkr ($1,000). Down suits are also expensive. A full kit will cost me 1.5 million pkr ($7,500) which would take me over three years to earn. If I buy these things, I cannot run my house."

Muhammad Hassan undoubtedly couldn't afford these things either. As the porter lay dying on the upper slopes of K2 on July 27, 2023, dozens of climbers who climbed over and around him for three solid hours on their way to the summit and back noted that he was terribly ill-equipped. Muhammad's priority hadn't been a down suit or sturdy mitts: it had been to earn money to treat his ailing mother. Shamefully, no one showed enough respect or compassion for this man to assist him to lower altitudes although such action may have saved his life. Muhammad Hassan's first foray into the Bottleneck to help fix lines was his last.

Ali Raza Sadpara, the mountaineer recognized by Little Hussain as one of the best in Pakistan, had climbed 8,000-meter peaks a staggering seventeen times—more than any Pakistani, living or deceased. Black hair—and lots of it—peeked out from under his hat, down the side of his face, culminating in an impressive beard. A wide grin softened his expressions.

An only son, Ali Raza was encouraged by his father to go to school and avoid the temptations of the mountains. But the school was destroyed by fire when he was in second grade, abruptly ending his education. Ali Raza joined his friends in the hills. "As children we were shepherds, which helped us acclimatize in the future," he explained. "Small peaks of 4,000 to 6,000 meters are located here, so we used to climb those hills on a daily basis tending to our livestock." One thing led to another, and when he was sixteen years old, he worked as a low-level porter on the Concordia Glacier. "Seeing K2 and Broad Peak made me think I could also climb these mammoth mountains," he said. The following year he carried loads on Gasherbrum II, and two years later, he got his chance.

"In 1986 I worked as a high-altitude porter on K2. . . . I did not even know how to wear a crampon or how to use the other equipment." He subsequently went on to climb with people from all over the world. "After working with us, the foreigners see that we are as good as the Nepalese," he said.

There is one area of high-altitude climbing he learned to avoid: winter. "With Muhammad Ali Sadpara—Sadpara's most famous climber—I went on a winter expedition to Broad Peak," he said. "We attempted it thrice but failed. The wind picked us up, and although we were on the ropes, it blew us away. Thankfully the ropes did not break. We lay there for two hours before the winds died down and we could finally reach Camp 2." Seeing the harsh winter conditions on Broad Peak, Ali Raza decided to forgo the pleasure in the future. Otherwise, as he succinctly said, "death becomes inevitable."

Optimistic about the field of mountaineering, Ali Raza encouraged three of his four sons to climb high. At fifty years of age, his only regret was his lack of sponsors. "Had I got them I would have climbed the fourteen 8,000-meter peaks," he said. "I only managed to summit mountains in Pakistan, and I did those seventeen times." In a 2021 conversation, he indicated that he had three to four more years of climbing left in him, and he had some specific plans in mind. "If I get a sponsor, I think I can climb all five of the 8,000-meter peaks in Pakistan in a single season." But he added that if that wasn't possible, he was happy to think of others in his village. "Making way for the next generation is critical," he said.

The following summer, Ali Raza was training for a K2 expedition when he was critically injured in a fall. He died in the Skardu hospital a few weeks later. Pakistan's mountaineering community was shocked by this premature death of one of Pakistan's finest climbers, a man committed to coaching the next generation.

Pakistan's young superstar climber Sirbaz Khan was devastated by the news about his friend, fondly referring to Ali Raza as *ustaadon ka ustaad*—teacher of teachers.

⁕⁕⁕

When you consider the number of world-class climbers hailing from small villages like Sadpara, and the amount of experience resting in people such as Ali Raza and others, it seems terribly unfair that Pakistani climbers still have to learn on the job. Yet that's the case, since there is little organizational or financial support for training programs.

Murtaza Sadpara started climbing in 2021. "I had no training whatsoever," he said. "I just had this desire to get into the field so I climbed Gasherbrum II with Ali Raza. He taught me as we proceeded up the mountain. Next year

I will summit K2. I will try to learn a few things by then." He added, "To stay fit, I break rocks for a living."

Imtiaz Hussain Sadpara, nephew of Muhammad Ali Sadpara, also started to make his living breaking rocks to build roads—a brutal job that paid poorly. His first job as a high-altitude climber was in 2017 at the age of twenty-nine on Broad Peak. He reached the summit with his uncle. When he returned to base camp, additional clients who had not yet summited asked Imtiaz to go back up with them. Ali Sadpara told him, "If you can do it, then go for it." So Imtiaz did, climbing Broad Peak twice on his first expedition.

When he climbed K2 in 2018, Imtiaz was surprised that the work was easier than on Broad Peak. "I was with the rope-fixing team, together with one Sherpa and two Pakistanis," he explained. "On Broad Peak, there were a lot of supplies that had to be carried up. On K2, we only had ropes to carry since we were with the fixing team."

To date, Imtiaz has climbed Broad Peak three times and K2 once, all without supplemental oxygen. But when asked about his real love, he said, "I want to go on routes where there is rock climbing." There are countless opportunities for first ascents or new routes on the steep, technical 6,000- and 7,000-meter peaks in Pakistan, but first ascents of more difficult, lower peaks don't pay. Sponsors don't exist. Consequently, and despite his personal passion, Imtiaz's workplace is on the normal routes of the 8,000-meter peaks.

Another of Ali Sadpara's nephews, Muhammad Sharif Sadpara, spent his youth with the Pakistani Army on the Siachen Glacier. After fifteen years Sharif was looking for something different; his uncle suggested mountaineering. In 2021 he summited K2, on his first attempt.

"I had heard about the Bottleneck and I asked the Sherpa 'What is this Bottleneck and where is it?'" he said. "He told me we had crossed it ninety minutes ago."

It's a shame that dozens of world-class climbers from places like Hushe, Machulu, Shimshal, Sadpara, and more are still unknown. These are strong, motivated, ambitious mountaineers. But their training is basic. Their secondhand equipment is outdated. Their families are poor. They look to their Sherpa counterparts in Nepal with envy. What they would give for the same training facilities, the same sponsorship opportunities, similar education levels—an equal playing field.

CHAPTER ELEVEN

Sadpara Climbers— Masters of Winter

My father is with Allah now. He is safe. I go only to find answers and to re-trace those last steps—to see what he might have seen. To see if he left any signs for me to follow. If there is anything he wants me to know.

—SAJID SADPARA, *Explorersweb.com, June 25, 2021*

Sadpara, as we have seen, has produced a strong showing of ambitious and talented high-altitude climbers. Is it the elevation? The difficult living conditions? The proud and honorable mountaineering heritage? Probably all of the above. But from that impressive group one climber stood out—Muhammad Ali Sadpara. Known simply as Ali Sadpara, he transcended local lore, regional recognition, and even his status as a Pakistani hero. When Ali Sadpara disappeared on K2 in February 2021, he became a tragic symbol far beyond his country's boundaries. The entire mountaineering world mourned his death.

Ali Sadpara was born on February 2, 1976, the youngest of eleven children, eight of whom didn't survive childhood. As a boy, he worked with his father, Haji Asad, and his older brother, Nemat Ali, in the pastures above the village, shepherding livestock. He studied the Koran with his sister, Malika, and mother, Fiza. He attended primary school in Sadpara, but since there were no other educational opportunities in the village, his father moved the family to the village of Sundus near Skardu so the children could continue their studies.

After finishing college, Ali Sadpara opened a little shop selling used climbing equipment. Soon, he put that equipment to personal use. On his first expedition in 1996, he traveled to Snow Lake on the Biafo Glacier with Sadpara legend Ali Raza, who immediately recognized the young man's natural talents. The following year, Ali Sadpara married Fatima, the daughter of Haji Muhammad Hussain, another Sadpara mountaineer.

Ali Sadpara's physical abilities and his natural intelligence were complemented by a temperament that was both inquisitive and sincere. He warmed to people, and they responded. His smile could light up a tent.

After some basic training from Ali Raza, Ali Sadpara landed his first high-altitude job on a Korean cleanup expedition to K2, removing garbage and old fixed lines from the mountain. Rescue work soon followed on Latok and Nanga Parbat. In 2006 he hoisted the green crescent flag on his first summit: 7,029-meter Spantik Peak. When he climbed Gasherbrum II later that year, his future was assured. Nanga Parbat—one of the deadliest mountains in the world—followed, then Mustagh Ata in China, Nanga Parbat a second time, and in 2010, Gasherbrum I.

In 2011, he decided to brave the thin, cold winter air at 8,000 meters. Decades earlier, Polish mountaineer Andrzej Zawada had launched the idea of climbing 8,000ers in winter. Throughout the 1980s, Polish climbers brought their strength, their climbing skills, and a level of toughness honed in the harsh conditions of postwar Poland to the Himalaya. They succeeded in making first winter ascents of most of the 8,000ers. But the Karakoram was another challenge altogether: farther north, with colder temperatures and terrifying winds.

The Karakoram winter had flummoxed the Poles, and all teams that followed them. But as the last Nepali 8,000er fell in the winter of 2009 to Russian Denis Urubko and Italian Simone Moro, Pakistan's mountains beckoned. And while Polish expeditions had been coming to the Karakoram since 1987, only in the twenty-first century did the area become "popular" in winter. As popular as you can get, at least, with temperatures dipping to −75°F.

A Polish expedition led by Artur Hajzer headed to Broad Peak in March 2011. This was intended to be next in a long line of winter triumphs for the

Polish "ice warriors." Two Sadpara climbers were with them on the trip: Ali Raza and Ali Sadpara.

Dr. Robert Szymczak, a Polish alpinist and high-altitude medicine specialist, hinted at the conditions: "Several hours spent in two small two-person assault tents, three people in each, penetrating humidity and no space, time or energy for cooking can suck out energy and motivation. It was a night when a man starts to chant a mantra, but it was not 'Om mani padme um,' but 'What the f . . . am I doing here?'"

The first summit bid began on March 7. When Artur, Robert, Krzysztof Starek, and Ali Sadpara arrived at Camp 2, they discovered both tents had blown away. "We sleep in what is left of the salvaged tents," Artur said. Rafał Fronia was monitoring the situation from base camp: "At the moment in C2 there is wind blowing with 100 km/h. . . . A hard night awaits them . . . but the motto of our expedition is: Hope freezes last."

It was a restless night, sitting up in the remains of a tattered tent abandoned by some previous expedition: no floor, drifting snow, and nearly –50°F temperatures. The climbers couldn't even crawl into their sleeping bags.

Ali Raza was the first to head back down the mountain, with frostbite in his toes. At 3 a.m., Ali Sadpara retreated as well, when frostbite crept into his extremities. The two Poles made a valiant attempt to continue up at around 5 a.m. but soon turned around.

Back in base camp, they waited—the all-too-familiar winter waiting game. Storm after storm pinned them down. On March 14 the weather cleared enough for another stab at the summit. Winds of thirty miles per hour battered the three Poles and two Pakistanis as they approached Camp 3, while above them stretched a spectacular lenticular cloud that could mean only one thing: even stronger winds at 8,000 meters.

Ultimately, the 2011 Broad Peak winter expedition failed. It was a harsh introduction to winter climbing for Ali Sadpara; his frostbite would bother him on every subsequent expedition. But he wasn't discouraged. If anything, he was even more intrigued with the unique "art of suffering" that winter provided.

The following February he joined Artur Hajzer's three-person team on Gasherbrum I. Working with Ali Sadpara and the Poles was Shaheen Baig. While Ali Sadpara and Shaheen were technically hired as high-altitude staff, they functioned as full members of the team. When Polish teams had first ventured to the Himalaya back in the 1980s, they had come with an army of climbers, enough to break trail, fix lines, set up camps, and make multiple summit attempts. Times were different now. More people in Poland had jobs—careers, even. They were less inclined to head off to the Karakoram for a couple of the coldest months of the year. Ali and Shaheen effectively expanded the Polish team from three to five.

There was another Sadpara climber on Gasherbrum I that winter: Ali Sadpara's friend Nisar Hussain. He was part of an international team led by Austrian alpinist Gerfried Göschl. Although both groups had their own objectives on opposite sides of the mountain, they shared base camp. During the first three weeks, the Poles pushed up the mountain to the base of the Japanese Couloir where they established Camp 3. There, while setting up the camp, Ali Sadpara sustained serious frostbite to his already compromised toes.

"Ali, I'm sorry, but it's the end of the expedition for you," Artur said when he saw his feet.

"I'm totally fine. I've had frostbite before."

"Listen, Ali, you have second-degree frostbite."

Ali said nothing. He didn't want to go down. He had his own climbing ambitions, and one of them was to summit Gasherbrum I in winter. But Artur refused to be swayed. After a few days, Ali gave in. The expedition was over for him. Adam Bielecki, one of the two Polish climbers who ultimately made the first winter ascent of the mountain, recalled the moment. "Ali was devastated. He was an exceptional climber. He was one of us. He wanted it so bad. Artur forced him to leave, for his own good."

The three Pakistanis brought considerable high-altitude experience to the two teams on Gasherbrum I that year, but the storm that hit the mountain in mid-February 2012 surpassed all their previous experiences. Wind speeds reached seventy-five miles per hour in base camp. Tents shredded, barrels filled with heavy equipment flew through the air, and at the nearby military camp, one terrific gust moved a 7.5-ton helicopter a distance of 20 meters. Adam recalled, "The things I experienced in the Karakoram were out of this world. In Poland, you can kind of imagine what -40 would be like, but -60 was kind of an abstract temperature." Exposed skin freezes in less than two minutes.

On February 25 the Polish team set off again, now without Ali Sadpara. They were hoping for a summit bid during a one-day weather window forecast for the twenty-seventh. But when they arrived at Camp 2, they found nothing. The camp had simply disappeared. They retreated to Camp 1 for the night, where Shaheen started throwing up. The Poles suspected stomach ulcers. Nevertheless, the following day Shaheen headed out with Adam. The wind was swirling so much snow around that they lost their sense of direction. They were shocked to cross their own footsteps after half an hour of climbing; they had wandered in a complete circle.

Relying on their GPS, they reoriented and climbed past the nonexistent Camp 2, all the way to Camp 3. The higher they went, the more ferocious the winds became. The gusts were so strong that, while climbing in the Japanese Couloir, they were actually blown upward. Staggering off-balance in the wind, they turned around and descended the mountain, discovering the cache of tents and equipment that *had* been Camp 2, a few hundred meters away from the original site. They retrieved everything and secured the camp to the mountain with ice screws in anticipation of the next summit bid. Adam had nothing but respect for his partner Shaheen. "He was super strong," Adam said. "He was modest and introverted . . . a huge asset on our team."

With another brief weather window forecast for March 8, the Polish team started moving up again. Adam, Janusz Gołąb, Artur, and Shaheen reached Camp 1 on the afternoon of the sixth. They planned to skip Camp 2 on the seventh and go directly to Camp 3, but the wind swept them back to Camp 2, where they sheltered for the night. That evening, when they learned there was a slight chance the weather window might last until the ninth, Artur announced a change to the summit strategy. He would stay at Camp 2 as backup; the other three would go to Camp 3 early the following day, but only Adam and Janusz would remain. Shaheen, after helping them set up Camp 3, would descend alone to Camp 2 to wait with Artur. Adam and Janusz would make their summit bid during the night of March 8—an outrageous plan, considering the nocturnal temperatures.

It was Artur's plan, so we assume he was content to remain at Camp 2, but Shaheen must have felt conflicted. He had worked as hard as anyone on the team. He had carried the heaviest load to Camp 3, and would now be heading home to Shimshal without the summit. Adam, however, is convinced that, deep down, it's what he wanted: "Shaheen was one of the strongest guys on the mountain, but his heart wasn't on summits; it was with his family."

At 8 a.m. on March 9, Adam reached the summit of Gasherbrum I, Janusz about twenty minutes later. When he radioed base camp, Adam learned that nobody had heard from the international team. Ten minutes later, there was a radio transmission from the other side of the mountain: Gerfried Göschl's team was camped about 300 meters below the summit, and Gerfried, Cedric Hählen, and Nisar were preparing to start up.

The two teams had hoped to meet on the summit, but Adam and Janusz were in no condition to wait for their arrival. They descended to Camp 3 where they rested a bit and rehydrated with tea. When they crawled out of the tent a couple of hours later to continue down, the front edge of a storm was already enveloping them, so immense it seemed to block out the rest of the world. By 5 p.m. the Poles were in Camp 2 with Artur and Shaheen. As the storm intensified, they felt a wave of dread for their friends, still high on the other side of the mountain.

The Polish team reached base camp, but there were no more messages from Gerfried, Cedric, or Nisar.

Nisar Hussain was the eldest of seven siblings. Because of his father's chronic illness, Nisar had taken responsibility for his entire family at a young age. He built roads as a teen and then worked his way up the porter ladder. High-altitude jobs provided him the best wages, but at much greater risk.

Muhammad Ali, whose company, Adventure Pakistan, handled the logistics for Gerfried Göschl's 2012 Gasherbrum I team, knew Nisar well. "Nisar was very strong, a highly professional and humble guy," he said. "On the mountains he was working like a machine; fixing ropes, breaking trails, making tea, etc., and in base camp working with the cook like a helper, helping clients manage their tents, repair clothes, etc. Mountaineering was his passion as he was doing it from his heart."

Muhammad had introduced Nisar to Gerfried in 2003. "Since we first knew each other, Nisar has been a close friend of mine," Gerfried said. "Nisar climbed all 8,000ers in Pakistan several times, always without artificial oxygen. . . . No doubt he is the strongest climber in Pakistan." In an interview with *Pakistan Explorer*, Gerfried seconded Muhammad's opinion about Nisar's genuine love of climbing. "Of course he climbs for money (as do all HAPs) . . . but it's also his passion. This winter for the first time Nisar will join a team not because of salary but because he wants to be part of the project. He knows GI very, very well!"

Despite his intimate knowledge of the mountain, Nisar and the international team didn't have much luck. As hurricane-force winds hammered the mountain, they hunkered down in base camp for the toughest job of all—waiting. After three independent meteorologists forecast a weather window on March 8, everyone mobilized to be within striking distance of the summit when the clear skies appeared. Nisar's team would tackle the mountain from the south side. The teams planned to meet on the summit, sharing the first winter ascent. This would require precision timing.

Nisar, Gerfried, and Cedric set off for their Camp 1 on March 6. On the seventh, they crossed the ridge of Gasherbrum South and reached the upper basin of Gasherbrum I, where they bivouacked at around 7,100 meters. Gerfried called base camp on the satellite phone that evening to say the night was bitterly cold, visibility was poor, but thankfully, there was little wind. "We will start at about 3 a.m., we hope to have reached the summit in the afternoon," he said.

The weather then turned, suddenly and ferociously. As the Polish team fled the mountain in the teeth of the storm, there was only silence from Nisar, Gerfried, and Cedric. Their bodies were never found.

The government of Pakistan gave Nisar Hussain a posthumous award—the *Sitara e Imtiaz*—which his younger brother Kazim accepted on his behalf. "He summited Gasherbrum I four times, Gasherbrum II four times, Broad Peak twice, Nanga Parbat and K2 once," Kazim said. "He summited 7,000-meter peaks as well and started the Baltistan Mountaineering Club in 2006 to empower the youth in mountaineering." The Alpine Club of Pakistan offered an official gesture of respect: "In him we have lost a great mountaineer, a good husband, a good father and above all a good human being. . . . May God Bless his soul eternal peace in the Heavens and give his family members strength to shoulder this irreparable loss."

Given the extensive list of Nisar's accomplishments, it seems astonishing that his government—or foreign sponsors—hadn't supported him more during his lifetime.

Louis Rousseau, a Canadian alpinist who shared the summit of Gasherbrum II with Nisar in the summer of 2011, called him a superstar climber. "He was so small, so strong, and because of his efforts, a lot of people got to the top of Gasherbrum II that season," Louis said. "When he talked to me about joining the Gasherbrum I winter team, he said he 'needed to take care of them.' It was his country, and his job."

Muhammad Ali, who had hired him for many expeditions, was deeply respectful of Nisar. "If he was still alive, I am sure by now he would have completed all fourteen 8,000-meter peaks," Muhammad said. "He was one of only a few who were technically strong and able to fix ropes in places like the K2 Bottleneck. Mountaineers often described him as a person who is difficult to catch once he is above 7,000 meters. Nisar himself told me that the higher he goes, the better and lighter he feels."

Nisar's widow, Nissa, eventually accepted his death with some level of peace. "God made the decision of his death; but he highlighted the name of Pakistan. He was punctual in prayers, honest, and didn't have any jealousy. He spent a simple life. He did not feel proud of himself." Nisar didn't realize he was a superstar climber. Or if he did, he didn't care. As the superstar legend faded into the background, a quieter narrative took its place, a story of muted conversations, sadness, and acceptance.

CHAPTER TWELVE

Ice Warriors

It's my passion and I cannot live without it.

—ALI SADPARA

Despite the tragic ending to the winter season of 2012, the lure of 8,000ers still unclimbed in winter remained strong. When the Poles returned to Broad Peak in 2013, they were with three Pakistani climbers: Shaheen Baig, Amin Ullah, and Karim Hayat. The team equipped the mountain with tents and supplies as high as Camp 4, and the four Poles headed up for the final summit attempt in early March. Team leader Krzysztof Wielicki, who was coordinating the expedition from base camp, directed Karim to climb as high as Camp 2 with oxygen, in case it was needed.

The Poles reached the summit late in the afternoon on March 5, 2013. Two of the four—Adam Bielecki and Artur Małek—survived a terrifying descent to their high camp in the dark. Throughout the night, Krzysztof and Adam engaged in a long, heartbreaking radio conversation with climber Tomasz Kowalski, trying to coax him off the mountain. Eventually there were no more responses from Tomasz. Only silence.

The fourth member of the Polish team—veteran winter climber Maciej Berbeka—hadn't been heard from since the climbers started their descent.

No one knew where he was, if he was in trouble, fighting for his life, or dead at the bottom of a crevasse.

At dawn a base camp cook thought he spied a flash of movement immediately below the start of the summit ridge, offering a glimmer of hope. Krzysztof sent Karim up from Camp 2 with the oxygen and directed Adam and Artur to begin searching for Maciej.

The two climbers started out, but turned back shortly after leaving the tent, citing exhaustion. When Karim arrived, having broken his all-time altitude record, they convinced him to go even higher, using oxygen. He did, against his better judgment. "I left Camp 4 and when I got to the catchment below the last serac it felt very lonely. In my mind, questions started to arise. What would happen if I fell into a crevasse or slipped off the mountain? At this altitude, nobody will help me. But I continued climbing as far as I could. I got to 7,700 meters or maybe a little lower but I didn't see anyone." He turned back. Maciej Berbeka's body has yet to be found.

Karim would go on to climb Broad Peak a year later, but in summer. In the winter of 2013, he had never climbed so high, and his willingness to do so while mounting a solo rescue operation, under deadly conditions, was certainly an act of heroism.

Now that Broad Peak had been climbed in winter, there were only two 8,000-meter peaks in Pakistan that had not seen a winter ascent. Nanga Parbat was one of them. Despite the worsening condition of his feet, Ali Sadpara continued to climb in winter, and Nanga Parbat beckoned. His next partner was Alex Txikon, a Basque alpinist with an impressive amount of high-altitude experience. Both men were itching for a first winter ascent.

Like Ali Sadpara, Alex came from a large family, the youngest of thirteen children. With a shock of black hair and a weathered face, Alex had arms as thick as the logs he annihilated in log-chopping competitions back home. He and Ali Sadpara could have been brothers.

In the winter of 2014–15, the two were joined by Muhammad Khan from Hushe for an attempt on Nanga Parbat. Ali Sadpara knew the mountain well, having already summited twice. But this time was different. Because of the 2013 massacre at Nanga Parbat base camp, they now had machine-gun-toting police escorts. The poor officers couldn't believe their bad luck—who wanted to hang around Nanga Parbat in winter with a bunch of climbers?

A severely exhausted Pasang Kikuli is escorted back to Camp 4 on Nanga Parbat after the disastrous summit bid of 1934. *(Peter Müllritter)*

A. Gyalzen Norbu Sherpa on the summit of Manaslu in 1956. It was the first ascent of the mountain. *(Toshio Imanishi)*

B. Four Sherpa survivors of the 1934 Nanga Parbat expedition: left to right, Da Thundu, Pasang Kikuli, Kitar, and Pasang *(Peter Müllritter)*

C. Hushe village is the home of many of Pakistan's leading climbers. *(Saqlain Mohammad)*

D. Mingma G and his sisters, Nima Jangmu Sherpa, Dawa Futi Sherpa, and Tshering Namgya Sherpa, in 2021, on the summit of Lobuche Peak, just before starting their successful ascent of Everest *(Gao Li)*

E. Standing on the summit of K2 in 2014: Maya Sherpa, Dawa Yangzum Sherpa, and Pasang Lhamu Sherpa Akita *(Al Hancock)*

A. Ali Sadpara and his young son, Sajid *(Sajid Sadpara collection)*

B. Sajid Sadpara at Camp 3 on K2 *(Sajid Sadpara collection)*

C. Mingma G, a leading Nepali climber from Rolwaling Valley *(Mingma G Collection)*

D. Nisar Sadpara on Nanga Parbat in 2009. One of Pakistan's leading climbers, Nisar disappeared in 2012 while on a winter attempt of Gasherbrum I. *(Louis Rousseau)*

E. Sajid Sadpara and Samina Baig in the Karakoram, their home mountains *(Sajid Sadpara collection)*

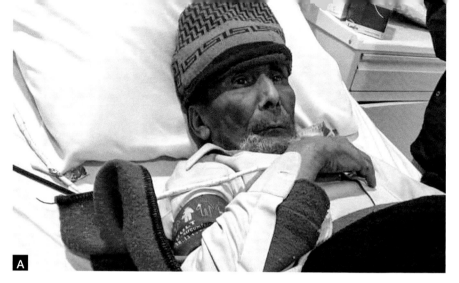

A. Pakistani climber Little Karim in the hospital shortly before he passed away in 2022 (*Saqlain Muhammad*)

B. Young boys and girls attend the mountaineering school in Shimshal run by Qudrat Ali and Shaheen Baig, with assistance from Simone Moro. (*Simone Moro*)

C. Pakistani climbing legend, Ali Raza Sadpara and two of the next generation Pakistani alpinists: Sirbaz Khan and Shehroze Kashif (*Sirbaz Khan Collection*)

D. Young Nepali mountain guide Vinayak Malla rock climbs in Bhartang, Manang. (*Photo courtesy Vinayak Malla*)

E. The Nepali team that made the first winter ascent of K2 on January 16, 2021. From left to right, back row: Pem Chhiri, Mingma David, Gelje, Dawa Temba; middle row: Mingma G; front row: Dawa Tenzing, Nimsdai, Mingma Tenzing, Sona, Kili (*Mingma G Collection*)

The true summit of Manaslu was clearly revealed by this drone image from Jackson Groves taken in 2021. Mingma G can be seen leading his team up past the fore summit toward the top. *(Jackson Groves)*

Ali and Alex started up the Kinshofer Route. It's known as the normal route on that side of the mountain, but it's certainly not a walk-up. "Ali worked his heart out," Alex wrote in his memoir. "We advanced meter by meter, keeping our eyes wide open, while our camaraderie deepened as we worked our way through that menacing and silent isolation." Italian climber Daniele Nardi, who was also on the mountain pursuing the unclimbed Mummery Spur, lost touch with his partner at one point and joined forces with Ali and Alex. But the weather did not cooperate. They languished in base camp waiting for a break in the cavalcade of punishing storms until March 8.

When the weather finally improved, the demoralized team loaded up their heavy packs and began slogging up the mountain. Wading through thigh-deep snow immediately upon leaving base camp, they took ten grueling hours to reach Camp 1.

The following day was spent drying out; everything was soaked from the snow. Alex was particularly intent on drying his favorite pair of socks—a gift from Ali, which he had received as a gift from Artur Hajzer. The laundry complete, they spent the rest of the day breaking trail toward Camp 2. The snow was so deep each climber could only manage 10 meters of trail-breaking before handing the lead to the next man. It was soul-destroying work.

Partway up the Kinshofer Couloir, the snow lessened, thanks to the steeper angle of the slope. Soon the climbers were on bare ice, crampons scratching, calves burning. Up and up they crept: Camp 2, Camp 3. The nights were cruel, but the days were improving, as were their spirits. Finally, at around 7,000 meters, they caught a glimpse of the sun. On March 12 they established Camp 4 at 7,200 meters and prepared for a summit bid the following day.

The alarm rang at 2:30 a.m. The temperature was nearly −50°F, and not a breath of wind. No one spoke. They knew what to do. By 4 a.m. three tiny orbs of light began advancing up the slope. Each climber was absorbed in his own thoughts, his personal fears, and his growing excitement. By 8 a.m. they were 500 meters below the summit. But they started to become disoriented: they chose the wrong way, climbed too high, were forced to descend, climbed back up, and finally had to admit that their decision-making was compromised by the altitude.

Dangerously depleted, they crept back to their tent. The sun came out, caressing them. They had blown it on a perfect summit day.

One year later, Ali Sadpara and Alex were back. And they weren't alone. Nanga Parbat was crawling with climbers, all intent on the same thing—the first winter ascent. Italians Daniele Nardi, Simone Moro, and Tamara Lunger were there, as well as the Polish duo of Adam Bielecki and Jacek Czech. The Poles were hoping to do a lightning-fast, alpine-style ascent of the Kinshofer Route. Tomasz "Tomek" Mackiewicz from Poland and French alpinist Élisabeth Revol were also there: Tomek for his seventh attempt and Élisabeth for her fourth. Not surprisingly, there was a certain amount of rivalry on the mountain that winter.

By this point, Ali Sadpara was well known within elite climbing circles as a strong and reliable partner. He, Daniele Nardi, and Alex were back on the Kinshofer Route, placing fixed lines and establishing a handline to the summit—they hoped. The other two teams were climbing independently on the Diamir (north-northwest) Face. As the season progressed, so did attrition. Daniele left the team because of conflicts with Alex. Adam and Jacek left the mountain after Adam was injured in a fall. Élisabeth and Tomek eventually abandoned their attempt, and soon after, Simone and Tamara joined Alex and Ali to continue as a team of four.

"Apo, rope is fixed," Ali would call to Alex. (*Apo* means grandfather in Balti.) Ali was the worker on the team, rigging 65 percent of the lines, and while he expected this would be his responsibility, he also expected something else—the summit.

Ali was moving faster than the others on the summit day. As he neared the top, he stopped and waited, banging his arms together, shuffling his feet, trying to stay warm. "As we closed in on that anticipated moment, each of us was fighting for our life," Alex recalled, "battling to keep the horrendous cold and the shrieking wind from piercing our skin." Alex finally reached the waiting Ali and they fell to their knees, embracing each other, 5 meters from the summit, waiting for Simone and Tamara.

"Just a few minutes before, when we were very close to reaching the peak, he had shouted at me: 'Alex! This time the unconquerable winter summit of Nanga Parbat will not get away from us,'" Alex later wrote. Simone eventually appeared, but Tamara had turned back. It was an international trio of Basque, Italian, and Pakistani climbers who touched the top of Nanga Parbat on February 26, 2016, making the first winter ascent.

In the following days, the entire country of Pakistan celebrated with them, perhaps the first time that crowds of people shouted, "Ali Sadpara, National Hero." It seemed like everyone—politicians, military officers, television hosts—wanted to honor Ali Sadpara and place a garland of flowers around his neck.

⁙

Ali was not yet done with Nanga Parbat. The following year, he summited again, his fourth time. He also made a winter ascent of Pumori in Nepal, and an unsuccessful attempt on Everest. He climbed K2 in 2018. Then, on March 1, 2019, he learned that two men were missing on Nanga Parbat: Italian Daniele Nardi and British alpinist Tom Ballard. They had been trying the Mummery Spur, a feature on the mountain that had not been climbed in any season, let alone winter. Their last communication with base camp had been February 24, so there was clearly something wrong.

Ali and his nephews, Imtiaz and Dilawar, joined Alex Txikon and his team, who had been climbing on K2, at base camp. With Pakistani military support, they planned to make an aerial search of the route with army helicopters. But a few days before, the Pakistani military had shot down a couple of Indian fighter planes, another incident in the never-ending war between the two countries. Flying in Pakistani air space was now severely restricted.

After some delicate arm-twisting, they gained permission for the search flights. The rescue party scoured the route, making pass after pass, spiraling downward from 7,000 meters, scanning for anything unusual—a flash of color, some movement, an unusual shape. They saw nothing and came to the conclusion that someone would need to climb the route to determine what had happened to the two missing climbers.

Since Ali and his nephews had done a reconnaissance of the route the day before, Alex peppered him with questions.

"How were the conditions, Ali?"

"The usual, no major problem."

"Any avalanche activity? How about the seracs? Any movement?"

"No, things were pretty quiet. There were two or three small avalanches, but nothing serious."

"Did you experience any rockfall?" Alex continued.

"No, it was fine, I think we are good to go."

Up they started: Alex, Ali, and Dilawar. Moving quickly up the Mummery Spur route, they carried little more than a drone, which they planned to fly higher up the mountain.

As they climbed, they talked. And as Ali talked, the truth emerged. He and his nephews had narrowly escaped an avalanche the previous day. Alex was shocked. "But Ali, twenty minutes ago I asked you if there had been any avalanches, and you said hardly any, as if it were nothing, and now you give me the details of one you barely survived."

The situation was so threatening and their nerves so on edge, they burst into laughter.

When they reached Camp 2, they discovered a partially destroyed tent. But destroyed by what? An avalanche? Rockfall? Wind? Was anyone inside? With a sick feeling, Ali attacked the half-buried tent, digging and clearing the snow. He was relieved to find nothing except sleeping bags and some climbing gear.

Out came the drone. Piloting it was tricky, as chunks of ice and snow hurtled down, threatening to toss the flying camera out of the sky. The three climbers cowered under a leaning serac, trying to avoid being hit by the icy projectiles. As daylight faded, the temperature plunged. They packed up the drone and the contents of the tent and sped down the rock-hard ice to Camp 1. One more day gone. The chances of anything more than a body recovery were growing slimmer by the hour.

The search continued, and with improved visibility the next day, the drone revealed a flash of color above Camp 2, but it was still inconclusive. The searchers descended to base camp. They tried again the following day, but avalanches scoured the route. Only later, when they focused the spotting scope on the spot where the drone had spied color, did the tragedy reveal itself. They could see two motionless bodies, hanging from the fixed line. The search was over.

⸻

As with many Pakistani climbers, Ali Sadpara wasn't completely honest with his family. Particularly about winter climbing. "Initially I told them only half-truth, and they believed it for a while," he admitted to Pakistani writer Raheel Adnan. "I told them that the risk of rockfalls and avalanches is lower in winter. They agreed at that time. But after we lost Nisar Hussain on GI, they stopped believing me. My wife has pressure from her parents. . . . My kids sometimes request me to give up this career. I tell them that it's my passion and I cannot live without it. My friends sometimes say that I am doing it for money. I tell them that if it was about getting rich, I would have been doing something safer, somewhere else. Pakistan is a country full of resources."

Thanks to his status as a national hero in Pakistan, Ali finally started to receive some financial support for his climbing aspirations. These funds allowed him to travel to Nepal, where, in 2019, he carried the green crescent flag to the tops of both Lhotse and Makalu, making him the first Pakistani to do so.

Inevitably, his eldest son, Sajid, wanted to be part of his father's exciting life. Ali discouraged him, urging him to study hard instead. Sajid insisted. So, Ali did what Sajid knew he would do: he took him to the mountains. Sajid's first summit was Nanga Parbat in 2017. He attempted K2 with his father in 2018 and reached Camp 4 before turning back. Then, in 2019, he reached the summit of Pakistan's highest mountain.

Sajid was soon working for Seven Summit Treks (SST), the thriving expedition agency from Nepal. Ali, Sajid, and SST would eventually and forever be tied to each other and linked with K2, but that story was still in their future.

Pakistani climbers gave their all for the winter attempts of their mountains. In some cases, they summited. In others, they took care of the others, as Nisar Hussain had expressed. Many endured debilitating frostbite injuries, and several never returned. Almost all are completely unknown not only outside their country, but also barely acknowledged inside Pakistan: they are recognized only in their home villages. Their efforts and accomplishments are shadow events. They weren't fêted. They weren't rewarded with sponsors or pensions. Instead, the lucky ones returned to their villages and families and livestock until the next season. The soft season—summer.

It's the mothers and wives, sisters and daughters, fathers and sons, who understand more than anyone the magnitude of their efforts and the dangers of winter climbing. Two years later, when Sajid Sadpara asked his mother's permission to continue climbing after his father's death on K2, her answer was clear. "Yes, son, but not in winter."

CHAPTER THIRTEEN

Day Job on Everest

They say we are nice guys, but I want to be the world's BADASS!

—GELJE SHERPA

While winter expeditions kept Pakistani climbers busy during the first two decades of the twenty-first century, Nepali climbers were chasing records of their own. Many of those records have to do with Everest—not surprisingly, since it's their signature mountain. Whether it's repeat ascents, speed ascents, heroic rescues, or bottled-oxygen-free ascents, Nepali climbers' reputations are often made on the highest mountain on Earth. And since the rest of the world is fascinated with this mountain and everything that happens on it, Nepali climbers benefit.

Ang Dorjee Sherpa is one of them. Born in 1970 in Pangboche, he grew up among Himalayan climbers. His father, Nima Tenzing Sherpa, was on Everest thirty separate times, though he never summited.

At the age of twelve, Ang Dorjee followed in his father's footsteps, starting as a porter. His mother tried to dissuade him, to no avail. Handsome and craggy-faced, he progressed from porter to climbing porter to climbing Sherpa to sirdar. He spent thirty years working with Adventure Consultants, the New Zealand company founded by his close friends Rob Hall and Gary Ball.

When Rob was trapped high on Everest in the infamous 1996 storm that killed eight climbers, Ang Dorjee and Lhakpa Chhiri desperately tried to rescue him. The two had reached the summit the previous day and had begun descending in the storm that enveloped the mountain.

During the night, Rob appeared to be in trouble. On the South Summit, his oxygen regulator had iced up and was useless. He spent the night out in the cold and seemed to be suffering from hypothermia and high-altitude cerebral edema (HACE), since his radio transmissions had become slurred and his thinking confused.

The following morning, Ang Dorjee and Lhakpa left their tent at Camp 4 and started up with extra oxygen and a thermos of tea for Rob, who was at least 1,000 meters above them. Their effort was courageous, because the storm was still raging and they would have at least eight or nine hours of climbing. It would be late afternoon, at the earliest, before they found Rob, and then they would face the most difficult task—getting him down.

At 3 p.m., when they were still 200 meters below the South Summit, they had to admit defeat. A few hours later, as they were descending to Camp 4 for the second time in as many days, Rob had his last telephone conversation with Jan Arnold, his partner back in New Zealand. He reassured her and wished her a warm sleep. His frozen body was discovered twelve days later, when an IMAX film team climbed to the summit.

As of 2023, Ang Dorjee had made twenty-eight ascents of 8,000-meter peaks, including twenty-two times up Everest. Ama Dablam, situated above his home village, is another of his trademark guiding routes. "One year on Ama Dablam I was on the summit and was able to look down through binoculars and see my father in our yard in Pangboche," he said, laughing.

He married an American woman in 2002 and immigrated to the United States, where he lives when he's not guiding. "I might retire in a few years," he said unconvincingly when interviewed for this book. "I would like to go back to the Karakoram—maybe climb K2," he added, more convincingly.

Ang Dorjee isn't the only climber with a notable Everest repeat record. Apa Sherpa, a slender, quiet man with a shy demeanor, has summited a staggering twenty-one times. Born in 1960 in Thame, deep in the Khumbu region of

Nepal, he was only twelve when his father died. He had to drop out of school and become a porter to support his mother, his two sisters, and his three younger brothers. After making his twenty-first ascent in 2011, he promised his wife he would stop.

"Everyone says twenty-one is a good number," he said. "I have to make my family happy." He not only stopped, but moved his entire family to the United States, where he began a second career in precision machining and injection molding. Much less dangerous than climbing, the work funds his children's education as well as his foundation, which supports educational and economic initiatives in Nepal.

In 2018 Kami Rita Sherpa broke the Everest record with his twenty-second ascent. He didn't even realize he was a record holder until the Guinness World Records people informed him. And then he broke his *own* Everest record. And again. In May 2021, he climbed it for the twenty-fifth time. "[Twenty-fifth] time was fun. God supported us," he said, as if blasé about his performance. "I used to get the opportunity to summit twice every year but because I was lazy, I would return home after just one summit. I did that many times." He climbed the Big E again in May 2022, but that still wasn't enough: in 2023 he created a new record with two more ascents of the mountain, for twenty-eight total for Kami Rita.

Born in 1970, he grew up in a one-room house in Thame. Perched high in the Khumbu at 3,750 meters, this tiny village produces a strong showing of young men with deep connections to Everest.

The son of Mingma Tsiri Sherpa, who was one of the first professional Sherpa guides after Nepal opened up in 1950, Kami Rita fell into the role naturally. In his early fifties, he shows no signs of slowing down. "If we have the will and your body lets you, yes, we can still climb at the age of sixty or seventy," he said. But there is constant pressure from home, which Kami Rita tries to ignore. "In mountaineering, you cannot think about your home and family because that could stop you." His wife, Lakpa Jangmu, has tried. "I keep telling him we could look for other jobs, start a small business. But he does not listen to me at all."

Kami Rita is candid about his role as a guide on Everest. "We cannot really carry them up, but we have pushed or pulled them up," he explained. "The thing we can carry for them is their oxygen. We swap the cylinders once they run out . . . then pushing, we pull them up with the help of rope."

Pushing and pulling to the top of the world—twenty-eight times—seems a lot, even for a second-generation climbing Sherpa from Thame. But it's not only the work or the records that motivate Kami Rita; it's the actual climbing. "If I have to say, it is like being intoxicated. For someone like us, if we stopped doing this job . . . it would feel strange." Despite his addiction to climbing, Kami Rita, as with so many other Sherpas, does not want his children to follow in his footsteps. His priority is to provide them a good education, ensuring they can choose occupations less dangerous than his.

⁕⁕⁕⁕

Preceding Kami Rita was the Granddaddy of all Everest summiters, Ang Rita. Born in Thame in 1948, Ang Rita spent his childhood herding yaks. He had neither a formal education nor training as a climber. His first porter job was at the age of fifteen. Five years later he topped out on Cho Oyu. During his impressive high-altitude career, Ang Rita probably climbed 8,000ers at least eighteen times. Nobody knows for sure. This singular human, with his wizened face, his quizzical look, and his lopsided smile, summited Everest ten times between 1983 and 1996, each time without supplemental oxygen, and once, in 1987, in winter.

Ang Rita had three sons and a daughter. His eldest son, Karsang, summited Everest nine times and died during an expedition in 2012.

During Ang Rita's last years, he suffered from a liver ailment and declined further in 2015 from a stroke. Some of his suffering was likely caused by his fondness for alcohol. He defended his drinking, saying, "Foreigners never find my drinking a problem. They know when it is time to work, I work." He died at his daughter's home in Kathmandu at the age of seventy-two.

Nepali author Deepak Thapa, in his 1996 article about Ang Rita, wrote, "Ang Rita Sherpa would have been an international celebrity if he spoke English, had fair skin, and concentrated on selling himself rather than grazing his yaks." Like many of the other climbers in these pages, he would also have been in a better position to promote himself if he'd had more opportunity for education. Instead, unable to read or write, Ang Rita was forced to rely on others to sell his services.

⁕⁕⁕⁕

Lakpa Rita Sherpa was born in Thame in 1966, almost twenty years after Ang Rita. Lakpa's father also climbed, and like Ang Rita, he was illiterate. The reason was simple: there was no school. Luckily for Lakpa, by the time he was school-age, Sir Edmund Hillary's Himalayan Trust had built a school in Thame, allowing him an education.

The eldest of eleven children, of which only eight survived, Lakpa stepped in to support his family once his father became incapacitated by frostbite while guiding. Lakpa tended the crops of potatoes, spinach, and chives, and he carried the produce for three hours down to Namche Bazaar's Saturday market to sell and trade. He also took care of his family's yaks, trading milk and meat across the border in Tibet for other essentials.

Even as a child, Lakpa was infatuated with Everest, thanks to Edmund Hillary's annual visits to the school. When his cousin offered him work hauling loads for an expedition in 1984, he jumped at the chance. "Commercial expeditions were very rare," he told podcaster Mark Pattison. "But I was always keen to work hard, try to do my best, and since I had been to school a little bit, I spoke a little bit of English . . . that helped me too."

His next big opportunity was with the Yugoslavian team on Everest in 1990, where he not only hauled loads, but fixed lines and pushed out the route. After fifteen ascents of Everest, and countless ascents of other Nepali peaks, he became the first Sherpa to climb the Seven Summits, the highest mountains on each continent. After that, Lakpa was given an offer he couldn't refuse: a chance to move to the US and work full-time with Alpine Ascents International, a guiding company owned by American Todd Burleson. Now two dreams were coming true: he would get paid to climb and he would live in America.

His financial future assured, Lakpa could relax, confident that his kids would be educated and he could continue doing what he loved—climbing. Within Nepali guiding circles, Lakpa is well known, and Alpine Ascents promotes him as their top guide.

Less recognized, but equally accomplished among Nepali climbers, is Pasang Dawa Sherpa. Often called "Padawa," he had even humbler beginnings than many Sherpas of his age. He was born in 1976 in a yak shed in the high pastures above Chhuking in the Khumbu region. His parents wanted him to become a monk, but Padawa had other plans. Coming into the world at approximately 4,800 meters prepared him well for climbing. He worked his way up from kitchen boy to porter to climber, then ran into some good luck when he guided famous British television personality Bear Grylls to the top of the dominant mountain in his own backyard—Everest. Padawa had no shortage of work after that, and he has climbed Everest so many times he isn't sure of the number; in a recent interview he thought it might be twenty-three, but some years there were two ascents, and he can't remember how often that happened. One season he climbed it twice in a week. When that happens today with some of the superstar guides, the feat goes viral on social media. Not so much in Padawa's time. Twice in a one week was simply a busy week (and a good one for tips).

He's climbed Ama Dablam at least thirty times, including once as a day climb from his house, and he has been to other Himalayan giants more than fifty times. However, almost no one outside the climbing community has heard of him. Why? He hasn't immigrated to the United States, isn't active on social media, and doesn't give lectures. When not guiding clients up the Khumbu giants, until recently he tilled his fields above Pangboche with a handheld plow and did a bit of handyman work around the village.

In 2021 Padawa's life was torn apart by a family tragedy that took the lives of both his mother and son. He retreated into alcohol and a depression so severe his life came close to ending. Local residents along with his intended client for the year, Jon Gupta, did what Padawa had done so many times for others—they rescued him. After what Padawa described as two brutal and humiliating months in a rehab center, he emerged somewhat intact. "The place of legendary mountaineers like Padawa is on the mountains and history books, not in rehab," said his friend Suraj Paudyal. "Padawa should be giving lectures and signing autographs to the kids in schools. . . . Padawa has done his job . . . without expecting any returns from the society and nation. We need to do ours and that is to honor him and his achievements."

Padawa moved to a Kathmandu apartment with his wife, Pasang Jamu. The heat and pollution were a far cry from his life in Khumbu: climbing into the death zone every season, meeting clients from around the world, breathing the sharp, thin air. His friends wondered if he would return to guiding or if this would be a kind of retirement. In May 2022 he guided clients to the top of Everest for the twenty-fourth time. And then once more that season, and twice again in 2023. He became the fastest in the world to summit the five highest 8,000-meter peaks: Everest, K2, Kangchenjunga, Lhotse, and Makalu. He then joined Dawa Ongju Sherpa, guiding the young Norwegian woman Kristin Harila in her race to climb all fourteen of the 8,000ers in record time. Still, Padawa almost certainly will never be famous, will never be rich, and isn't even entirely sure of his Everest ascent record. But he will have survived an extremely dangerous life.

......

Not all the climbing stories within the Sherpa community are about breaking records. Many come with harder, sadder endings. When they are young and fit, performing at their top level, socializing with mountaineers from around the world, and acting as role models in their villages, high-altitude climbers and guides can seem invincible. But as every high-performance athlete knows, at some point your fitness levels off, then dips. If you spend your life in the harsh conditions of the most challenging mountains on Earth, you may also suffer from the long-term effects of frostbite or injury. The only logical response is to lower your expectations, perhaps transition to trekking or teaching, or operate a teahouse. Many Sherpas find that transition difficult, sometimes turning to alcohol for support.

Sungdare Sherpa was a legendary climber from Pangboche whose first time on Everest was with Chris Bonington's 1975 Southwest Face expedition. A newcomer at the time, Sungdare carried loads to Camp 5 at 7,772 meters on the forbidding face. Later, when Canadian mountaineer Roger Marshall interviewed him about the climb, he asked, "Did you like it?"

"Yes, I liked it."

"Why?"

"Because I got new equipment."

When he chose to stay with his client, Hannelore Schmatz, as she was dying on the upper slopes of Everest in 1979, Sungdare lost most of his fingers and toes to frostbite. When Roger pressed him to explain why he continued climbing after that, he said: "Because I have no school, no good writing, and no good speaking. That is why I climb." He was one of the early repeat-summiters on Everest, with five summits to his name, but he couldn't resist the lure of the potent local drink, rakshi.

When Sungdare succumbed to alcohol addiction, he was hired less often and could no longer support both his family and his drinking problem. He drowned in the river below his village at the age of thirty-nine, apparently by suicide, leaving his widow, Bhing Phuti, to manage on her own.

......

Babu Chhiri Sherpa's story ends badly as well, but he was a harbinger of the future for Sherpa climbers. His first 8,000-meter success was on Kangchenjunga in 1989 when he was twenty-three years old. Hired as a climbing Sherpa on a Russian expedition, he reached the summit with no bottled oxygen. "It was like an exam," he told British journalist Ed Douglas, one that he clearly passed.

A strong man, almost square in shape, Babu Chhiri was instantly likeable, exuding optimism and cheer. Despite having no formal education, he spoke four languages: Sherpa, Hindi, Nepali, and English.

He used his amiability and language skills to convince his sponsor, California-based outdoor equipment company Mountain Hardwear, to design a tent that would withstand a night on the top of Everest. Tent designer Martin Zemitis described the meeting. "I remember this guy comes by who's pretty much all lungs and chest. He says he wants to spend the night on Everest, which is pretty wacky. But, hey, we're near Berkeley. We hear all sorts of wacky ideas." As wacky as the plan sounded, Babu Chhiri pulled it off, spending twenty-one hours on top without bottled oxygen, chatting and singing through the night to avoid falling asleep, ensuring his place in history. He then made a speed ascent of the mountain in sixteen hours and fifty-six minutes.

He was better known than some of his fellow Sherpas because he understood the newsworthiness of his feats. But Babu Chhiri's good fortune ran out in 2001. He was on his eleventh Everest expedition when he fell into a crevasse near Camp 2 while taking photographs. He was thirty-five years old, with a seemingly limitless future ahead of him, when he lost his life.

Since he was highly respected in Nepal, his body was brought to Kathmandu and draped in flowers and ceremonial scarves. Many dignitaries, including the prime minister, paid their respects. Tributes poured in, even from King Birendra. But in the end, his wife, Puti, was left to support their six daughters on her own.

Babu Chhiri was a trailblazer for the generation that followed, a cohort that carefully studied what made headlines, how to make those headlines, and how to leverage them once they were made. That next wave of Nepali climbers would perfect this strategy, chasing records while tweeting their way into the minds and hearts of people around the world. No longer content to operate in the shadows as their predecessors had done, unwilling to accept substandard wages and nonexistent insurance policies, fed up with foreign superstar climbers strutting about on their mountains, the next generation changed the game forever. But that change would not be without considerable turmoil.

CHAPTER FOURTEEN

Big Mountains Are Big Business

I see the view from up high—it's beautiful. But I do it for the money. It's the most dangerous job in the world.

—ANG DORJEE SHERPA

April 27, 2013. A team of Sherpas was fixing ropes between Camps 2 and 3 on Everest for clients who planned to use them the following day. In a meeting at Camp 2 the previous evening, the clients and Sherpas agreed that nobody would climb near the fixing team. "Fixing ropes is a sensitive and huge task," Tashi Sherpa, one of the fixers, later told journalist Deepak Adhikari. "So, we strictly alerted everyone not to go high up."

At 6,700 meters they noticed three people climbing toward them. Tashi radioed down to Camp 2 to ask who they were; he was told they were Russian climbers with a permit for nearby Lhotse. They kept approaching the Sherpa fixing team since this part of the route is shared by both mountains.

But the climbers were not Russians. They were Swiss alpinist Ueli Steck, Italian Simone Moro, and British climber and photographer Jonathan Griffith. The three famous climbers had an ambitious objective—the elusive Everest–Lhotse traverse, and they were on the Lhotse Face for an acclimatization round up to their tent at Camp 3. The Sherpas in Camp 2 had asked

Ueli not to climb that day, but he reassured them that they would not touch the lines and would be extra careful not to knock any ice onto the fixing team.

The three sped up the face much faster than the Sherpas since they were merely climbing, not working with the ropes. The optics weren't good for the fixers. "I think the leader felt like he was losing face," Ueli later told writer Tim Neville. "They had been fixing ropes for four or five hours, and then we climb up on the side of them without using their ropes in one-and-a-half hours."

When they caught up to the Sherpas and crossed over the fixed line, the tension erupted. The details are murky, but Tashi maintained that when the Europeans traversed past Mingma Tenzing, the lead fixer, ice tumbled down, hitting one of the Sherpas below him. Ueli denied the charge, insisting his group was being extremely careful. He pointed out that fixing lines without dislodging bits of ice is impossible, and he suggested that ice could easily have been loosened by the lead fixer, hitting one of the Sherpas below.

Regardless, Mingma was angry and decided to call off the job. He set up a belay and began rappelling down. Insults were lobbed back and forth. Then there was some physical contact, though nothing serious enough to knock anyone down.

Simone was a bit behind Ueli, but when he arrived on the scene, the situation worsened. Furious, Simone yelled to Mingma in Nepali, "What are you doing, motherfucker?"

The fixing team descended in disgust, and the three Europeans took over the job of fixing the lines, intent on making amends. They were fully aware of the dozens of clients in Camp 2 expecting the lines to be ready first thing the following morning; they would be blamed if the ropes weren't in place.

Before the three climbers began descending, they informed Greg Vernovage, one of the foreign guides in Camp 2, that they wanted to discuss the incident with the Sherpas when they arrived in camp. "Greg knew it was not a good situation," Ueli said. "He said it's really bad . . . The Sherpas were really pissed about Simone swearing." There were dozens of Sherpas standing around in the camp when Ueli and his companions arrived, perhaps as many as one hundred. Many had face coverings, lending an ominous feeling, according to Ueli. Tashi scoffed at that idea. "It was natural for Sherpas to wear scarves to protect from cold. I was also wearing a scarf."

Scarves or no scarves, a serious brawl ensued on the slopes of Everest: flying rocks, shoving, kicking, and punching. American guide Melissa Arnot threw herself into the fray, positioning herself between the Sherpas and the

Europeans. She calmed everyone down enough to prevent injuries, but the tension remained.

Ueli's team fled to their tents, and the Swiss alpinist was convinced his life was in danger. "That's false," Tashi said. "If Sherpas had really wanted to kill them, would they be alive now?" He has a point: the odds were one hundred to three, with only Melissa in the middle. Simone crawled out of his tent to apologize, but he managed only to antagonize the Sherpas even more. Eventually, the three Europeans slipped away and descended to base camp. Shortly after, they left the mountain entirely.

Ueli was traumatized. "I lost something I really love in my life," he later told Tim. "It's done. I'm not saying I'm never coming back, but give me time. I need to figure it out." Tashi was bitter about the subsequent media coverage of the event, claiming they talked to everyone *but* the Sherpas who were involved. "Not a single journalist or blogger approached us," he said. "They were simply not interested on [*sic*] us. Even the government-appointed liaison officer didn't bother to talk to us." Although this was Tashi's personal experience, staff from several outdoor publications had, in fact, been trying to contact some of the other Nepali eyewitnesses to the event, without immediate success.

As shocking as the incident was, players on both sides later admitted that some kind of confrontation was probably inevitable. Resentment between foreign climbers and Nepalis had been building for decades. Nepali climbers had tended to swallow their pride, suppress their feelings, be thankful for the work, and sometimes take their frustrations out on the rakshi bottle once the work was done. But on April 27, 2013, the insolence reportedly shown to the line-fixing Sherpas outweighed their traditional sense of hospitality; the result was violence.

Despite his anger, Tashi remained hopeful about the future. "I think the relation between Sherpas and foreign climbers is still good," he said. "It has been strong and cemented over the years working together for a goal. But this incident was waiting to happen, and it will happen again as long as Sherpas are humiliated." Ueli agreed. "This is not over," he said. "It will be a big problem for commercial expeditions in the future. . . . You can feel the tension."

In the summer of 2014, *Alpinist* magazine published an article by Tashi Sherpa (not the same Tashi as referenced above) that offered a nuanced reflection on stereotyping.

> *"Much has been written about the infamous brawl between Sherpas and European climbers on Everest last spring, where, typical of the hyperbole of the*

> *Internet, those voices that spoke loudest and first got heard and believed. And suddenly the pedestal that the Mikaru ('Westerners') had placed the Sherpa on started tumbling. The act of punching and kicking someone is inherently reprehensible to all Buddhists, but neither violence nor nonviolence is an attribute that belongs solely to any religious group or nationality. I'm not sure what a trigger-happy citizen of some other country might have done to me had I pushed my way into his backyard and accused his ancestors of sexual depravity. . . . We do not ask to be treated like someone's immaculate knight, so it is not fair to condemn us because, on occasion, we are not confined to the comforting image you have built."*

Years later, most professional Nepali climbers are still reluctant to comment frankly about that day at Camp 2. Sareena Rai, who works with the Himalayan Database—the official record of Himalayan climbing—in Kathmandu, understands why. "These guys have way more to lose by talking about this incident honestly and openly than any Western climbers," she rightly pointed out.

Pemba Sharwa Sherpa was at the scene that day. He comes from Phortse, the Khumbu village with the highest density of Mount Everest summiters: more than eighty of the current inhabitants have stood on the summit. And he comes from Everest royalty: his father, Lhakpa Dorje, reached the summit in 1987 and worked on a total of more than thirty expeditions; one of his grandfathers supplied yaks for the 1953 Everest expedition, and his other grandfather supported nearly twenty expeditions in the high Himalaya. Pemba has his own reflections on the Everest brawl. "There is an imbalance with the media," he said. "The incident in 2013 was their [the Westerners'] wrongdoing. They were trying to go ahead without communicating properly. And then sharing a one-sided story in the media. What can I say—it is about mutual respect. The mountains are about mutual respect."

Anthropologist Sherry Ortner made a similar observation more than twenty years ago. "Himalayan mountaineering was originally, and is still, for the most part, defined by the international mountaineers. It is their sport, their game, the enactment of their desires," she wrote. But she added that, to understand the actions of Nepali climbers in any conflict situation, it's important to remember that the one overriding desire is for *respect*.

Prakash Gurung, who has guided on many Himalayan giants, was careful with his comments as well. "They made a mistake," he said of the European team on Everest that day. "The fixing team is working for hundreds of people.

They could have waited." He added, "There could have been a communication issue. But we are in Nepal. We have our way. They should have discussed the issue and come to a consensus decision, which they didn't; they just decided they had the right-of-way.... We would never be allowed to do that in their country if there was a fixing team." And then the *respect* word appeared again. "It's about mutual respect of one another's ways.... We would have politely asked or stayed back and waited."

Once again, determining the truth from multiple viewpoints is difficult. Nevertheless, the years of suppressed resentment can't be ignored. Nepali climbers living in impoverished or humble circumstances had watched Westerners traveling, climbing, spending money, making money, getting sponsors, becoming famous. Ueli, a consummately professional alpinist during his brief yet spectacular career, summed it up nicely, although he needn't have limited his observations to Everest: "Climbing Everest is so big now, with so much money involved, and the Sherpas are not stupid. They see this, and they want to take over the business and kick out the westerners."

⁕⁕⁕⁕⁕

Local climbers haven't "kicked them out," but the squeeze is on. Twenty to thirty years ago, foreign companies had a much greater say in expedition operational matters, with less influence from the Nepali side. Today the tables have not only turned; they have flipped over completely. At first, the surge of 100 percent Nepali-owned and operated companies was driven by the benefits of local Nepali knowledge and access to the many bureaucratic doors that foreigners didn't know existed, never mind had access to. Many of those early Nepali companies undercut the foreign operators, and clients responded in kind. Why spend $60,000 to climb Everest when you could do it for $40,000?

Not every aspiring climber knows to peruse the smaller print to understand the pricing. There are tangible differences between a $40,000 climb and a $60,000 climb, regardless of who owns the company: the amount of bottled oxygen, the quality of the tents, even the training and experience of the guides. Guided clients on an 8,000-meter peak should want the best, most experienced guides and the highest guide-to-client ratio they can possibly find, because their lives depend on it. And it's important to have the equipment required in worst-case scenarios—specialized rescue gear, medicines, reliable communications devices—and people who know how to use it.

With more than two thousand expedition agencies operating in Nepal, however, the choices today can be mind-boggling. Some Nepali guides with an astute business sense have evolved from porters to Icefall Doctors to high-altitude guides to expedition company owners. The availability of first-class infrastructure, equipment, helicopters, and qualified guides has given the Nepali agencies the edge over western operators. Rodolphe Popier, a member of the Himalayan Database team, has watched the transition. "Nowadays, Sherpas perfectly know that they are the key craftsmen on the high peaks," he said. They are turning the business of guiding in Nepal on its ears. Few are still offering the $40,000 budget alternative, and many are exceptionally qualified to cater to today's clients.

It's likely that at this point, neither foreign nor Nepali companies could fully function without the other; the foreign agencies generally assemble the clients while the Nepali operators provide all other services. However, even this scenario is changing. Nepali operators are increasingly able to do it all, including finding clients without the intervention of a third party. Celebrities such as Nimsdai, as well as Mingma G and other rockstar Sherpas, are attracting their own clients through many avenues, including social media. It's likely that all aspects of the expedition industry in Nepal will soon be delivered by Nepalis.

⸻

April 16, 2021. Pasang Lhamu Sherpa Akita posted a photo resembling a conga line of climbers, buried in down and oxygen tanks, plodding their way to a summit. It was a scene common on Everest, but this peak didn't look like Everest. In fact, it was Annapurna—the deadliest of all the 8,000ers in Nepal. What was going on?

The story behind the photo revealed that a total of sixty-eight guided customers summited Annapurna just two weeks after they were brought to base camp via helicopter. Virtually everyone used bottled oxygen. Fixed lines were in place from bottom to top. When the fixing team ran out of ropes at 7,400 meters, both clients and fixers descended to Camp 4 to await more ropes. But how to get them up there? Another helicopter appeared out of the sky with plenty of ropes, plus extra oxygen for the stranded clients. The fixing team continued their work while the clients waited, hoping that a storm wouldn't arrive. It didn't, and a couple of days later, everyone topped out.

Welcome to Mass Market Climbing—quite a contrast to that historic first ascent by the French in 1950, where the summit climbers paid the cost of adventure with their fingers and toes. The 2021 climb, on the other hand, had no intention of writing Himalayan history. This was strictly a business venture, where risk was exactly what the organizers and clients hoped to avoid.

Climbing agencies like SST are increasingly offering an "industrial version" of the high Himalaya. Calling it Himalayan "climbing" might be a stretch, though of course, it still includes the need to go up. A more accurate term might be a Himalayan "experience." As Little Karim declared the Karakoram peaks to be "like gold" for Pakistanis, Nepali companies have likewise learned to offer a valuable product based on the natural wonders of their country. And as the clients evolve, so must they.

Foreign mountaineers of the 1930s, '40s, and '50s had required support from local Sherpas, but in those early days it was the Westerners who explored the possibilities of summiting the high mountains, and who pushed out the routes. Most modern clients look much different. Some wait to receive the most elementary instruction at base camp from Nepali guides, practicing with their crampons and ascenders and ice axes. These clients don't have months at their disposal to trek to a mountain and acclimatize to the altitude. They have weeks, at most. But they have money, and they have ambition. Flying to base camp, breathing bottled oxygen, and clipping in to lines from bottom to top, works for them. As well as a holdover from earlier times—being accompanied by their personal Sherpa.

For alpinists still trying to climb independently, the scene can be shocking: air traffic jams, equipment drops, tents full of oxygen cylinders—and the equivalent of introductory climbing classes taking place at the foot of the mountain.

·······

It's easy to be cynical about this approach; many climbers are. But SST and other agencies, are merely responding to the market. They know what clients want: a stress-free summit delivered within the time constraints of their vacation, with the least amount of danger and discomfort. As Angela Benavides of Explorersweb observed, "The strategy doesn't take a miracle, just hard work, a huge Sherpa staff, kilometres of rope, and enough oxygen to colonize Mars."

The chairman of SST is Mingma David Sherpa, the first Nepali to claim all fourteen of the 8,000ers. His brother, Chhang Dawa Sherpa, was the second Nepali to do the same. And the third partner, their brother Tashi Lakpa Sherpa, has climbed Everest eight times as well as several of the other 8,000ers. Perhaps most significantly, he is associated with Nepal's Ministry of Culture, Tourism and Civil Aviation as a mountaineering expert.

SST has been in business since 2006, but their name didn't resonate outside of Nepal until the winter of 2020–21 when they set up shop at the base of K2. After a financially devastating year in Nepal, during which no expeditions took place because of the COVID pandemic, SST was keen to make up time in 2021. Part of their strategy was to offer "double-headers," an attractive option for 8,000-meter-peak collectors. In the spring of 2021, for clients willing to pay a large sum, SST offered the chance to summit both Annapurna and Dhaulagiri in quick succession.

To save time, SST flew them from Pokhara to Annapurna base camp in company helicopters. The short flight eliminated days of porter costs, and because of the shorter time frame, fewer supplies were required. The strategy was not without risk, however. The clients were not acclimatized; two weeks isn't enough. But the guides and clients were lucky with the weather and avalanches, and by utilizing the helicopter for the last-minute rope and oxygen drop, the fixing team was able to lace up the route. Clients—each guided by a personal Sherpa—needed only to follow the fixing team, clip in to the fixed ropes, adjust their oxygen, plod to the top, and take their selfies. The 2021 Annapurna season lasted only two weeks, and all those who reached the summit did so within a couple of hours.

With all that helicopter activity, it's tempting to dismiss the season as some kind of high-altitude circus. But one of those helicopters ended up saving at least three lives, possibly four. When three Russian climbers became stranded high on the mountain, unable to descend on their own, a rescue helicopter carried Gesman Tamang (nicknamed Dr. Annapurna) up to execute a series of high-altitude longline rescues—where the rescuer swings in at the end of a cable—and saved both digits and lives. Gesman had already worked as a fixer on the mountain and had summited without supplemental oxygen earlier that season.

A helicopter also plucked Taiwanese client Lu Chung-han from Camp 3 because he was worried about descending on foot through the avalanches that occurred several times a day on the route between Camp 3 and Camp 2. He flew to Kathmandu to rest and treat his mild frostbite, and then heli-shuttled on to his next 8,000er—Dhaulagiri.

A few weeks after Dhaulagiri, the SST teams moved over to Everest and Lhotse for another double-header. For expedition agencies, Everest offers endless opportunities. For a period of time, SST offered a VVIP (Very Very Important Person) Everest experience for the heady sum of $130,000. The service included a private, internationally qualified guide, a private chef, side-trip helicopter flights to Namche Bazaar and Dingboche, and fresh fruits and vegetables flown in on a regular basis. Their website described it: "If you want to experience what it feels like to be on the highest point on the planet and have a strong economic background to compensate for your old age and your fear of risks, you can sign up for the VVIP Mount Everest Expedition Service."

But even with all the luxury and planning, things sometimes go wrong. On May 7, 2021, twelve SST Sherpas reached the top of Everest, including Kami Rita Sherpa on his twenty-fifth lap. They had finished fixing lines from bottom to top, and it was now up to the clients, partying and acclimatizing at base camp, to give the summit a try. It was as if the COVID pandemic had not yet arrived in Nepal. Or perhaps it had already left. Multiple teams co-mingled at the parties, some of which included live music. Dawa Yangzum Sherpa posted a fun photo on Instagram of herself celebrating "with legend brothers" Mingma G and Nimsdai. Nimsdai shared video footage of jamming with all of his "brothers," "the big guns," and the "best mother-fucker on the planet"—Mingma G. The revelry looked like a lot of fun, but even thirty seconds of footage revealed some questionable behavior in what had become a COVID petri dish. The partygoers included several climbers who had recently come from Dhaulagiri, where COVID had struck the teams. Not surprisingly, COVID came with them. Most teams had clients who had recently tested positive, and many had already been flown out of base camp for treatment.

As bizarre as it might seem for the remote Khumbu region to welcome foreign climbers and trekkers during a pandemic, it makes economic sense. For many Nepalis who work in mountain tourism, there is no financial support system for the months or years when earthquakes or wars or pandemics strike, and visitors cancel their trips. "Namche Bazar is among the very wealthiest parts of the whole country, despite not having a road," Ed Douglas wrote. "Yet for every pilot or doctor, there are still a hundred more Sherpas, not born on the trekking route to Everest, desperate to get their foot on the first rung of the tourism ladder, even if that ladder is bridging a crevasse." For many of those starting up that ladder, the issue is more than a season of lost profits; it's survival. Anthropologist Pasang Yangjee Sherpa shed light on the situation: "Families are weighing anxieties about COVID-19 against other survival needs. This is why it is not surprising to see people still working in the mountain tourism industry despite the risk of illness. The lack of sufficient vaccines, medical resources and health care professionals in rural Nepal is a known fact. What those of us watching from the West often fail to recognize is that for many local people in roadless regions—who are literally carrying the mountaineering tourism industry on their backs—merely getting to health care facilities can be a challenge."

Despite the apparent disregard of the COVID situation, many Everest operators tried hard to do the right thing; isolating their clients in base camp, providing extensive testing opportunities, and climbing as far as possible from other teams. Their concerns were warranted, because COVID is a pulmonary virus. Experiencing COVID symptoms at Camp 3 or even higher could be disastrous, and helicopter rescues only go so high. "I could not live with being responsible for the death of a Sherpa or client because of a COVID infection that became problematic during our summit push," expedition operator Lukas Furtenbach said. "We all know that there is a massive outbreak in Base Camp. All teams. Pilots know, insurance [companies] know, HRA [Himalayan Rescue Association] knows. Still sending people up is negligent from a legal point of view and inhuman from a moral point of view."

Lhakpa Nuru Sherpa was evacuated from Everest base camp on May 29, 2021, to a hospital in Kathmandu, allegedly suffering from high altitude pulmonary edema (HAPE). The forty-two-year-old Sherpa died a few days later of cardiopulmonary arrest, leaving behind his wife and son. Many wondered if the cause of death actually derived from complications connected to COVID. A highly experienced guide, with multiple ascents of Everest and Manaslu, single ascents of Annapurna and Lhotse, and a winter Everest attempt with Basque alpinist Alex Txikon, Lhakpa Nuru would likely have noticed the signs of HAPE before they became so severe. Nevertheless, his death certificate stated HAPE as the cause of death. And the Nepali government continued to claim there was no COVID at Everest, despite clients describing it as a "total shitstorm."

Nepal's mountain community had been ricocheting from disaster to disaster for years. The Khumbu Icefall avalanche of 2014 killed sixteen Nepali climbers, triggering a strike by Sherpas who were working on the mountain. It was a pivotal moment in terms of Sherpas insisting on their safety, their voices, and their rights, but it also resulted in a serious loss of work for that season. The massive earthquake that occurred the following year destroyed entire villages. Guides who had retired from their dangerous profession were forced to return to work to pay for repairing or rebuilding their homes. Families pulled their children out of school in Kathmandu. Bookings by foreigners dropped sharply as a result of the infrastructure collapse following the earthquake. Phurba Tashi Sherpa, head Sherpa with Himalayan Experience, who has made over thirty-four summits of 8,000-meter peaks, described the scope of loss experienced by the community. "Everything I worked for was destroyed in a minute," he said, pointing at the rubble that used to be his home in the village of Khumjung.

Then COVID hit, and the 2020 season didn't happen at all when Nepal closed its doors to tourism. But given the overwhelming economic and political pressure, no one was surprised when the country opened wide in 2021. Pandemics care nothing about political and economic decisions, though; many local guides and porters returned to their villages from the 8,000ers with the virus. Who knows how many more people they infected? And that's to say nothing of the optics: thousands of oxygen cylinders were being used on the mountains while Nepali hospitals desperately needed bottled O2 for the sick and dying.

Nepali guide Prakash Gurung sees several issues with the current guiding situation in Nepal. "Nowadays, anyone can climb Everest," he said. "Whoever has money—even if they can't climb—summits. And the credit doesn't go to the ones working hard. Only those at the top get it." But the problem is more complicated than that. As a freelancer, Prakash works for a number of guiding companies. "The pay scale is all over the place," he said, adding, "We need a standard." And not only a standard pay scale, but standards in safety, hiring, and ethics.

Ang Tshering Lama, a veteran guide who accomplished one of the most spectacular rescues in Everest history from the South Summit in 2017, understands why companies like SST operate the way they do. "It's the clients who want that fast turnaround time, so the companies respond," he says. Big mountains and fast summits are good business.

⸺

Nepal's business model doesn't work as well in Pakistan for a number of reasons. While Nepal has two main climbing seasons, spring and fall, Pakistan has only one—summer. While Nepal has eight 8,000ers fully within its borders, Pakistan has five, and those are notoriously difficult to guide. While Nepal has training programs and dozens of internationally qualified guides, Pakistan is years behind and sadly lacking in both. While Nepal has two thousand registered guiding companies, Pakistan has only forty-five companies registered in the Baltistan area. There are plenty of Pakistani climbers working hard and climbing high on the mountains, but many clients still want better-known Nepali Sherpas to guide them, even in Pakistan.

Taiwanese climber Grace Tseng hired seven guides for her K2 attempt in the winter of 2022. All were Sherpas from Nepal. The expedition company Grace used was SST from Nepal. Muhammad Ali, founder and managing director of Adventure Pakistan, believes Nepali companies will continue to dominate. "They use lots of marketing tools and are well educated," he said. "Nepalis use their Sherpa name and expertise to grab adventure business. It seems in future almost 99 percent [of] expeditions will be run by Nepalis in Pakistan."

As recently as ten years ago, most in the climbing community shuddered at the sacrilege of K2 being guided. It's common now, in both summer and winter. But often by Sherpas.

CHAPTER FIFTEEN

Gaps in the Line

When we see people in trouble we help them, even if our lives are at risk.

—AZAM BAIG

Fura Diki felt as if her life was collapsing. When her father Ang Nima, the famous Icefall Doctor, died of cancer in 2013, she rushed to Dingboche, the tiny Sherpa village located at 4,358 meters in the upper Chukhung Valley of Nepal. She needed to be there in time for the puja ceremony. Her husband Mingma joined her, but he was soon leaving for Everest base camp where he was scheduled to work in the Khumbu Icefall. Like his late father-in-law, Mingma's job was to install ladders and fixed lines in the treacherous jumble of ice.

British mountaineer Chris Bonington once described climbing through the Icefall as "a cross between a medieval assault on a fortress and crossing a dangerous minefield. The first time through, everything seems to be full of lurking threats, of toppling seracs and hidden chasms, but once a trail has been broken, with all the obstacles laddered, one can quickly be lulled into a dangerous illusion of security, for the risk is always there." He was describing the experience of climbing *through* the Icefall, something climbers do only a few times during an expedition. Imagine working *in* that threatening terrain, day after day, as Mingma was about to do.

At 1 p.m. on the day of the puja, Mingma left for Everest. "He called me from base camp at 5 p.m. to tell me he had arrived," Fura Diki recalled.

She and Mingma owned six yaks, which she used to transport supplies up to Everest base camp. Twelve days later, Mingma sent a message asking her to bring a load of potatoes. She did, but Mingma wasn't there when she arrived; he was in the Icefall.

After delivering the potatoes she took the yaks down to the small settlement of Gorakshep at 5,164 meters. "On the way down, I got a call from my husband," she said. "I told him to be careful—it is something I never used to tell him at all. He told *me* to be careful instead, because one of our yaks, when tired, sometimes head-butts people. He told me there was only one day's work left, and to bring *chhaang* next time." The pale-colored alcoholic beverage, made with a variety of grains, is popular throughout the Khumbu area of Nepal.

Fura Diki stayed in Gorakshep with her yaks that night, descending to Dingboche the following day. She rested the yaks, fed them, and helped prepare a potato field with a friend. In two days she would head back up to base camp with *chhaang* for her husband, who would then be finished with his Icefall work.

"I had a terrible nightmare that night," Fura Diki said. "I was climbing Ama Dablam, and a black snake was chasing me. I turned back and that's when it attacked me. I begged the snake to leave me, but suddenly it stood huge in front of me. I bowed three times and asked for forgiveness for all the wrongs I had done so far. It let me go. I woke in a panic." She lit incense, did puja, and prayed.

At 4 p.m. her brother called. "Fura Diki, go to the helipad. Go now." She started running, and then remembered to call the Sagarmatha Pollution Control Committee (SPCC) in Namche Bazaar, since they would have more information about what was happening. "They told me my husband had an accident in a crevasse," she recalled. "They didn't know if he was still alive but told me to go to the helipad. I asked them which helipad. When they said Dingboche, I knew my husband was no more. If they had indicated Pheriche's helipad, I would've thought he was still alive; there's a hospital there."

Mingma was cremated in Dingboche in April 2013. "After the puja ceremony ended, I vowed to never return," Fura Diki said. "I don't like that village. I endured hardship since I was little. It became difficult to live there.

When I'm there, I see my husband's belongings. I see places we visited, and it hurts me," she said, brushing tears from her face. Within the span of forty-six days, she had lost both her father and her husband.

⸻

Fura Diki was born in Dingboche, the eldest of six children. The closest school was five hours' walk away in Khumjung. "My parents weren't educated, and they didn't know the importance of being educated," she said. "My task, being the eldest, was to help with the housework. Since my mother kept having children every year, I helped look after the house, and because of that, I did not go to school at all." Fura Diki looked after their naks (female yaks), grazing them and stabling them. At the age of nineteen, she married.

"I had my first daughter at twenty-one and all three daughters before I turned thirty," she said. "My mind wasn't mature at that age. I felt like a child with children." Mingma worked as a carpenter, but Fura Diki's father was convinced he couldn't make a good living in that field, so he brought him into the Icefall Doctor fold. They worked together in the Icefall for eight years.

After the puja for Mingma, Fura Diki returned to Kathmandu to be with her two youngest daughters; the third daughter was studying in the United States. Her emotional life in tatters, her financial situation began to unravel too. "When I think about it now, I had lost my mind," she said. "I did not have an income. I did not have any skills." After a year of struggling, she placed her two younger daughters for adoption. It seemed the best solution for their future. "For about eight or nine months after my daughters left, I wandered around aimlessly. Whenever I was alone at home, I would have negative thoughts, like consuming rat poison or hanging myself." A cousin kept an eye on her and tried to keep her safe.

Then, in 2015, Nepal was struck by the devastating earthquake. People who were lucky enough to save their houses were afraid to sleep inside them, for fear of aftershocks. Fura Diki decided it would be safer to sleep in the open field near the Hyatt Hotel. She and a few friends lived there for a month until her aunt offered her work as a cook at a lodge in the village of Phortse. Back up in the Khumbu Valley, she began to return, emotionally, to the land of the living, meeting people, getting to know trekking guides, and working through her grief.

She became close friends with two other young Everest widows—both named Nima Doma Sherpa. One husband had died within sixteen days of

Fura Diki's husband. The other was buried in the avalanche near base camp in 2014. One day, over a cup of tea, the widows joked about climbing Everest—a crazy, impossible idea. But Fura Diki wasn't joking. Shortly after, she was invited to a family dinner that Everest guide Ang Tshering Lama attended. "I considered him a brother created by God," Fura Diki said. She told him about what had happened to her father and husband.

"So, what are you doing now with your life?" he asked.

"Nothing. I'm not doing anything at all. I have no skills and no education."

"Well, what do you want to do?"

"I want to climb Everest. Can you help me?"

"Sure, I can help you, but you have to prepare yourself. And more important, you have to commit to giving back to your community once you climb Everest."

He would know. Ang Tshering has been giving back ever since he achieved enough success to earn a voice in the community. When he isn't guiding, he does humanitarian work in Nepal. After the 2015 earthquake, his teams of volunteers rescued people buried in rubble throughout the country and helped to rebuild entire villages. An instructor at the Khumbu Climbing Center (KCC), he is a symbol of leadership wherever he goes. Fura Diki chose well when she floated her Everest dream with Ang Tshering Lama.

He advised Fura Diki and Nima Doma on how to get fit, and he enrolled them at the KCC in Phortse to learn some basic climbing skills. He even paid their way. With borrowed equipment and oodles of enthusiasm, they trained hard. "After KCC we did a 6,000-meter peak," Ang Tshering said. "Their skills weren't great, but they live at high altitude so they had no problems with that. At the end of March in 2019, we left for the Khumbu and we climbed it [Everest]."

Climbing Everest doesn't pay the bills. And one ascent is not a career path. But it was a start. Since then, both women have climbed Ama Dablam, and Fura Diki plans to climb the Seven Summits. She hopes to acquire enough funding from overseas companies to realize her long-term objective—to become a professional guide. She already has a trekking guide's license, but she wants more, and she is willing to train. "Whatever Nima Doma and I have achieved as a team has been great so far," she said. "Five or six years ago when we became widows, it seemed as if we didn't exist in this world. Now I would like to help women here who are interested to get into this field; they usually don't get any support from their family and they are financially not capable. If they could just head out and be independent, that is much better—to build their confidence." Fura Diki's confidence is growing, but her road is long and difficult. Now in her mid-forties, she needs much more advanced training before qualifying as a guide. "My thinking is that I can keep up until fifty-five years of age."

Ang Tshering can see the difference in their confidence. "Before Everest, they were scared to even go down to Thamel. They were afraid to speak in public." But he's monitoring the "giving back to the community" promise he extracted from them before helping them. Climbing and guiding in Nepal is still predominantly a man's world. Nima Doma and Fura Diki's success on Everest elevated their profile in the country, offering them the chance to act as role models for other young Nepali girls. Ang Tshering sees this as not only an opportunity for them, but a responsibility. He expects a lot from the young women he helped to climb Everest.

⁂

Unlike Fura Diki, Jangmu Sherpa doesn't find much that excites her. Born in Phortse Village, she left school after the fourth grade to help her parents. She entered an arranged marriage with Dawa Tenzing at the age of nineteen. "My mother just said, 'You're going to marry this man.' I didn't know him," she said.

Like most young men in Phortse, Dawa Tenzing worked as a farmer during part of the year and in the mountains during the climbing season. Jangmu knew his job was dangerous, and as a young mother, she was nervous. "I was scared," she said. "When he was gone, if I heard bad news I was scared. If there was snow or wind or bad weather, I was scared. It was like two different worlds. I never felt scared when he was at home. When he was gone, I was scared all the time."

One day she received a call from her brother-in-law; Dawa Tenzing had been transported to a Kathmandu hospital from the mountain where he had been injured. By the time she reached him, her husband had passed away.

His company provided her with some life insurance, and a few clients and a Sherpa support organization collected a bit of money for her and her two young sons. But the puja ceremonies were expensive, and then came the biggest worry of all: education for her boys.

She felt lonely, unfulfilled, and depressed. Phortse's tight community expected her to remain alone, to stay in her husband's house, and to commit everything to her sons. But Jangmu is intimately knowledgeable about the

Phortse area. After ten years of widowhood and with the encouragement of her friend Sareena Rai, she is finally taking preliminary steps to independence. She enrolled at the KCC, hoping to learn enough skills to work as a trekking guide. She has no interest in climbing, but she wants to share her knowledge and love of the mountains with foreign visitors. "We see *bideshis* [foreigners] like gods," she said. "If there was no bideshi there would be no money—in trekking, in the mountains, in hotels. It's because of them we can survive."

Yangji Doma Sherpa didn't lose a husband, but from the age of thirteen she knew about tragedy firsthand, because her father—a veteran of fifteen Everest expeditions—died on the mountain. His body remains there. "Things change when the main breadwinner is gone," she said. As she watched her mother struggle to support the family, Yangji made a decision. "I thought, Mom is working so hard it's not fair. . . . I'll make sure my sisters finish school . . . so I left school." That was the end of Yangji's education and any dream she might have had of creating a different kind of life for herself.

When her mother found another partner, Yangji moved in with her grandmother and began working as a trekking guide. But she dreamed of being a climber like her father, a man whom she admired and loved. So, in 2013 she climbed Manaslu, becoming the first Nepali woman to do so. She wants to climb Everest someday because she's sure that would bring her closer to her father.

Sherki Lamu lost her husband to an avalanche in 2007, five years after marrying him. His body was never found. At first, she found work in local hotels, farmed and did a bit of trekking. But even before marrying she was interested in climbing, so she began to pursue guiding as a profession.

In 2021 Sherki worked on her first Everest expedition, in the kitchen at base camp. She has much higher goals, but she's patient. "I'm happy," she said. "Last year at this time I was farming and doing housework. Here I am working and healthy. I'm getting paid."

There are many climbing widows in Nepal. When Nima Doma first moved to Kathmandu two years after her husband was killed in an avalanche, she met almost thirty-five other widows. They gave her energy, hope, and support.

Of course, this is nothing new in climbing communities. There were widows in Darjeeling in the 1940s and '50s too. But they were so focused on survival that most of them had neither time nor inclination to think about creating lives for themselves. They barely had time to mourn. Today's Nepali widows are often less patient. They are more confident, more exposed to other cultures. Many are tired of being perceived as helpless. They want to rejoin society, not be isolated from it. For some, surprisingly, getting into the same game that killed their husbands seems to be the answer. They are navigating the trauma of widowhood as best they can.

In some ways, they are lucky. Their Pakistani sisters in widowhood do not have the same opportunities or freedom to launch out on their own. Their responsibilities are equally daunting, but because of different cultural norms, they must rely on the support of their extended families to survive.

When Nissa Hussain's husband Nisar disappeared on Gasherbrum I, she was left with three young children. Nissa described what it had been like to be married to a high-altitude worker: "Oh God, we were always worried about his coming back home." Together with his parents, she had tried to dissuade him from continuing this line of work. His fatalistic answer wasn't encouraging. "He replied that a person has to die in the world regardless, so it does not matter where he dies . . . so there is no problem to go to the mountains."

Nisar's younger brother, Muhammad Kazim, who was also an experienced high-altitude climber, had discussed the details of the climb with Nisar before he left for the mountain. Kazim understood the significance of what the team was trying to do: a new route in winter. "I told him winter is risky," he said. But Nisar reassured him that they had examined the route carefully and they would be able to handle the technical difficulties. "I advised Nisar not to take any risk, health is first," Kazim said.

The two brothers stayed in contact throughout the Gasherbrum I expedition. The last time they spoke was three days before the final summit push. Kazim tried to call on the satellite phone several times, but there was no answer. "Then my stress increased. In base camp, people waited for them for seven days. It was a difficult time for us. We knew this field had risk, but our brother was responsible for our house and household expenses. I cannot express in words how those moments were on us."

The family waited, hoping he was still alive. "Two years of waiting and we were still hopeful he would contact us and come back," Kazim said. "I even converted his number to my name hoping he would call on his number because he remembered it." Kazim's spirits jumped every time his phone rang. "My mother was hurt a lot. When a door would open, she would stand up quickly, thinking her son had come. When she heard the sound of vehicles, she would open the door and look outside, hoping her son had come."

Kazim then did the honorable thing; he married Nissa and assumed responsibility for the family. His family was firm after Nisar's death, though: no more climbing for Kazim. He accepted his new role, but he was disappointed that the Pakistani government did not support Nissa's children. "There is no proper insurance system in place," he said. "They get PKR 200,000 [about US$1,000] if any casualty happens, which is nothing." Luckily for the family, there was some financial support from the agency that hired him as well as from the estate of Gerfried Göschl—leader of the tragic expedition.

Wedding a younger brother is an accepted solution for climbing widows in Pakistan. With Nissa and Kazim, the union worked out well. But for many, the prospect of widowhood is one of extreme poverty, isolation, and loneliness.

Spouses aren't the only ones left behind when a climber or porter loses his life on a mountain. When Azam Baig learned the details of his father Jehan's death on K2 in 2008, he was confused and angry. "I had heard that my father's task was to return from the Bottleneck after carrying up ropes for the clients," he said. "When he returned, one foreigner got into an accident and my father, together with two other members, helped to rescue him. Above 8,000 meters it is difficult to rescue a person, especially in an area such as Bottleneck. A person's energy is already so low. How can he rescue someone else? My father's foot slipped." Azam was only nine years old when his father perished on K2. "At the time no one raised a voice for this accident," he said.

Azam recalls vague promises of compensation for his education, but those promises were not kept. He remembers that his uncle Ijaz Karim left the mountaineering field after the accident, as a result of pressure from the family. He has not forgotten that his mother wouldn't let him go outside for months, afraid he would be hurt or killed in the mountains. And he remembers leaving school after tenth grade to support his family.

Azam remains bitter about the accident that took his father. "My father's job was not to rescue people on K2," he said. "He could have left the rescue to others and come down alone, but he decided otherwise, and he died." Azam clarified that this was not a personal decision, but a cultural tradition of his home village. "When we see people in trouble we help them, even if our lives are at risk," he said. "This is what Shimshal is all about. In Shimshal if someone is in trouble, we support them. I have no words to express Shimshal."

Back in Nepal, Jemima Diki Sherpa, a young writer from Khumbu, painted a heartbreaking portrait of the losses endured:

> *I picture next year, at gatherings around Khumbu, when the women sit with the women and the men sit with the men, when the children dart about and pull faces at each other from behind their parent's backs, and the cups of tea are poured and served first to the patriarchs, then to the householders, down the young fathers and husbands. In each line there will be gaps, like missing teeth— if remaining teeth could all shuffle forward, the way that the adolescents, now a little less awkward than last year, will move a little closer to the fire to fill the spaces of the ones that are missing.*

CHAPTER SIXTEEN

The Nimsdai Effect

Game is on, folks.

—NIRMAL PURJA

I t's rare to encounter someone with such relentless self-belief as Nirmal Purja. In his autobiography, *Beyond Possible*, Nirmal, also known as "Nimsdai," crowed about his "freakish physiology . . . taking seventy steps at altitude where normal climbers can only take five." Most people, no matter how experienced and fit they are, need time to recover after climbing an 8,000-meter peak. Not Nimsdai. He ricocheted from one to the other in fast succession.

Even Nimsdai struggled to explain the phenomenon: "Well, you've got to roll into it, brother. You've got no other options. . . . Even my friends from special forces, when they came and climbed Everest and they're like 'Damn, Nimsdai, it's been nearly two months and I haven't even recovered properly: How the hell do you climb those three mountains back-to-back in 48 hours?' So, yeah . . . we should get some scientist to do tests on me."

Nimsdai doesn't just climb. He parties, stays up late, suffers from hangovers, promotes himself on social media, manages a business, and still functions at altitude. "Nothing could hold me back, no matter the circumstances."

Nimsdai looks younger than his forty-one years. His face is round and smooth—he actually looks a bit soft. But he's not. And speaking in clipped, direct sentences, tinged with British and Nepali inflections, he is rarely at a loss for words. Grand ideas, like, "Don't be afraid to dream big," or "This is about inspiring the human race," roll off his tongue as easily as his military-affected quips: "It's life or death, mate."

Where on earth did this self-confidence originate? Nimsdai wasn't brought up in a world of silver spoons and he didn't even grow up at altitude, as so many Sherpas have. Born in 1983 in the village of Dana in western Nepal, he was the youngest of four brothers, with one younger sister. His father served in the Indian Gurkha regiment, but five kids was too much for his modest salary, so his mother worked on their farm to supplement their income, a child strapped to her back while she tilled the fields. They moved to the Chitwan—the hottest, flattest part of Nepal—when Nimsdai was four.

His older brothers joined the Gurkhas and sent part of their salaries home each month for their little brother's education. When Nimsdai was five, he was bundled off to Heaven Higher Secondary, an English-language boarding school. He hated it. Sick with tuberculosis and asthma, he fought with his classmates on a regular basis, generally raising hell. "There wasn't a single day when I wasn't beaten by my teacher," Nimsdai recounted, "because I was a very naughty boy."

He had one ambition—to follow his father and older brothers into the Gurkhas—and one backup plan—to work as a government official. Either way, he could "steal from the rich and give to the poor," as he put it.

As a Gurkha, he would have not only a salary, but respect, since Nepali soldiers are known for their skills, their endurance, and their bravery. Becoming a Gurkha soldier seemed exciting, prestigious, and profitable.

When Nimsdai first applied for Gurkha training, however, he was rejected. Disappointed, but not defeated, he trained harder, and was accepted on his second attempt in 2003. He moved to England for training, including the All Arms Commando Course—a course so difficult that nearly 50 percent of the applicants drop out. Nimsdai finished it and was deployed to Afghanistan, where he conducted door-to-door patrols, searching for stashes of ammunition and drugs, and swept vast areas of terrain for improvised explosive devices (IEDs). "My day-to-day life was about the battle, and the risks were clearly defined," he wrote. "Somebody had to die."

When Nimsdai married his wife, Suchi, in 2006, she became the support system for his ambitions, their home a base camp from which he could launch his adventures. Nimsdai pursued more specialized units of the army, including the Special Boat Service (SBS). He trained relentlessly. Suchi described his routine in the film *14 Peaks: Nothing Is Impossible*. "He used to wake up at two or three in the morning, run for twenty kilometers carrying seventy-five pounds on his back, work all day, and then head off to the gym and come back at eleven," she said. "That's how it was for six months."

The SBS is an elite unit responsible for maritime counterterrorism. Their activities are highly classified and rarely acknowledged, due to their sensitive nature. Nimsdai became a "Grey Man"—someone who was expected to fade into the background while doing what was required on their secret and dangerous missions. In retrospect, it's hard to imagine him assuming a persona that deflected attention, considering the global public profile he created for himself in the years that followed.

His first trips to the high mountains were for training opportunities connected to his work: Everest base camp in 2012, Dhaulagiri in 2014, and Everest in 2016. A complete novice at high-altitude climbing, he proved to be a quick study.

Nimsdai watched as a lead Sherpa plowed through the deep snow for a predetermined amount of time, breaking a trail for those who followed. At the end of his stint, he would step aside and the second Sherpa would take over. Then, the third and fourth, at which point the first Sherpa would fall back into the lead, having recovered from his time at the back of the line. This is basic protocol for anyone who travels on foot or on skis in deep snow, but it was breaking news for Nimsdai. Marveling at the way the team worked together, he understood that collective effort was key to a successful climb.

⋯

Nimsdai's first attempt of Everest was in 2016, when his sergeant major unexpectedly granted him a month's holiday from military service. With both time and financial limitations, he thought it best to climb it quickly—and solo. That effort ended when he developed HAPE, but after enlisting the help of Pasang Sherpa, a young porter from the Makalu area who was at Everest base camp, Nimsdai made it to the top. His next exploit was to lead a team of Gurkhas to the summit the following year. With each success, his vision expanded. Why not try three peaks in a two-week period? Everest, Lhotse, and Makalu seemed like good choices.

His Special Forces buddies weren't quite as keen as he was to climb peak after peak, and they were happy to retire to Kathmandu to celebrate after Everest. Not Nimsdai. He headed back to Everest, summited for the third time, climbed Lhotse, descended to Namche Bazaar for some more partying, and finally headed to Makalu. "I blasted to the peak, all 8,485 metres of it in one hit, leading from the front with my small team and trailblazing through heavy snow, high wind, and disorientating cloud cover until I'd reached the top," he declared.

He was awarded an MBE (Order of the British Empire) by the Queen, and he scoffed at the mountaineering community's criticism of his use of bottled oxygen. "Nobody was in a position to dictate to me why or how I climbed the mountains, in much the same way that I didn't have the right to dictate to others," he stated. Besides, he insisted he wasn't climbing for fame or his ego. "It was about service." He was climbing "Nims style."

Emboldened by his success, he decided to tackle the five highest peaks in eighty days. But he needed extra time off for an eighty-day expedition. When his military bosses refused his holiday request, Nimsdai quit. He not only quit, but ratcheted up the plan several notches. Why only five peaks? Why not climb *all* the 8,000ers in record time? Seven months seemed like a good time frame—one that would shatter any previously held record.

"I just said, 'You know, let's climb all 14 8,000-meter peaks. And let's do it in seven months, because "Project Possible, 14/7" sounds cool.' Everything has to be cool."

Nimsdai knew enough mountaineering history to appreciate that Korean climber Kim Chang-ho had climbed all fourteen of the 8,000ers in seven years, ten months, and six days. He had even heard of Polish alpinist Jerzy Kukuczka, who had done the job in a similar time of seven years, eleven months, and fourteen days. What he perhaps didn't know was that Jerzy had done all but one without supplemental oxygen, several in winter, and several by new routes, and that Chang-ho had managed all fourteen without supplemental oxygen. Nimsdai was attracted to the time frame rather than the style—the speed record. He loved the idea of "ripping up the rulebook."

Ignoring the rules can be a great way to change history, but it can be argued that Nimsdai exhibited some insensitivity when he compared himself to those early practitioners of the 8,000ers. They had used inferior equipment, faced greater unknowns, had smaller budgets, and in some cases, they had climbed alone. Many of them climbed without supplemental oxygen.

Nimsdai prided himself on creating his own set of parameters, but oranges and apples are simply different fruits.

He soon learned about the inflexibility of some rulebooks. Eight thousand-meter peaks require permits, which are issued by national tourism departments. Tourism departments report to government officials. And everything costs money. Back in 1990, Polish alpinist Artur Hajzer, Jerzy Kukuczka's protégé and frequent climbing partner, announced he was going to try to climb all the 8,000ers in a year. He and his team were in the process of raising the million dollars they would need when they received a blunt refusal from the Pakistani authorities to climb the five peaks within that country's borders. End of plan.

For Nimsdai, the pursuit of permits was only the beginning. An even bigger problem loomed—money. Since he had resigned from his job with the military, his salary had evaporated. He had little brand recognition and almost no credibility within the mountaineering community, so sponsorship from that sector was unlikely. "I spent a year fighting to raise the money. . . . Most of my time went to trying to tell people that 'It is a great idea, and you should be part of it, and can you give me some money?' But everyone was like, 'Who even are you? The previous record is nearly eight years, and you want to do it in seven months? Are you on crack or something?'"

He eventually convinced Suchi to remortgage their home to kick-start the first phase of what he called "Project Possible," since nobody believed it was. Suchi's support was unwavering. "I understood the risk. But I knew it was going to be life-changing for him," she said. Nimsdai bowed his head in gratitude. "Suchi is an amazing human."

He developed strategies for his project, studying weather patterns in Nepal and Pakistan, then more specifically for each mountain. He concluded that the climbs would have the greatest chance of success if he grouped them into three distinct phases. Phase I would be all the Nepal 8,000ers except Manaslu and Cho Oyu. Phase II would cover the five Pakistani peaks. Phase III would circle back to Manaslu and Cho Oyu, in addition to Shishapangma in Tibet.

Nimsdai's next step was to assemble a top-notch team. He was smart enough to know he could not pull this project off on his own, so he hired a professional high-altitude Sherpa climbing team to form the core of Project Possible.

Mingma Gyabu Sherpa, known as Mingma David, was leader of the team. He had the most experience as a climber, and he had performed more than a hundred high-altitude rescues. Born in 1989, Mingma David is a compact bundle of muscle and sinew; his face exudes quiet determination. "I will support you as a brother," he told Nimsdai. Like most Sherpa climbers, he began as a porter, but by the end of Project Possible he had set a Guinness record as the youngest person, at the age of thirty, to claim all the 8,000ers.

Lakpa Dendi Sherpa came to Project Possible with a Guinness record already in his pocket. In May 2018, he had set a speed record by climbing Everest three consecutive times in ten days, eighteen hours, and thirty minutes. In each case, he was either fixing lines or guiding clients. If Nimsdai was interested in speed, Lakpa would be a strong partner, and as Nimsdai observed, "He can carry the side of a house."

Halung Dorchi Sherpa brought even more strength and vision, with multiple successful ascents of 8,000ers. Gelje Sherpa was the youngest member of the team and, according to Nimsdai, was "the best dancer on the planet." He had raced up almost as many 8,000ers as Mingma David had.

The final member of the core team was Mingma David's friend Gesman Tamang. Like Mingma, he'd been to Everest, Lhotse, and Makalu and was trained in avalanche and high-altitude mountain rescue. He later explained his role on the team and his responsibilities: "I carried part of his [Nimsdai's] weight, cooked, and pitched the tent, as I would do with any other client."

Nimsdai approached the project as he would a deployment in the Special Forces, in which each team comprised expert warriors with specialized skills. Nimsdai's job was to get them to operate as a unit, to solve problems and to look after each other in the crises they would inevitably encounter. "With a superior level of unity, I wanted us to trailblaze through the deepest snow and into the hardest weather towards the fourteen summits," he declared. "I wanted us to become elite—to be regarded as the Special Forces of high-altitude mountaineering. And from there, I wanted that respect to shine favourably upon the entire Sherpa community."

There was no question about the quality of the team. But many in the mountaineering community wondered: Why do it? Nimsdai claimed the project wasn't about him—it was about bringing attention and respect to the Sherpa community. But his next statement seemed to negate that assertion: "I was showing humankind what was achievable if an individual put their mind and body to reaching a seemingly insurmountable target—and that was a big deal." It was the phrase *an individual* that seemed contradictory. He continued in a more altruistic tone. "Re-establishing the Nepalese climbing community as being the best in the world . . . was important, too." At different times he listed additional reasons: statements about climate change, the fact that he was a "bloody Special Forces soldier." Despite inconsistencies in his rhetoric, he insisted, "Project Possible was never just about me."

Project Possible began on March 28, 2019, with an unlikely choice for a first summit—Annapurna. The notoriously dangerous mountain's unavoidable avalanches almost killed them at Camp 2. Nevertheless, they were on the summit on April 23, where Nimsdai announced, "The clock starts now."

After descending, they learned that Malaysian doctor Chin Wui Kin was stranded high on the mountain. They were too exhausted to start back up on foot but agreed to take a look from a helicopter. After several passes, they spotted the stranded client high on the mountain, and in a tricky spot. He waved as they flew by, which meant he was alive.

Back at base camp the rescue team regrouped, stripping everything out of the helicopter, including the second pilot. Nimsdai, Mingma, Gesman, and Gyalzen piled in. It's hard to imagine the self-discipline required to go back up onto a mountain you have just climbed, knowing the risks. But they did so, willingly.

They were dropped at 6,500 meters and immediately started up toward the immobile doctor, 1,000 meters above them. By now he was in rough shape: suffering from HACE and out of bottled oxygen. They bundled him up, strapped on an oxygen mask, and started lowering him down the mountain. They reached Camp 3 at dawn. A helicopter whisked the Malaysian doctor to base camp and then to a Kathmandu hospital where he was reunited with his wife. Despite all their efforts, he did not survive.

The effort had delayed Project Possible's next objective—Dhaulagiri—and the team members who had already fixed the lines on the mountain were frustrated that the climb had been derailed. With ready access to helicopters (thanks to the funds raised from his mortgaged house), Nimsdai did what he often did in a tight situation—he partied. To raise the team's spirits, he picked up the Dhaulagiri climbers and flew everyone to the city of Pokhara for a few days of drinking and dancing.

Back on the mountain they started their summit push at 9 p.m. in a full-blown storm. Twenty-one hours later, they reached the top. Even Nimsdai admitted the effort was a stretch: "It was one of the hardest things I have ever done."

Two days later, they were back in the helicopter on their way to Kangchenjunga—but not before some more partying. In fact, too much partying. According to Nimsdai, he was still hungover when he arrived at base camp. But they were on a tight schedule, so instead of moving up the mountain one camp at a time, they sped up in a day. "'We'll fucking climb this mountain as fast as we can, brothers!' I shouted, excitedly," Nimsdai recalled, "When you're panting, you can't sleep!"

They used fixed lines already in place, thanks to a number of other teams on the mountain. He and Mingma summited on May 15, with Nimsdai shouting "Bloody hell!" from the top.

And then the problems started. During their night descent they ran into two climbers from other teams who were suffering from HAPE, out of oxygen, and collapsing in exhaustion. Nimsdai and Mingma gave them their own bottled oxygen and started helping them down. After descending for eleven hours, Nimsdai began stumbling, losing his concentration, and hallucinating. The group's calls to Camp 4 for help and oxygen went unanswered, and both of the rescued climbers eventually died, one of them in Nimsdai's arms.

Shattered, he called Suchi. She was unsettled by the desperation in his voice, but she rallied. "If I am constantly worrying about him, then it's not gonna do any good to me," she later explained. "I would break down. I would never want to deviate him from his dreams, from his goals." So, she simply urged him to descend safely, and carry on with his plan.

....

While they had climbed three of the fourteen 8,000ers in short order, the project was starting to look more like a series of rescues than climbs. Even Nimsdai began to question the viability of the plan, he said later, but he kept his thoughts to himself at the time. The clock was ticking. Everest was waiting.

It was almost a bygone conclusion that Nimsdai would get up Everest; after all, he had already climbed it three times. But Everest would give him something more valuable than one more summit. He took a photograph of around 150 climbers inching along the fixed lines, some edging upward, others creeping down. Navigating around them required intense concentration, since each time Nimsdai passed someone, he had to unclip from the fixed line, scuttle around the climber, and clip back in, only to repeat the maneuver minutes later.

Even so, he managed to pull out his camera, look back up toward the summit, and capture an unsettling image that went viral on social media. Much to the annoyance of the Nepali government, the world gasped at the crowds and tsk-tsked their disapproval at what was happening on Everest. Nevertheless, the image became Nimsdai's calling card. Here he was, on his fourth 8,000er in less than two months. Nobody had believed that his project had any possibility of success, but it looked as if they had misjudged him.

After summiting Everest on May 22, the team headed over to Lhotse, which they summited. They then took a helicopter to Makalu, where they reached the top two days later.

Boom! Phase I was complete.

Nimsdai now faced a problem. With the publication of the Everest photo, his project was awash in attention, including details about his background. His next stop was Pakistan, but the Pakistani government wasn't keen on having a former Special Forces guy poking around the sensitive corners of the Karakoram. Who knew what he was up to? Pakistani climbers also knew of his fondness for partying, and they were concerned. Ali Sadpara warned him: "Nims, I've been told about your reputation. . . . I know you like to party. . . . You drink; you play loud music. But in Pakistan that won't happen. This is not Nepal. No messing around!"

The team slipped into Pakistan on several different flights and trekked quietly to Nanga Parbat base camp. There was no drinking, no partying. They drew no attention to themselves. After summiting on July 3, they left the mountain as silently as ghosts.

From Nanga Parbat, the most easterly and northerly of the Himalayan 8,000ers, they traveled to their first Karakoram peaks—the Gasherbrums. At only 8,080 meters, Gasherbrum I might suggest a comparatively moderate objective, but the mountain is unforgivingly steep. Nimsdai chose to climb it quickly with Mingma and Gelje, and without a rope. They summited without problems, but while descending, the two experienced Sherpas were able to down-climb the difficult terrain confidently, while Nimsdai, shaking and wobbling, longed for a rope. "Self-doubt hit me like shrapnel," he later said.

Still, there was no time to waste. They were off to Gasherbrum II next door, which they summited on July 18.

The plan was working. Only K2 and Broad Peak remained in Pakistan, and the Karakoram summer season was still young. Unfortunately, it had been storming for weeks on K2. The climbers who were already there were marooned in base camp, frustrated and despondent due to the weather and the dangerous avalanche conditions. Canadian alpinist Louis Rousseau was one of them, having survived a 40-meter fall while fixing lines near the top of the Bottleneck.

In walked Team Project Possible. Flush from their recent successes and raring to give K2 a go, they were cheery, optimistic, and downright annoying. "No problem. Here we are!" Nimsdai announced. He urged the other climbers on: "Guys, one life, eh? We live it!" The climbers in base camp were skeptical, so Nimsdai elaborated on his strategy: "When you feel you are totally fucked, you're only 45 percent fucked."

With that frame of mind, and with a change in the weather, Nimsdai and his team sped up K2 on the fixed lines. They finished fixing lines above the Bottleneck section and summited on July 24. Nimsdai later seemed to gloat about single-handedly re-energizing the climbers at base camp, enabling their subsequent ascents. Some of those alpinists rejected his claim, pointing out that 95 percent of the line fixing had already been done. However, there is no denying that twenty-four people summited K2 in the days following the departure of Nimsdai and his team, crediting their unwavering encouragement as well as improved conditions on the mountain.

Nimsdai ambled over to Broad Peak, expecting to knock it off in a day. Not so fast. Broad Peak almost defeated them with thigh-deep trail-breaking, no fixed lines near the top, and not quite enough bottled oxygen. Plus, the team was wearing out. The pace was almost too much. But not quite. "I'd finished the Pakistan 8,000-ers in 23 days." He was on top of the world, shouting, "I am the Usain Bolt of the mountains—no one can defeat me."

Thanks to the famous Everest picture and his astonishing success thus far, Nimsdai was swamped with attention and funding. It was time for Phase III. But now an even bigger problem loomed. Phase III included Shishapangma, a mountain entirely within Tibet. And the Chinese government wasn't interested in Project Possible.

Nimsdai worked the phones, but as he moved up the bureaucratic ladder with his pleas, the doors remained closed. To add to the pressure, his mother was gravely ill in a Kathmandu hospital. He was juggling so many balls he felt he could explode. But the clock continued to tick. Even without permission and with an ailing mother, Phase III was waiting.

He had planned to start his final push by guiding clients up Manaslu with his company Elite Exped. But when it was rumored that Cho Oyu permits would expire on October 1—earlier than usual—he sprinted out from Manaslu and flew to Cho Oyu.

He summited Cho Oyu on September 23. Then back on the heli-shuttle to Manaslu in time to reach the top on September 27. Except it wasn't the top. He was on a subpeak of the summit ridge that many before him had claimed as the summit—and that many after him would as well. Although a number of climbers and mountaineering historians were well aware of this discrepancy, it would take fellow Nepali climber Mingma G to finally clarify to the world the exact location of the highest point of Manaslu.

Gesman filmed Nimsdai's summit speech: "The earth is our home. We should be more serious about it, more cautious, more focused about how we look after our planet." His words were said with good intentions but were greeted with skepticism, even laughter by many who saw them on social media. Here was a man who was commuting by helicopter every few days, consuming countless bottles of oxygen that could be used in Nepali hospitals, traveling the globe in search of sponsors, and still talking about looking after the planet? Not many bought it. But the world couldn't help showing interest in Project Possible, which was looking more than possible—it looked probable. Only Shishapangma remained.

After all the meetings, phone calls, and high-level politicking, the Chinese Mountaineering Association eventually agreed to open the mountain for Nimsdai's team. But Shishapangma wasn't the cakewalk they had anticipated. Storms, snow, wind, avalanches all played their part. In the end, Mingma David and Geljen Sherpa summited with Nimsdai on October 29, crawling along the endless summit plateau in fifty-five-mile-per-hour winds.

Relieved, Nimsdai called his mother, Purna Kumari Purja, from the summit with the news.

Project Possible was done. Six months. Six days. Fourteen 8,000ers.

The jubilation in Kathmandu was reminiscent of Everest 1953. There were parades, speeches, awards, and receptions. Touching reunions between team members and families. Endless parties. Who could blame them? Relieved, Suchi admitted, "I had so many grey hairs. . . . It was a roller coaster."

Nimsdai's life became even more frenzied than it had been during the previous six months. He delivered lucrative speeches around the world, answered endless questions from the media, paid off the mortgage on his house, and bought his mother a house in Kathmandu. Sadly, she died shortly before the move-in date. He ramped up his guiding business, wrote a memoir, and produced a film about himself.

Amid all the hype there were plenty of critics. "With his coolness, he has made himself the superstar of a very specific expedition clientele," journalist Stephanie Geiger wrote. "Nirmal Purja gives you the feeling that willpower is the key to success on the mountain, and that everything is very easy if you just want it. No gratitude, no humility, no trace of respect for the mountain. Instead, the Shaka gesture popular with Hawaiian surfers. . . . Everything cool, everything easy."

Forced to defend himself countless times to the mountaineering community, Nimsdai befriended influential people, including Italian alpinist Reinhold Messner. Messner had consistently decried the use of oxygen in the past, insisting on a "fair means" approach toward high-altitude climbing. Yet he defended Nimsdai. "I like people that do, not chat," Messner said. "He has all my respect."

Nimsdai's cockiness was undeniable. But what was also undeniable was the effect he had on many Nepali citizens; they felt inspired, empowered. Nimsdai claimed that Project Possible had advanced the careers and self-confidence of Nepali climbers. He railed at the historical habit of Westerners referring to their Sherpa companions simply as Sherpas—as if they had no names. "You are a ghost," he said. And on that point, he was right.

There was a noticeable uptick in the public profile of other Nepali climbers following Nimsdai's meteoric rise in popularity. They were more confident and successful in promoting themselves: with photos, blogs, videos, and postings. "The bottom line is, we [Nepali climbers] can't compete with our Western friends on technical 6,000-meter and 7,000-meter peaks, but 8,000-meter peaks are our home, it's our playground," Nimsdai told journalist Stephen Potter. "No one is better than us, you know?"

But the Nepali climbing community is more nuanced, according to Billi Bierling, a German alpinist who works with the Himalayan Database. "What makes the international news is what happens on the big mountains. But within the Himalayan climbing community, young Sherpa climbers have been recognized for some time. There are now over 70 internationally qualified Nepali mountain guides and more and more Nepali operators are running expeditions." So, it wasn't only Nimsdai who was creating this groundswell of pride.

He was *part* of the story, but not *all* of the story.

In one of his more generous moments, Nimsdai stated, "It wasn't my project—it was the people's project. So many people played a role in some form, from getting the political permission to go to Shishapangma to giving five or 10 pounds here and there." Not to mention the support he received from his wife, his mother, his teammates, his sponsors, and countless other climbers whose fixed lines he used.

So, what to do for an encore? When an interviewer asked the question, Nimsdai looked straight into the camera. "Just wait and see."

CHAPTER SEVENTEEN

Rolwaling's Mingma G

I'm not ready to quit alpinism until I feel that I've helped change mountaineering in Nepal.

—MINGMA G SHERPA

K hang Tagri is the original name of the mountain now known as Chobutse. At 6,686 meters, hidden in an upper corner of Nepal's Rolwaling Valley, few climbers from outside the region have seen it. Waves of rock and ice rise on the northern and southern flanks, but the sheer west face rears up boldly and mysteriously. Unclimbed, it was this face that intrigued Mingma G.

The west face is two hours' walk from Mingma G's childhood home. He watched the mountain for years, tracing the light gleaming gold on the snow, carving a line on the indigo sky. He dreamed of an ascent. A new route. A solo climb. No one from Nepal had yet done such a thing. It would be good for his village. "Once I began the climb, I just focused on staying alive," he wrote in *Alpinist* magazine.

When Mingma G focuses on a task, it's something to behold. His days in the mountains are etched onto his face, which, together with his mop of long, untamed hair, exudes a sense of power. Even when he's freshly shorn and looking well kempt, his gaze remains intense. He commands respect wherever he goes, whether he's punching through deep snow while fixing lines or navigating a press conference. He has a sharp tongue, and his smiles must be earned.

Mingma G headed out alone on October 27, 2015. The only person who knew of his plan was his little sister. "I didn't dare tell my mother," he explained. "She wouldn't have let me go."

At 3 a.m. he stuffed his pack with one coil of rope, draped another around his shoulder, and started up. The night was so luminous he could see every detail of the face. Every crevice stood out, every handhold and foothold clearly outlined in the moonlight. It was a perfect climb in the dreamy pre-dawn glow, each movement made with ease and confidence. Rocks clattered down the face, but none touched him.

He transitioned from rock to snow-covered ice, his crampons biting into the crystalline surface. Calves burning, he eventually stopped to chop out a small resting place. Only then did he notice the dawn creeping over the ridge. It would be hours before the sun touched him directly on the west face, but when it did, he basked in the warmth, and reveled in the rhythm of climbing the last few hundred meters. After thirteen hours, he emerged on the flat summit of Chobutse. He savored the view of the surrounding peaks, bathing in the caress of the late afternoon sun.

Almost immediately after starting down, however, he was blinded by a full-blown whiteout. It was too dangerous to continue, so he dug a shallow cave in the snow and hunkered down to wait out the storm, rubbing his body to keep from freezing. He had no bivouac gear.

The storm continued through the night. The following morning, Mingma G called his cousin in Kathmandu on his satellite phone to say he might be in trouble. A few hours later, the clouds thinned a bit, so he started down again, only to be engulfed in mist and fog. He rappelled, then tumbled down an ice cliff, landing in a shallow snow hole. When an avalanche slithered over top of him, he scrabbled along, searching for shelter. He discovered a small cave tucked under a serac and crawled in. Shortly after, he received a message that a helicopter had landed in the Rolwaling Valley but could fly no higher because of the murk.

Mingma G enlarged his cave and settled in to wait for the fog to lift. When night fell, his mother called, weeping, begging him to come home safely.

At 8 a.m. the following morning he emerged to discover a clearing sky, so he stomped out a landing pad in the snow and scanned the horizon, listening for the sound of helicopter rotors. It landed lightly—almost hovering—on the makeshift helipad. Mingma G scampered inside and was flown to the valley bottom where he was encircled by friends who fussed over him, scolding him for his foolhardy adventure.

His mother was relieved. "Why do you have to climb mountains where others have failed? . . . Without you . . . I'd have no reason to go on living." Mingma G was the sole provider for her, his siblings, and his cousin. Her husband had died of cancer earlier that year, and Mingma G had assumed all the responsibility.

Flooded with guilt, he remained silent. "My mother never wanted me to be a climber," he said. "She is always worried. . . . But my father was proud of what I was doing." Mingma G named his climb "Dorjee Route" after his father. "It was the first soloist climb done by a Nepalese so I know my father is proud. He always wanted to climb Everest but never got the chance to go to the summit. If he was alive, I would have taken him to the summit of Everest with his proud son and daughters."

·······

Mingma G was born and raised in Na village, at 4,100 meters in the Rolwaling Valley. Completely overshadowed by the glittering peaks, a scattering of stone houses dots the alpine meadows. His official date of birth is April 14, 1986, but it's incorrect: April 28 of the following year is when he actually first appeared in the world. The Rolwaling Valley in 1987 was much like it is today: remote, poor, and sacred. Known as a *beyul*—a hidden valley in Tibetan culture—it lies on the southern slopes of Gaurishankar, a mountain holy to both Hindus and Buddhists. According to scholar Frances Klatzel, "A beyul is more than just a place, it is a state of mind. . . . Beyul are reminders to prepare ourselves for challenges ahead by developing a calm and steady state of mind that becomes our inner beyul, our inner sanctuary." Rolwaling beyul is more a gash than a valley, less than a mile wide by five miles long, surrounded on three sides by 6,000- and 7,000-meter giants.

There are three villages in the valley that is Mingma G's ancestral home: Ramding, the lowest at 3,000 meters; Beding, in the middle at 3,600 meters; and Na at 4,100 meters. Above Na, there are only yak pastures, rock, and ice. Perched high in the valley is Tsho Rolpa, the world's largest and deepest glacial lake. Today, it is dangerously full of water and frequently overflows, thanks to glacial melt sped up by climate change. If the lake ever lets loose, the entire valley will be flooded.

Visitors can only drive to within a day and a half's walk of Rolwaling and then must travel on foot. Needless to say, the population of this special place isn't booming: 85 percent have left for Kathmandu. According to Janice Sacherer, an anthropologist who has studied the area for years, it's now mostly "the old, the poor, the alcoholic, the incapacitated, and those with no close relatives in Katmandu—the very people who could least afford to lose everything."

Rolwaling was unpopulated until about 1870, when hunters from the Tibetan town of Kyrong and Sherpa families from Thame began filtering in, initially living in caves and rock lean-tos. When Sacherer conducted interviews with the valley's elders during the 1970s, she learned that their ancestors had fled to the valley to escape feuds, debts, and tax collectors. "For many of the original settlers, Rolwaling truly was a hidden land of refuge, and [they] paid for their splendid isolation by being the poorest of all Sherpa communities," she observed.

The first Western visitors to the valley were Edmund Hillary and Earle Riddiford when they crossed into the area via the hazardous and glaciated Tashi Labsta Pass after their 1951 Mount Everest reconnaissance expedition. A few other groups trickled in over the 5,755-meter pass during the 1950s, and in 1959, a Japanese expedition wandered through and altered the modern history of the valley.

When the Japanese climbers illegally crossed the Menlung La—the traditional but permanently closed trading route into Tibet—in order to climb Tseringma Khangri (the Tibetan/Sherpa name for Gaurishankar) from the Tibetan side, they were robbed. "The Nepalese government, unable to patrol Rolwaling because of its remoteness, and fearing international repercussions from further illegal border crossings, decided to put the entire valley off limits," Sacherer explained. The area was opened again only in 1973, shortly before she arrived to do ethnographic fieldwork. Due to these unusual circumstances, she was able to study a Sherpa community whose members were still living a traditional life. "It was the men of the poorest families who did the hundreds of kilometres of portering and are consequently the best travelled and most interesting storytellers," Sacherer observed. "The richer inhabitants of the valley, by contrast, stayed at home enjoying the comparative leisure of following their yak herds from place to place within a 20 km radius of the valley proper, knowing very little of the outside world."

The young Rolwaling porters who worked the Tashi Labsta Pass quickly morphed into the role of cultural brokers for their community. A few intrepid trekkers began infiltrating the valley in the 1970s, but the doors closed again in the '80s, when the Nepali government limited permits to climbing expeditions. Spring and autumn employment migration become an accepted way of life for the younger generation of Rolwaling men. Women became the bedrock of society. As in most rural communities in Nepal, matriarchal households were the norm, but education for these women was a rare luxury, since they were busy grazing animals high in the hills.

One of six children, Mingma G arrived midstream, between an older sister and brother and three younger sisters. He comes from a true mountaineering heritage. His uncle climbed Everest via three different routes, and in 1997 he climbed K2, becoming one of the first Nepalis to reach the summit. Mingma G's father, Dorjee Sherpa, was one of the highest-earning Rolwaling guides. But he suffered the consequences, losing eight fingers to frostbite while guiding a Japanese team on Everest in 1982. "His client's crampon strap had loosened and my father removed his gloves to help him tighten it. His fingers became seriously cold and later he lost eight fingers to frostbite." Despite the loss, Dorjee continued guiding until 2012.

As a child, Mingma G and his friends would listen to older villagers share stories of adventures on the 8,000-meter giants. "We played climbing games on nearby rocks and sang the popular song, 'Hamro Tenzing Sherpale Chadyo Himal Chuchura,' about Tenzing Norgay Sherpa's first ascent of Everest," he recalled.

His family sent him to a Kathmandu school at the age of eleven. "Even today, we still don't have good schools, no transportation, no hospitals, no electricity, no internet and other modern facilities in our valley," he said. His sister Dawa Futi reinforced this reality for students in their home village: "Government teachers hardly came to us, or they got altitude problems, and were generally irregular. They would teach for about one to two months and then just disappear."

The Hillary Foundation's schoolhouse in Rolwaling opened in 1974, but prominent members of the community initially viewed secular education with mistrust. Their influence waned by the late 1970s, and the school heaved with students. By the 1990s, however, when Mingma G was a child, the numbers had dwindled. Increasingly aware of the value of a modern education—and of the deteriorating quality of teaching in the valley—the more affluent Rolwaling families began sending their children to private schools in Kathmandu. Hillary's school decayed. A new building, sponsored by Norwegians, remains an empty shell due to lack of students.

Mingma G's Kathmandu studies didn't start well. "I left Rolwaling as a student in Class V," he recalled. "Because of my lack of English knowledge, they relegated me to Class I in Kathmandu. Yet this was still too high. I soon found myself in the Lower Kindergarten and finally in the nursery, where the kids around me started laughing before I even opened my mouth."

Soon after finishing high school, Mingma G landed a job with his uncle working as a porter on a Japanese expedition to Manaslu. "I joined just because of my curiosity, because all my male relatives have been doing this job," he said. "I never imagined I would be a climber; rather I dreamed of being a doctor."

He reached 7,000 meters on that inaugural trip, then reached 8,300 meters on the South Face of Lhotse, and the summit of Everest from the Tibetan side—all within one year. "I found it an interesting and happy job. I could travel, meet new friends, and enjoy myself." But Mingma G hadn't given up on his studies completely. He continued to toy with a future in science, and then gradually shifted to commerce, graduating with a college degree in business. He also modified his name. There are many Mingmas in Nepal, and Gyalje is not that easy for foreigners to spell or pronounce, so Mingma simplified it to Mingma G.

For any aspiring guide in Nepal, Everest seems to be a ticket of some sort: get to the top and the job offers appear. Mingma G was twenty-one when he first summited Everest, so his future already seemed rosy. But he had bigger plans.

Becoming an internationally accredited mountain guide, regardless of a person's nationality, is a long, hard road. The Union Internationale des Associations de Guides de Montagnes (UIAGM) is the international umbrella for mountain guides. It regulates the profession on a global scale and determines the mandatory guiding standards. Those standards are extremely high. Most take years to complete the training. Mingma G began in 2010 with the Basic Mountaineering course offered by the Nepal Mountaineering Association. "Physically I was very strong on the mountain, but I had little knowledge of climbing," he said. "In fact, I knew nothing about climbing techniques and advanced equipment." Two years later he did more advanced training, and a year later, after passing a series of tests, he was awarded his Aspirant

Mountain Guide license. Shortly after, he led a team in late November on the first ascent of 6,400-meter Mount Bamongo, one of the toughest climbs of his life. It almost certainly gave him added experience and confidence in approaching the high mountains in the colder seasons, something that would define his future career.

His next climb was K2. And then, an all-Sherpa first ascent of 6,257-meter Chekigo, which he led. The climb attracted little attention from the media, but it signaled a growing trend of young Nepali alpinists making first ascents in their country.

After that, he set out for his solo ascent of Chobutse. "It was my most dangerous climb and my biggest mistake," Mingma G said later. The Himalayan Database confirmed that it was the "first technical solo climb by a Nepalese Sherpa."

Confident that he was ready for the final level of training, in 2016 Mingma G enrolled in the twenty-day UIAGM guides' course. All the instruction happened above 4,000 meters in the Rolwaling, Langtang, and Manang regions of Nepal. He passed.

Now that he was a fully certified UIAGM guide, with an impressive résumé of climbs plus a degree in commerce, it was inevitable that Mingma G would start his own guiding company, Imagine Nepal. But he is not a doting guide, pampering his clients to the top of the 8,000ers. He leads his clients without coddling them.

Most Nepali guides, as much as they love the mountains, still view climbing not as "fun" or "personal challenge," but as work. Mingma G understands this reality too, and he has stated that as much as he would like to do cutting-edge Piolet d'Or-level climbs—the Oscars of alpinism—he has responsibilities that come first. He needs to make a living. Nevertheless, Mingma G is among a few Nepalis who do both personal ascents and guided climbs.

Perhaps more than anything, Mingma G is a patriot, committed to advocating for Nepali climbers. When he and other members of the Nepali team made the first winter ascent of K2 in 2021, his dream of ensuring their rightful place in history was realized.

After the K2 ascent, Mingma G had little time to bask in the limelight. He had work to do. First came a guided ascent of Annapurna, widely reported in the climbing media as one of the most commercialized endeavors ever seen in the Himalaya, outside of Everest. From there, he went to Everest, where he had the pleasure of leading his three younger sisters to the summit on May 12, 2021. Nima Jangmu, Tshering Namgya, and Dawa Futi became the first three sisters to climb Everest together. The siblings dedicated their ascent to their father.

The sisters were already experienced climbers by that point. Nima Jangmu held the record as the fastest female "triple header," having climbed Everest, Lhotse, and Kangchenjunga within twenty-five days. Dawa Futi had climbed Ama Dablam and had taken several climbing and mountain rescue courses. And as a threesome, they had climbed Lobuche earlier that season. But three sisters on the summit of Everest? The record will likely change their lives.

Mingma G is a stickler for details. He announced that his guided expedition to Manaslu in the fall of 2021 would be going to the "true summit"—as identified numerous times in the past by mountaineering historian Eberhard Jurgalski and others—rather than to a secondary summit traditionally reached by autumn climbers. Many people, including a number of climbers, were confused. Their confusion was justified, since the true summit isn't visible from the secondary summit, which—while standing on it—appears to be the highest point.

Jackson Groves, a Manaslu client with another company, was celebrating his summit moment with a drone video of himself and others. He was surprised when the footage revealed that they weren't at the highest point at all. The true summit was farther up, along a narrow, corniced ridge. The video also showed a small group of climbers breaking trail along an exposed traverse, then punching steps up and up to the real summit of Manaslu. The person out front was Mingma G.

"Once I fixed the final anchors to the summit, our team came up one by one and returned [the same way]," he explained to Angela Benavides of Explorersweb. "We had a single line of rope and the anchors were completely new, so I didn't take the risk of bringing them all together. Also, our final anchors were placed in snow which I kept holding almost till the end."

It was a triumphant moment, but what a can of worms Mingma G had opened. How many guided clients now realized they hadn't reached the true summit of Manaslu? How many mountaineers claiming the fourteen 8,000ers now had to admit that one of their summits was missing? Even Nimsdai realized that in order to claim all fourteen of the 8,000ers honestly, he would need to return to Manaslu and Dhaulagiri, neither of which he had summited within the six-month period. After long discussions between Mingma G and the Himalayan Database, a compromise was reached. The past was the past; no revisions would be made to previously claimed ascents of Manaslu. But according to the Himalayan Database—the gold standard for Himalayan climbing ascents—anyone who claimed the summit of Manaslu in the future would need to go where Mingma G went: to the actual summit of Manaslu. "There won't be any more excuses in the future," he said with satisfaction.

⸺

In Rolwaling today, not much has changed. If anything, the valley is even more deserted than it was in Mingma G's childhood days. Most who had the opportunity to leave have gone, either to Kathmandu or abroad. There are only fifty-four residents in the entire valley, many of them elderly, including Mingma G's mother. The villages still don't have roads or proper schools, health clinics, or dependable electricity. Since the average elevation is 4,000 meters, the growing season is short, best suited to potatoes. "We do go back to the village every now and then—during lockdown in 2020 we were there for seven months," his sister Dawa Futi said. "My memories of village life include playing a lot; helping mum with the cows, sheep and goats; working in the fields." Although her description sounds idyllic, she pointed out the downsides: no electricity, no internet, no social life. "It's fine for getting refreshed, but I prefer it here in the city."

During the pandemic lockdown, Mingma G retuned to Rolwaling to spend time with his mother and to climb. He remains convinced it is one of the best places in Nepal for ice climbs and rock routes and, if developed and promoted properly, could be an exciting attraction to visiting alpinists. Unlike the Khumbu region, Rolwaling would be focused on technical climbing, rather than the 8,000ers. He envisions a climbing and trekking community living and working in the valley, bringing prosperity to Rolwaling. He foresees a day when that change will happen, and he wants to be part of it.

But for now, Mingma G lives in Kathmandu with his sisters, tending to his business, responding to media requests, and guiding big mountains. His typical schedule includes leading groups on Annapurna, Dhaulagiri, Everest, Lhotse, and Kangchenjunga in the spring season, K2 and Broad Peak in the summer, and Manaslu in the fall.

On a personal level, he wants to climb Shishapangma without supplemental oxygen, which would make him the first Nepali to climb all fourteen 8,000ers without bottled O2. He intends to do more new routes and first ascents of 6,000-meter peaks in Nepal. And in his spare time, he's writing a book.

In short, Mingma G is a busy man. He feels responsible to himself, to his family who depend on him, and to his nation. He understands his position within the Himalayan climbing community and he wants to make a difference. "I think we should do what we can do to make our own community proud, to test human limits and to make oneself better and better," he said. "Sherpas and mountains are synonymous to each other." He is confident and hopeful about the future, and equally committed. "Our future generation will be far better than us. I'm not ready to quit alpinism until I feel that I've helped change mountaineering in Nepal."

It's clear he already has.

CHAPTER EIGHTEEN

K2 in Winter

The Goddess K2 accepted us this time.

—MINGMA G

Pakistan's highest mountain, never before climbed in winter, was suddenly swarming with people: a spiderweb of fixed ropes, unlimited ambition and drive, and wildly differing levels of skill and experience, all facing hurricane-force winds and sub-zero temperatures. The possibility of a first winter ascent of K2, the "Savage Mountain," had captured the attention not only of the mountaineering community, but of the world. While speculation swirled about the sixty individuals, their skills, their motivations, their style, and the incredible risks they were willing to take, the drama ricocheted between a high-stakes human chess game and a Greek tragedy, all fueled by the power of social media.

The first to arrive at base camp, on December 6, 2020, was Icelandic climber John Snorri, making his second winter attempt of the mountain. With him was Pakistan's leading high-altitude climber, Ali Sadpara, and his twenty-one-year-old son, Sajid. Both had previously summited K2 in summer. The trio began working on the mountain immediately, fixing ropes to Camp 1.

Mingma G came next, with his three-person team that included Dawa Tenjin Sherpa and Kili Pemba Sherpa. He admitted it had been a struggle to assemble a team. "My two partners' wives didn't want to send their husbands on such a mountain, particularly in winter," he said. The three Rolwaling climbers, with dozens of expeditions to their names, fully understood the seriousness of tackling K2 in winter. Their arrival on December 18 signaled something new and exciting: an independent Sherpa team with no client responsibilities attempting a first winter ascent of K2.

On December 21—the first day of the official calendar winter season—they sped up the fixed lines placed by the Sadpara team, climbed to Camp 1, and on the following day, fixed lines to Camp 2.

The Seven Summit Treks (SST) team, led by Chhang Dawa Sherpa, began trickling in on the twenty-first. Suffering after a lack of clients during the previous pandemic year, the SST entrepreneurs from Kathmandu welcomed Pakistan's easing of entry restrictions for foreign climbers, and they were now offering a unique opportunity for K2 winter aspirants: a large-scale commercial expedition, complete with porters, kitchen staff, and Sherpa guides. Dutch climber Arnold Coster and Catalan alpinist Sergi Mingote would coordinate the climbing strategies. The SST approach provoked spirited conversations among climbers about the future of winter alpinism in the highest mountains—particularly since some of the clients came with little or no winter experience. Clients such as Colin O'Brady, a controversial adventurer with limited experience at altitude but a knack for self-promotion. Commercialism had apparently now crept into the last exclusive realm of mountaineering—high-altitude winter climbing—a niche that had traditionally been reserved for the very best. It was a sharp contrast to the first winter ascent of Everest in 1980, which had signaled a genuine adventure into the unknown.

It's worth noting that not all the SST clients were expecting to be guided. Italian alpinist Tamara Lunger—who had reached within 100 meters of the summit of Nanga Parbat in winter and summited K2 in summer without supplemental oxygen—had also joined the expedition. She planned to take advantage of the infrastructure SST provided while climbing independently with her experienced partner, Romanian Alex Gavan. Others, such as Poland's Magdalena Gorzkowska, had climbed at high altitudes before, but not in winter.

Sergi had a word of caution: "Without risking, I don't think you can go up to K2 in winter. . . . I do not consider myself reckless, but there are mountains that you cannot climb without that decision point. I am sure that if we have the option of the summit, it will happen by taking risks." His words were chillingly prophetic.

Arriving fashionably late on Christmas Day was Nimsdai. Describing the climb with typical fanfare on his blog as "one of the last remaining grand prizes in mountaineering, a feat regarded as impossible," he brought five veteran high-altitude climbing Sherpas: Mingma David, Dawa Temba, Pem Chhiri, Gelje, and Mingma Tenzi. British filmmaker Sandro Gromen-Hayes would document their adventure. The ever-exuberant Nimsdai announced his intention to make the first winter ascent of K2 without oxygen and then paraglide off the summit. "Game is on, folks," he tweeted. After one day in base camp to assemble their tents and communication systems. the team headed up. Within three days, they were at Camp 2.

They weren't alone. Mingma G and his team had set up Camp 2 at 6,800 meters on December 28 and began fixing lines up to 7,000 meters. On the twenty-ninth, they moved their camp to their high point to acclimatize but realized they had only 900 meters of rope remaining—not enough to fix lines to Camp 3 the following day. This presented a problem, but also an opportunity: Mingma G contacted Nimsdai, and by December 30, the two teams were collaborating, fixing lines to 7,300 meters.

"We spoke for a few minutes only," Mingma G wrote, "but that was the moment that made Nims's team and my team one team on one mission because we both were climbing for our Nation."

"We had never worked together before," Nimsdai explained to British writer Natalie Berry, "but I knew Mingma G was a great climber, and to be honest, between us we were little like rivals." According to Mingma David, the lead climber on Nimsdai's team, that rivalry was more than "little." The first thing he did when he reached base camp on Christmas Day was head over for a chat with Mingma G to float the idea of cooperation. "My first attempt failed because we were in tough competition," Mingma David said. "But we got back down, we had a chat and realized that our vision, our aim and our objectives were the same," Nimsdai explained. "[Mingma G] wanted to do something for the climbing community here in Nepal and for future generations. More importantly, there was no selfishness or agenda. That's why we decided to collaborate."

Bad weather kept everyone in base camp for over a week, but on January 10 Nimsdai climbed up to Camp 2, only to discover that high winds had blown all their equipment—including the paragliding apparatus—into oblivion. The setback was serious, but they had a backup plan: "We plan for the worst and hope for the best."

Everyone was glued to the weather forecasts. As usual, they varied. Mingma G was using a forecaster from Nepal, whereas Nimsdai's and Ali Sadpara's teams were following European experts. Ali Sadpara's team opted to wait for better weather, but Nimsdai and Mingma G decided to launch a summit attempt. There would be ten Nepali climbers: three from Mingma G's team, six from Nimsdai's team, and Sona Sherpa from the SST team.

Nimsdai and his group headed up as far as Camp 2 on January 12. Mingma G delayed his own departure until January 13, when his team climbed all the way to 7,000 meters. Even though they were heavily loaded with equipment for the upper part of the mountain, they reached 7,350 meters at Camp 3 on the fourteenth and continued fixing lines an additional 300 meters. On the morning of the fifteenth, Mingma G, Mingma David, Mingma Tenzi, and Sona began fixing lines up toward Camp 4.

Mingma G described what happened next: "We followed the way to Camp 4 the same way we do in summer." But this wasn't summer. At this point, Mingma G was fixing and the others were assisting. After fixing 400 metres of rope, they were approaching the steep wall below Camp 4 when a problem arose: "We found a big crevasse, which was impossible to cross. . . . We tried more on the right side, still the same. Then we descended back a little and tried to find a way on the left side—again it was the same so we descended all the way back to just above Camp 3." This was a devastating situation since they essentially had to start all over again. Using what was left of the beautiful day, they persevered and fixed a completely new line up to Camp 4. Luckily, a serac had collapsed over part of the gaping crevasse, providing a tentative bridge. Exhausted from breaking trail and fixing lines, Mingma G stepped aside while Mingma Tenzi took over the lead.

At around 4 p.m. they arrived at Camp 4, the route fully equipped below them. "Our first reaction was winter K2 will be ours, and we hugged each other because we knew we would make the summit next day," Mingma G said. Their efforts had been immense. The route from Camp 3 to Camp 4 usually takes two to three hours; they had taken eight. Still, he was elated. "We talked a little bit about our luck and hard work before descending. Whenever we are on the mountain, we pray to the mountain for our safety and we also pray for her to accept us. The Goddess K2 accepted us this time." They rushed down to Camp 3 and began preparing for the summit bid, which would begin in a matter of hours. The forecast for January 16 was even better than expected, so instead of starting at 11 p.m., their original plan, they felt comfortable delaying the start to 1 a.m.

Camp 3 began stirring at midnight. After the usual ordeal of lighting the stoves, boiling water, double- and triple-checking the contents of their packs, and then stuffing their feet into their high-altitude boots, they emerged from the tents, one by one. Nimsdai, Kili, Dawa Tenjin, Sona, Dawa Temba, and Mingma Tenzi left first. Mingma G came to the sad realization that his previous day's efforts had so exhausted him that he didn't feel strong enough to climb without oxygen. Disappointed, he fiddled with his oxygen regulator, which didn't fit properly. He eventually found a spare regulator but chilled his fingers dangerously in the process of attaching it. By the time he was finally ready to start up, the others were already nearing Camp 4. It didn't look like a promising summit day for Mingma G.

He left Camp 3 with Mingma David, Pem Chhiri, and Gelje. They reached Camp 4 two hours later and were shocked at the chilling effects of the wind. When Mingma G stopped for a few moments on the upper side of a crevasse while waiting for Mingma David, he became so cold he considered turning around. "I almost gave up there because I was worried to lose my toes."

He checked his watch. It was 5 a.m. In another hour the sun would appear above the horizon, so he decided to continue, at least until dawn. At the same moment that he felt the first warming rays of the sun, the wind miraculously dropped. The four climbers stopped to soak up the rays and warm themselves before climbing up to the Bottleneck. The heat from the sun had given them extra energy and hope.

The first group was fixing lines up the Bottleneck, Mingma Tenzi leading the way. Mingma G's group climbed toward them, finally catching up before the traverse. Nimsdai urged them on: "We all had that common pride, a common goal. This was for Nepal." When they reached the small plateau 200 meters below the summit, they stopped to brew some tea. After resting a bit, Mingma Tenzi resumed fixing. They were still four hours from the summit.

They planned to stop around 10 meters from the top and continue as a group to the highest point. "We all started moving together and our 360 GoPro was on," Mingma G said. "We then started moving towards the summit singing the National Anthem. This was my third time summiting on K2 but this time it was connected with the pride of the nation. . . . It was a thrilling moment. I had tears in my eyes and my body was shaking itself, bearing goosebumps. No member in the team can explain the moment we had there."

The ten Nepali climbers stepped onto the summit at 4:43 p.m., January 16, 2021. First winter ascent of K2.

The video of their final steps to the summit sped around the world, delighting millions. What a sight: their faces lit up by the low-angled sun, the distinct curvature of the earth as their backdrop, their crimson and gold suits as bright as jewels, and that magnificent indigo sky. They strode up those last few steps to 8,611 meters—singing!

But the summit scene hadn't been completely spontaneous. Mingma David later explained to Angela Benavides that they had terminated radio communication with base camp that day. "Our policy was to make zero contact so that no individual members could give information on their own. Our plan was to relay news of the success through a proper channel. We finally reached the top, but only later we [released the news] through our UK PR Team."

Nimsdai acknowledged the day had been difficult, and that there had been close calls where team members nearly turned around due to extreme cold. Out of the ten, eight sustained varying degrees of frostbite. "I cannot describe in words how tough Saturday night was," Mingma G admitted. "It really tested the limit of Sherpas."

The team descended to base camp over the next couple of days and flew to Skardu for the first of an extended round of celebrations. The whole world rejoiced with them. Veteran winter alpinist Simone Moro weighed in: "Today the Sherpas have rightly received a well-deserved place in history as they have helped hundreds and thousands of mountaineers and their ascents for decades."

But the joy of an all-Nepali winter climb of K2 was tinged with sadness, because at the same moment they were scratching their way up the Bottleneck, Sergi Mingote fell while descending from Camp 1. Tamara described the event to Italian journalist Alessandro Filippini. "When Sergi fell I was forty meters from where he ended up. I was afraid to approach. I didn't want him to suffer, instead he breathed for another hour while we . . . did everything possible. . . . We stood beside him, I held his hand, we talked to him. Then it took four or five hours to prepare the body and the Sherpas to bring it back to base camp." Those at base camp regrouped, huddled in their tents, mourned, and waited. There would be another weather window. They were confident. A short window opened near the end of January. Ali Sadpara, together with his son Sajid and John Snorri, made a summit attempt but turned back because of high winds. More waiting. Then some good news arrived for Ali: the Pakistani government announced they would support him financially for his dream of completing all fourteen of the 8,000ers. Finally, a victory for Ali, and for all Pakistani climbers; the government was taking them seriously.

When a three-day window appeared in early February, independent climbers and the Sadpara trio all headed up. By the evening of February 4, Camp 3 was heaving. Trying to rest before their final summit attempts, six people stuffed into tents designed for three. The situation was bad: temperatures of −60°F, little rest, poor hydration, and no space to cook or eat. Several people descended because of ill health; even more retreated because of the terrifying temperatures. But Ali, Sajid, John, and Chilean alpinist Juan Pablo Mohr headed up.

Their plan was to summit on February 5, directly from Camp 3. The winds were predicted to increase to thirty-seven miles per hour on the afternoon of the sixth, with gusts of sixty-two miles per hour expected above 7,500 meters. The weather window was perilously short, and not nearly as favorable as the mid-January window, when the winds had been light, almost calm.

Sajid recounted the events that followed to Spanish journalist Isaac Fernández:

> We started the ascent at 11 or 12 at night. . . . At about 8,200 meters, at the Bottleneck. . . . I was not feeling well, I was lacking oxygen [up to that point Sajid and his father had ascended without using bottled oxygen]. My father told me to use the oxygen from the client [John Snorri] because there was enough. When I was putting the regulator on, the oxygen started to leak because it didn't fit well. As I was not feeling well, my father told me to go down, while they continued up. At 12 I started to descend towards Camp 3, which I arrived at 5 in the afternoon. I spoke with the base camp and explained that my teammates were trying to reach the top and that the next day we would descend together. They did not carry a satellite phone or walkie talkie. I made tea and hot water and then left a light on so they could find the [tent]. I was all night without sleep, waiting for them. In the morning I called base camp to say that no one had arrived and the leader told me that, please, I had to go down because the weather was going to get worse, I was tired and it could be worse for me. He told me that he was going to send a rescue group from base camp.

While Sajid waited, unbeknownst to him, Bulgarian climber Atanas Skatov fell to his death descending from Camp 3.

Now Sajid had to make the most difficult decision of his life: Should he wait for his father or go down? After repeated calls from base camp urging him to come down, he began his long, solo descent. Two Sherpas from the SST camp began ascending toward him, and two helicopters left Skardu to retrieve Atanas's body and to pick up some frostbitten climbers from base camp, as well as make a flyby in the hopes of spotting the three mountaineers still high on the mountain. Despite reaching 7,000 meters, they saw nothing. Sajid arrived in base camp, physically sound yet emotionally destroyed.

Two more helicopters showed up the following day. There was no sign of the missing trio, but the rescue team took high-resolution images to be examined at base camp. A second flyby—even higher—again revealed nothing. Still hopeful, Pakistani climbers Imtiaz Hussain and Akbar Ali, the cousin and nephew of Ali Sadpara, set off in search, but reached no farther than Camp 2 before the weather shut them down.

Sajid left K2 and flew to Skardu, where—though obviously suffering from shock—he was assaulted by the media clamoring for a firsthand report. "They must have had the accident on the descent because at night it started to get very windy," Sajid said. "They have been [at] eight thousand meters for two days; at that height in winter, I have no hope that they are alive." He added, perhaps hopefully, "I think that they summited." He expressed hope that the search would continue for his father's body. Amid all his sorrow, he summoned the grace to thank the families of Juan Pablo Mohr and John Snorri, the Pakistani army, the Sherpa expedition, the other mountaineers, and the media. Sajid then left the press conference and returned to his grieving family.

Mingma G later reflected on Ali Sadpara. "He was an amazing man. . . . Ali was like our brother, and he visited our camp almost every day. He knew our tentative plan on K2 but he was there guiding. . . . If he was alone then I think he would definitely have been with us on the K2 summit. I still feel very sorry for this man."

And so, the 2020–21 K2 winter climbing season ground to a close. A mixture of elation and pride paired with loss and grief. Sixty climbers arrived at the mountain of their dreams. Some retreated. Some prevailed. Ten were victorious and five lost their lives. Once again, wives and partners, sons and daughters, were left to ask why. Despite the climbers' expertise, their strength and determination, the improvements in equipment and tactics and accurate weather forecasts, mountains don't become smaller or easier to climb. They are simply rock and ice structures of unimaginable beauty. They symbolize freedom, they inspire the imagination, but they tolerate human presence for only brief moments in time.

The victorious team was fêted everywhere: Skardu, Islamabad, Kathmandu. Receptions, parades, awards, speeches, parties, and press conferences. Regrettably, jealousy from other climbers was part of the aftermath, and Mingma G, among others, was left to defend their success. "It is sad and at the same time funny to see the reactions of some climbers who just returned back without success. They are blaming Nepalese team saying Nepalese Sherpas might have cut the rope after their summit, proper information was not given, kept their plan secret etc.?" Not one to mince words, he added: "Remember why K2 is called SAVAGE Mountain and Why it remained unclimbed for 34 years after the first winter try in 1987/1988????"

He dismissed the accusations as sour grapes, insisting that when the Nepalis began heading up the mountain as a group on the twelfth and thirteenth of January, it should have been obvious that they weren't planning to stop. He was even more direct in his criticism of those who complained about fixed lines. "We are thankful to Apo Ali, Sajid, and John for fixing rope till Camp 1. When we fixed rope from Camp 1 to the summit, none of these climbers were there to help us . . . and now they are shamelessly speaking as if we were paid to fix the line for them. What I call them, 'Parasite Climbers': Those who use other climbers' works (i.e., fixed ropes) unpaid and blame them shamelessly if they fail to reach the summit."

And how about the accusations from some of the K2 climbers that the Nepalis were secretive about the route, not sharing information with those in base camp? Mingma G pointed out that Sona remained in base camp until February 9 after having summited. Did anyone ask Sona for the information that might have helped them? "Everyone on K2 this winter was aiming to be first and so were we," Mingma G added. "Everyone had their own plans and no one shared their plan with us. We also kept our plans to ourselves like in any other sport." He pointed out the strategy they had used with the weather forecasts: start in bad weather, gamble on good weather up high, but accept that the so-called "summit bid" would also be a rope-fixing exercise. This was an important difference because on most summit bids, the ropes would have already been fixed by high-altitude workers. In this case, they *were* the high-altitude workers. Mingma G insisted the Nepali team was the only one strong enough to do both. "We took the risk and we got success. . . . Football world cup is the most popular sport. The coach of the team shares his tactic and plan with his players, not with players from other teams to win the trophy. It was the same with us." He continued, "They are jealous because we made a successful ascent and they couldn't make it—in spite of the fixed line all the way to the summit."

There were even some who accused the team of removing the fixed lines as they descended, making the climb more difficult for anyone who might follow. Mingma G scoffed at the idea. "We reached the summit at 4:43 p.m. exactly and we started descending by torch light 200 meters from below the summit with a fully exhausted body. A mistake could cost our lives. It was getting colder and colder and we were trying to descend as fast as possible. . . . In such a condition, how will a climber be able to cut rope?"

Another debate swirled around the topic of bottled oxygen. The previous attempts at climbing the mountain in winter, all made by Western climbers, had been without supplemental oxygen. And this was the twenty-first century—using bottled oxygen for such an important ascent should have been a thing of the past. Legendary Himalayan alpinist Denis Urubko, who had reached 7,650 meters on K2 in the winter of 2003, was typically blunt about the use of supplemental oxygen: he called it not merely "doping," but "powerful doping." He elaborated in an interview with Explorersweb: "I may forgive its past use during first ascents at 8,000m, but not now. I find it shocking that sports' authorities are fighting against doping in all other sports, while the mountaineering community applauds O2-doped athletes. As I see it, this is unethical. Supplementary O2 is now a supplement used by people who are too weak for the goals they have set. They use gas to simulate achievements."

But it's important to ask: Is there a cultural context missing with this statement? Nepali climbers are fully aware of the difference between climbing with or without bottled oxygen, and some are adding oxygen-free ascents to their résumés. But they traditionally use oxygen above 8,000 meters because they are working: breaking trail, fixing lines, setting up camps, guiding clients. Both Mingma G and Nimsdai had planned to climb K2 in winter without bottled oxygen, but as we have seen, Mingma G was exhausted from the previous day's efforts. In the video, Nimsdai appeared to summit without oxygen, but the news was slow to emerge.

Mingma David—often the concertmaster to Nimsdai, the conductor—shed some light on the puzzling delay: "Our plan was to announce this news about [the No-O2] summit later, in the movie about K2. But after we had too many controversial comments, we informed the world a few days later."

"I seem to have a genetic advantage at dealing with altitude," Nimsdai explained, in an effort to clear up any doubts. "But my training also helped. The British Special Forces has the hardest training regime in the world, and I was trained by the best. When you combine that with physical ability and hard work, it's possible to achieve anything." Denis flatly didn't believe him. "Well, that's what he said. But I saw his pictures and the summit video. It is impossible to be like that on K2's summit without O2. Least of all to keep pace with a crew of climbers on O2."

Despite all the doubts, the jealousy, the sadness, and the tragedy of the 2020–21 winter season on K2, the climb remains a beacon of pride for Nepalis. "K2 was the only remaining 8,000er left to be climbed in Winter," Mingma G said. "Nepalese Sherpas—being synonymous with Mountains and yet no 8,000 metre first winter ascents—it was shameful for us. We got the chance to climb it, but our future generations won't get this chance. If we hadn't done it now; then it would have been climbed by foreigners. Our future generation will be proud to see Nepalese on this list."

If Mingma G seems genuinely proud for his country, Nimsdai seems equally proud of himself. When asked by journalist Thomas Pueyo why K2 hadn't been climbed in winter by Nepali climbers long before 2021, he replied: "Because I wasn't there!"

⸻

Less than a year later, Sajid was back on K2, searching for his father. The helicopter flights that had circled the mountain after the disappearance of Ali Sadpara, John Snorri, and Juan Pablo Mohr had revealed nothing. Part of the problem may have been their use of technology. According to Rashid Ullah Baig—a famous Pakistani helicopter pilot who had rescued Slovenian alpinist Tomaž Humar from close to 6,000 meters on the Rupal Face of Nanga Parbat—John's choice of a Thuraya rather than a Garmin inReach mobile satellite device was unfortunate. The inReach could have sent a live signal of their location with a single press of the button, saving hours of useless flights.

And who knows—it might have saved a life. "The difference between the two is like someone calling you saying, 'Help! I have got a heart attack in Islamabad' and the other sending you live location with Google Maps along with the declared emergency," Rashid said. While impossible to know if it would have made a difference, he shook his head in disbelief at the loss. "We lost our friend with the most contagious smile; Ali Sadpara would be missed forever."

Sajid was determined to find out what had happened, and he knew how to continue the search—on foot. "I had one of the most challenging and traumatic experiences in life," he said. "I don't want to remember the time of despair and fear. I am healing myself and I try to heal the whole family as well. . . . I am recovering my strength and my rationality with the passage of time. And I decided to lead the search and recovery of my father Ali Sadpara, John Snorri, and JP Mohr. . . . My family and I will leave no stone unturned to recover them and give the right rituals as per everyone's faith." Accompanied by Canadian filmmaker Elia Saikaly and Nepali climber Pasang Kaji (PK) Sherpa, he headed off. "We want to find out what happened to them and try our best to recover their remains."

The press conference with Sajid before his departure was heartbreaking. He described his last moments with his father when Ali advised him to descend to Camp 3. "That is the last time I ever spoke to him," Sajid said. "I don't know what happened to them. That is why I am here now. It has been 4½ months. Of course, I know he is not alive. I was grateful to [those] who used technologies I wouldn't begin to understand to look for them from afar. And now, it is my turn—to go back and see for myself."

He speculated about the possibilities. Perhaps they had summited and one of them had become injured on the way down. They could have been hit with bad weather. Or perhaps exhaustion. "But speculation does not help," he said. "My father is with Allah now. He is safe. I go only to find answers and to re-trace those last steps—to see what he might have seen. To see if he left any signs for me to follow. If there is anything he wants me to know." It boggles the mind to imagine the trauma, the stress, the sadness, and the self-discipline this young man must have rallied to manage the constant media attention and summon the courage to return to the mountain that claimed his father.

He ended the press conference with this tribute: "If I do not find my father, then I will place his plaque with pride at the Gilkey Memorial in honor of my father, whom I loved more than anything, who taught me mountaineering, and who is, to this day, one of the greatest, if not *the* greatest Pakistani mountaineer of all time."

Sajid summited K2 on July 26, 2021, with Elia and PK Sherpa. But before they did, they discovered what they were looking for. Russian alpinist Valentyn Sypavin had alerted them to the location of three bodies on the route. The first was below the Bottleneck, a solitary corpse that, after examination, was almost certainly Juan Pablo Mohr. Valentyn discovered two more bodies higher up: Ali Sadpara and John Snorri. His descriptions of their positions suggest that both were descending and had likely experienced problems while doing so, which under normal circumstances might have been easily solved, but at night, under duress, and completely exhausted, would have been impossible. Since they were too high to be removed, Sajid and his team relocated their bodies to less traveled areas on the mountain.

Later, at base camp, Sajid and his partners visited the Gilkey memorial. "Perched high on a cliff just outside of K2 base camp, there is a mirror of dreams gone wrong where loved ones are honored and remembered," Elia posted on his Facebook page. He watched as Sajid paid respect to his father. Together with Ali Sadpara's memorial were the others from the previous winter season: Atanas Skatov, Sergi Mingote, Juan Pablo Mohr, and John Snorri, all taken far too soon.

Having done all he could to honor his father, and to help with his own and his family's healing, Sajid Sadpara, son of Muhammad Ali Sadpara, began his long journey home. "Salute to Sajid for your courage," Mingma G said.

CHAPTER NINETEEN

The Maoists Are Coming

I feel I'm not really scared of anything now.

—DAWA FUTI

G uiding is a dangerous job—regardless of country or mountain range. Guides accept that reality, but in most places their passion for climbing outweighs their concerns about the inherent risks. In Nepal and Pakistan, the motivation to enter this profession is still driven primarily by economic necessity. Many local mountaineers talk about starting their own companies, taking greater control over when they guide, whom they guide, and how much profit remains with them. But launching a company isn't easy. Like any business start-up, it involves red tape, regulations, insurance, unforeseen costs, and the risk of failure.

There are certainly success stories. Seven Summit Treks has exploded in size and influence. Nimsdai's Elite Exped company is wildly successful. Mingma G's company, Imagine Nepal, is equally well known and respected. There are dozens of others. Of the approximately two thousand adventure companies and agencies officially registered in Nepal today, 100 percent of them are at least partly locally owned and operated, thanks to a Nepali law forbidding foreigners from owning more than 49 percent of a company.

But these companies are more than headliner names. Many of the real stories are found in the young guides who do the work, day in and day out.

⎯⎯

The Rolwaling Valley has produced dozens of world-class climbers, and they haven't all been men. Dawa Yangzum Sherpa is young, strong, and determined, and, as of 2024, is the only female Nepali UIAGM-certified guide; the international standard qualifies her to guide anywhere in the world. She has summited thirteen 8,000ers, including K2, and is a role model for countless Nepali girls.

Like most climbers from Rolwaling, her beginnings were humble. Born into a farming family in 1990, she spent the first few years of her life hauling water, cutting grass for the yaks, and digging potatoes in her village of Na. Her home had neither running water nor electricity.

At the age of six she moved to Kathmandu to live with her uncle and attend school. But when her aunt and uncle divorced, she returned to Na, where Dawa found it awkward to make friends with the local kids. "They were shy towards me," she told Swiss writer Ruedi Baumgartner. "I looked too different in my Kathmandu clothes. I could not speak proper Sherpa, and they hardly knew any Nepalese. . . . I must have been a rather useless daughter at the beginning; often my attempts to light the first fire in the darkness of early mornings failed and I felt ashamed when I had to fetch fire from the hearth of a neighbour's house."

There was no more schooling for Dawa. Instead, she watched the seasonal parade of local men packing their rucksacks, bidding their families goodbye, leaving the valley to work on expeditions, and a couple of months later, most of them returning, flush with tales of adventures, fancy new clothes, and cash. She was intrigued, even envious. But she couldn't imagine herself in that role. She was a girl.

Finally fed up with the grind, and having tasted the bright lights of the city, she ran away from home when she was thirteen. But she did so "Rolwaling style," signing on as a porter with a trekking group that was headed over the steep and glaciated 5,755-meter Tashi Labsta Pass into the Khumbu Valley. Carrying a load of more than sixty-five pounds for six days earned her enough money to fly back to Kathmandu.

Her life changed again at the age of fifteen when her mother passed away. Dawa returned to the valley to help her elder brother raise her siblings, since her father had turned to the bottle to drown his sorrows. "When he came home drunk, we were afraid of getting beaten," she said. "I felt jealous of friends whose father only drank during festivals!" To supplement the family income, she guided a few treks and, with some of her earnings, enrolled in a mountaineering course sponsored by the Nepal Mountaineering Association. There were forty-two students, five of them girls. Dawa was the youngest, at eighteen.

Dawa was strong, fit, and ambitious. She soon set her sights much higher than a local climbing course and, in 2012, enrolled in the first level of training for the international guides' program. Even though she trained hard, she failed the course. Discouraged, she turned to her friend, Maya Sherpa, for support.

Slightly older than Dawa, Maya had already amassed a lengthy climbing résumé, but she had been out of the game for a few years, having recently given birth to a daughter. She was itching to get back in the mountains, so she suggested to Dawa that the two of them team up with another female climber, Khumjung native Pasang Lhamu Sherpa Akita, and do something outrageous. Why not climb K2?

⸻

Pasang Lhamu knew she would be a climber ever since she was a child; after all, she had the same name as the first Nepali woman to climb Everest. Back on April 22, 1993, a team of five Sherpas, three of them from Rolwaling, had helped Pasang Lhamu Sherpa reach the summit. When a violent storm hit the group on their descent, Sonam Tshering, her personal guide from Rolwaling, stayed with her at the South Summit while his younger brother left to get help. Both Pasang Lhamu and Sonam Tshering perished. But while Pasang Lhamu became a Nepali icon, Sonam Tshering faded into obscurity.

The younger Pasang Lhamu Sherpa Akita was fully aware of all this history. Then, after the 2014 avalanche killed many of her friends on Everest, she began having second thoughts about attempting K2. She considered pulling out, but Dawa and Maya consoled and encouraged their friend, and ultimately, the three women climbed K2 on July 26, 2014, to great acclaim.

When the earthquake destroyed much of Nepal the following year, Pasang Lhamu paused her career—she was already well on her way to climbing all the 8,000ers—to help rebuild some of the most remote areas. She began training other young women to climb, as well. "In the patriarchal Nepalese society, opportunities for women to explore the outdoors industry are almost nonexistent. Even as a Sherpa woman, I personally faced many such challenges. . . . Therefore, I consider it an honor to put together a fifteen-day training program that provides the skill sets and the experiences to women which could potentially provide them a road map to the outdoor world of climbing and guiding."

Dawa didn't allow her K2 success and newfound fame to derail her professional ambitions—she still wanted to be a certified mountain guide. She trained. She rock climbed. She worked on her ice-climbing technique, practiced alpine climbing on lower Nepali peaks. She made a number of impressive, alpine-style first ascents, like 6,357-meter Langdung, completed in December of 2018. And she started passing the tests. Four years later she qualified as an internationally accredited mountain guide and considers it her greatest achievement. This, coming from a woman who has summited Everest and Makalu, climbed Manaslu and Annapurna without supplemental oxygen, is the only Nepali climber to be sponsored by The North Face, guides clients around the world, and is an ambassador for the luxury watch brand Rolex. She credits her mentors for helping smooth the way: her brother, Dawa Gyalje, David Gottlieb, and American alpinist Conrad Anker, who not only helped her with training at the Khumbu Climbing Center but made introductions for her at The North Face.

Maya, in turn, credits her father for supporting her alpine aspirations. They aren't modest. She's climbed seven of the fourteen 8,000ers, including Everest three times and Kangchenjunga twice, and has her eye on all fourteen. She isn't oblivious to the dangers; she knows enough climbing widows in Kathmandu to understand the risks. But Maya is pragmatic: "If something happens to me, my daughter has her father and my family to take care of her. . . . People will not sit and cry about someone their entire life. They will mourn for a couple of years and slowly things will get back to normal." She feels that climbing the fourteen 8,000ers, on the other hand, would be an inspiration for young female Nepali climbers for generations to come.

Maya's aspirations are admirable, since everyone benefits from mentorship. Gelje Sherpa was fortunate to be invited by Nimsdai to join his Project Possible. Born and raised in Khumbu, Gelje started as a lowly porter, graduated to the dangerous job of Icefall Doctor, and then moved up to what he considers a much less risky occupation—guiding clients at 8,000 meters. He climbed eight of them with Nimsdai, and then topped it off with the first winter ascent of K2 in 2021.

It may sometimes appear that he was unfairly overshadowed by Nimsdai, given all the expertise and hard work he contributed. Gelje disagrees. He was so grateful to see his name in Nimsdai's *14 Peaks* film that he broke into tears. As for lack of personal fame, he claims, "It is our weakness that we are not able to express ourselves well. We only know how to climb mountains." To help improve his communication skills, Gelje took Nimsdai's advice and enrolled in a public-speaking class.

But public speaking isn't Gelje's first priority. For the moment, he has to earn a living, guiding British climber Adriana Brownlee on a race to become the youngest woman to climb all the 8,000ers. Some of Nimsdai's bravado may be rubbing off on Gelje, however, judging by a recent post on Instagram: "They say we are nice guys, but I want to be the world's BADASS!"

⸻

Tenji Sherpa may not have had Nimsdai as his benefactor, but he had the good fortune to train with one of the best. Born in the Rai village of Gudel, Tenji commuted ninety minutes on foot each way to school as a child. "Sandals were a luxury and running shoes were unheard of," he said. As soon as he was old enough, he began working as a porter to earn money toward a college education. One of his earliest encounters was with Swiss climbing legend Ueli Steck. Although Tenji had little climbing experience, he was fast. Ueli was *famously* fast. With Tenji, he found an ideal partner, someone he could coach and someone who could keep up with him. Together they climbed in the Alps, they climbed Everest, and they climbed the renowned North Face of Cholatse, a difficult route that improved Tenji's technical skills.

Tenji was at Everest base camp on the evening of April 29, 2017. He and Ueli were planning an acclimatization round to the South Col the following day in preparation for the Everest–Lhotse traverse. But Tenji had frost-nipped his fingers a few days earlier and was recuperating. Ueli, who was at Camp 2, sent a text message: "Tenji, I have decided that tomorrow I will go to climb Nuptse for acclimatization. I will come down to base camp in the evening. See you then."

Tenji was a bit surprised, but answered, "Are you going to climb alone or with friends?" He didn't hear back from Ueli.

The following morning, Tenji was still in base camp when he received a call from a friend at Camp 2. Someone had witnessed a lone individual fall approximately 900 meters down the North Face of Nuptse. Sickened, Tenji waited for more details. He soon had them: Ueli Steck—his friend and partner, his mentor and teacher—had fallen down the face and lay dead in the Western Cwm.

Tenji is now one of Nepal's leading alpinists. He performs well, both as a UIAGM guide and as an independent climber, organizing Sherpa-only expeditions in all seasons. He resists being typecast as either a guide or an independent climber, saying, "My preference is fast and light.... I like alpine-style climbing at 8,000 meters." But he is perfectly clear about Ueli's impact: "His mentoring is undoubtedly the most significant reason why I am where I am today. His energy and expertise motivated me to complete my UIAGM certification.... Ueli was like a brother to me."

Tenji is part of a growing community of young Nepali climbers who guide 8,000-meter peaks to finance their personal climbing objectives. One of his friends with a similar strategy is Vinayak Malla, known as Vinny. Hailing from the Annapurna valley, he spent his childhood playing in the forest, gathering firewood for his family, cutting grass for the livestock. "Soccer fields, climbing gyms, and organized sports did not exist," he said.

He was less influenced by stories from porters and mountain guides than by army officers returning to his village. "Guerrillas would come through to ask for teenage recruits from every family to help with their revolution during the civil war. My family immediately sent me to Kathmandu to continue my studies for fear I'd be taken away." After graduating from college, Vinny interned at an investment firm, but didn't enjoy it, so he started rock climbing. It whetted his appetite for more. So began the long process of qualifying not only as a UIAGM guide but also as an examiner, a trainer, and a helicopter longline rescue specialist. Coming from outside the Khumbu region, and initially seen as an "outsider," his profile within the Nepali climbing community is unusual.

It was Vinny who discovered Ueli's body. He had been walking up the Western Cwm from Camp 1 with a group of clients on a sunny, "bluebird" day. Earlier that morning, Vinny had noticed a lone climber on the slopes of Nuptse. A bit later he heard a sound that indicated a fall. But until he reached the body, he had no idea who he'd seen on the mountain.

He recognized Ueli immediately and got in touch with Tenji at base camp. Together with several other guides, Vinny then carried Ueli and his belongings to Camp 1 to be retrieved by helicopter and transported off the mountain. When asked by Leo Montejo if Ueli might have taken something with him that day that could have prevented this tragic accident on Nuptse, Vinny answered: "More than anything else, a climbing partner is perhaps what would have been most valuable." When asked to speculate about what could have caused such an experienced alpinist to fall, he said, "If you have been to the Himalayas, you will often see Bharal, blue sheep, very high on the mountains," he said. "They are very agile and fast so as to protect themselves from snow leopards. But sometimes, blue sheep fall off from cliffs. Each time they do, there is a different reason. Sometimes they fall due to rock fall, other times, they have perhaps run too fast, etc. Perhaps we must think of Ueli as such—as a Bharal, as one of our blue sheep of the Himalayas who one day fell for an unexpected reason but was otherwise a master."

Vinny continues to climb—with a partner and a rope. He guides on the 8,000ers but his personal projects are not on 8,000-meter standard routes. "I am definitely not a 14 × 8,000-meter climber. My strength and preference is technical climbing," he said.

⸻

Dawa Gyalje Sherpa demonstrated a similar outlook when he started thinking about possible first ascents in Nepal. A Rolwaling native with more than forty-six expeditions to his name, Dawa Gyalje credits Mingma G as his role model and best climbing partner. But it wasn't Mingma G whom Dawa Gyalje teamed up with for a remarkable trilogy of first ascents within a three-day period. Joining him instead were fellow guides Nima Tenji Sherpa and Tashi Sherpa. The trio climbed 6,224-meter Raungsiyar, 6,220-meter Langdak, and 6,152-meter Thakar-Go East, all alpine style.

Before they set out, Dawa Gyalje had already made two winter attempts on the South Face of Lhotse. He reached over 8,000 meters in 2003, and in 2006 he was forced to descend with a hand so injured by falling ice that he could barely operate his descending device. It's worth noting that his efforts on those winter attempts are not mentioned in any of the official reports. Not in the *American Alpine Journal*, the *Alpine Journal*, or the *Himalayan Journal*. Not even in the Himalayan Database. Likewise for his role model, Mingma G, who was with him on that formidable face in the coldest season.

Acknowledgment and recognition of the Sherpa climbers who contributed to those impressive and dangerous efforts still had a long way to go back then.

None of that mattered to Dawa Gyalje, whose trilogy of first ascents wasn't about working for foreign expeditions—it was about a group of Nepalis climbing for fun. They embody the transition of Nepali climbing culture from a "vocational to an avocational one," as American alpinist Conrad Anker described it.

But Kami Rita, the famous Sherpa guide with twenty-eight ascents of Everest, still retains an outdated view of climbing opportunities in Nepal. In an interview with Nepali journalist Bhusan Dahal in 2021, he said: "To talk about Nepal, there aren't any mountains that can be climbed alpine style... As far as I know, in Nepal, not just the 8,000ers but also 5,000-, 6,000-meter peaks, there are no records of people climbing mountains alpine style. You have to climb the mountains on fixed rope." He and Dawa Gyalje might have an interesting conversation should they sit down together for a coffee and talk about climbing.

⸱⸱⸱⸱⸱

Since sponsorship is still a rarity for Nepali climbers harboring personal climbing aspirations, guiding remains their main funding source. Two or three expeditions a year pays the bills, but there isn't much left over for pleasure climbing. Most guides have families to support. And it's impossible to ignore the risks of their day job, despite many insisting that Everest is the safest 8,000er to guide.

One of the most important benefits of the UIAGM certification is that qualified Nepali guides now have more authority and confidence to say no to their clients. Countless accidents and tragedies have occurred because clients insisted on a summit attempt when everyone, including their guide, was begging them to go down. Sange Sherpa's story is a terrifying example.

On May 21, 2017, eighteen-year-old Sange was above the Balcony at 8,440 meters on Everest with an SST client. Several more experienced guides had refused to guide this particular person, citing him as "difficult." But Sange, an inexperienced but strong and hopeful teenager from a small village in the same region as his employer, leapt at the chance. And his employer let him.

"Everything was going good, but my client was very slow and using a lot of extra oxygen," he said. "We were close to the summit. . . . I was quite comfortable without using oxygen at that point, so I planned to use my bottle of oxygen as a backup when we returned." The weather suddenly changed. When Sange could no longer see through his goggles he asked his client to turn back. The client refused. He had paid a small fortune for his permit and his travel; he wanted the summit. "If I wanted, I could have returned by myself, but I didn't," Sange said. "His life was equally important for me."

Once they summited, the client began using Sange's oxygen, leaving him with none. They were both in trouble at that altitude: dizzy, with impaired vision, and stumbling. When they stopped to rest, Sange realized his client was no longer responding to his voice. Unwilling to desert him, Sange fell asleep at 8,700 meters.

At 12:30 a.m. the next rotation of Everest climbers started passing by on their way to the top. "Luckily, I was awakened by the noise of other climbers, otherwise they would have considered me dead," he said. "I was feeling very hungry and thirsty, my water bottle was frozen, and no matter how hard I tried I was not able to move my hand and body at all; there was no feeling in either hand. . . . I closed my eyes and could have easily become a permanent member of the mountain. It would have been very peaceful. I was waiting for death."

But this would not be the day that Sange Sherpa became a permanent part of Everest. Many climbers walked by Sange but were unable to assist because of their own limited resources. Ang Tshering Lama did stop, however, shocked by the sight. "We gave him some O2. I found his pulse—he was just a kid—I couldn't leave him," At great risk to themselves, a group of Sherpas dragged Sange back down to the Balcony—one guy at the front, one guy at the back. When the traveling conditions improved, they lowered him on a fixed line. "As we came down, we heard a noise from him—the *first* noise from him," Ang Tshering said. "A few feathers were flying out of his down suit as we dragged him along." They skidded him to Camp 4 where a doctor—Ellen Gallant—administered a shot of dexamethasone and did her best to make him comfortable. She did not expect him to live after that kind of exposure. He was eventually airlifted from Camp 2 to a hospital in Kathmandu.

Sange lived, and has called his survival a miracle. But the miracle was a long and painful one. He lost all his fingers to frostbite and, along with them his dream of becoming a mountain guide. Neither his company nor the Nepali government provided any assistance. But Sange's story caught the attention of a Sherpa in Denver, Colorado, who helped to find funding for Sange's extensive medical treatment and rehabilitation in the United States. After eleven surgeries, a life-threatening infection, and the reconstruction of "new hands," Sange's heartfelt appeal to clients remains simple: "Please listen and obey the instruction and decision of Sherpa Guides during your climbing. . . . Your life and family is more precious and important than the summit. Mt. Everest will always be there."

Sange's rescuer, Ang Tshering, understood what could have happened. He's been guiding for decades and has seen every type of client and every possible kind of guide. "The clients have different levels of experience," he said. "I have the power to say 'Turn around,' but the younger guides don't always have the confidence." What concerns him most is the lack of rescue skills, even among experienced guides. "They know how to get their clients up the mountain, but not necessarily back down. There is also economic pressure to get to the top—even if sometimes they should turn around."

Sanduk Tamang, a guide from Pangboche, grew up among climbers, including his father who lost his life on Everest. He undertook his first Everest expedition, for which he was woefully unprepared, at the age of twenty. "I was strong enough," he said. "I went nine times carrying loads from Camp 2 to Camp 4 . . . [but] I didn't know how to climb, how to use the equipment. I didn't have any idea. It was crazy." Sanduk survived his first expedition and kept climbing, learning a bit more each time, but always on the job. With a family to support and no formal education, he saw this career as the best way to take care of his kids.

In 2014 he almost lost his life near Camp 1 on Everest in the catastrophic avalanche that killed sixteen Nepalis. He subsequently enrolled at the Khumbu Climbing Center (KCC) in Phortse for some badly needed technical skills and avalanche awareness training. In the following years he has made twelve Everest ascents from both sides of the mountain. His experience and KCC training have given him enough confidence to recognize and avoid potentially dangerous situations as well as the authority to say no to an overly ambitious client.

As a Gurung from the Tanahun district of Nepal, Prakash Gurung is not a part of the elite Sherpa group that most people associate with climbing and guiding in the high mountains. There aren't many people from Tanahun who climb, but Prakash is obsessed with climbing, is educated, and knows that in order to sustain his climbing life he needs to "professionalize" his passion. He now has full UIAGM certification, all of which has been funded by his work on the 8,000ers as well as guiding rock climbing and teaching with the Nepal Mountaineering Instructors Association. Prakash is clear about his priorities. "Everyone always talks about summits. I would like to be seen as a guide—with a focus on safety and security. I want to be remembered as one of the best instructors in Nepal." He may well be remembered as one of the first Gurung climbers to break into the Nepali guiding scene—a sign of the democratization of the business of guiding in Nepal and an emerging culture of diversity.

⸱⸱⸱⸱⸱⸱

Abiral Rai spent at least $25,000 on training required for his UIAGM status. Although he is from Solo Khumbu, Abiral is not Sherpa, but of the Rai ethnolinguistic group. His youth in Mukli Village was rudely interrupted by the Maoist civil war that devastated Nepal from 1996 to 2006. The war resulted in the deaths of over 17,000 people, and internally displaced hundreds of thousands more, mostly throughout rural Nepal—places such as Mukli Village. "My friends all became Maoists," Abiral said. "They tried to convince me to join but I didn't want to." Abiral solved the problem by stealing one kilogram of millet flour and fifty rupees from his mother and running away to Jiri. He was fourteen at the time.

The fifty rupees didn't last long, so he started working as a porter. His first job was carrying eighty-eight pounds of salt, rice, and dal from Jiri to Salleri—a one-week journey for which he was paid 600 rupees, equal to about US$5 today. For seven months he had no contact with his parents since the Maoists had cut all the phone lines to his village. His parents, he learned later, thought he had joined the Maoists.

Abiral soon landed a job hauling goods on his back from Jiri to Lukla, a twelve-day journey that paid him 2,000 rupees. The weight of the loads was staggering—88 to 110 pounds on a teenager's still developing frame. But Abiral thought he'd hit the jackpot. And in a way he had, because in Lukla he first observed foreigners and learned that carrying their packs was both less work and more profitable. "I thought this looked like an easier gig," he said.

His first season on the difficult Mera Peak trail didn't go well, however. "I didn't have good shoes. My load was thirty kilograms [about sixty-six pounds] for 275 rupees per day, and after four days I was told to return—I couldn't physically handle the work. I was too young; I was too small. They rejected me saying I couldn't keep up."

Back in Lukla he eked out a living with odd jobs, washing dishes, cleaning houses, and working as a cook's helper. When the budding entrepreneur wasn't hauling loads for foreigners or cutting wood, he broke stones in the jungle and lugged them to Lukla for building projects. He eventually found work at Island Peak base camp as a kitchen boy. "That's when I saw mountaineering for the first time. It was so interesting. One day the guides put their gear on me, and I tried it out. They encouraged me."

He graduated to "cook" at Island Peak but couldn't stifle his interest in climbing. Finally, in the spring of 2010, the guides invited him to join their last trip up the mountain. They not only guided him but also gave him some training, and advised him on a potential career in the mountains. Nine years and $25,000 later, he is an internationally accredited guide.

Abiral has guided Island Peak more than 250 times, has worked on various 8,000ers, and narrowly avoided the 2014 Everest avalanche by three minutes. "It was night and we were walking to Camp 2 with heavy loads from base camp. A bridge broke, so there was a traffic jam. . . . My friends sat around smoking. . . . I had an awkward load of tent poles and I couldn't just put them down anywhere. I had this urgent feeling to get out of there." He was in one of the most dangerous parts of the Icefall, with leaning seracs and gaping crevasses, when he heard a huge chunk of ice crashing down. Everyone around him was praying. Shortly after, "around nine or ten of us pulled the bodies out. My friends in front and behind me died."

The avalanche of 2014 that killed sixteen Nepalis in the Khumbu Icefall was an objective hazard that was probably impossible to predict. But Abiral believes that "subjective" accidents are less frequent now, thanks to better training.

As with so many from Nepal and Pakistan, his choice of profession is linked directly to education. "I am now helping to educate my brother, my two sisters, my wife, and my son, because education is the most important thing one can't do without. For work, for life. If I was educated, I probably wouldn't have been a guide! It's hard work! Education will fill the gap and make a balance for us."

Still, for a man who fled his village from the Maoists at the age of fourteen, Abiral Rai has done okay. "What I love about mountaineering most: it's beautiful being in nature. I find it is sacred to go to these places."

Other Nepali climbers have chosen different models of survival. Tenzeeng Sherpa is an internationally qualified guide, but he is also a clever entrepreneur. When the pandemic hit Nepal in 2020, virtually closing the country to foreign travelers, he took advantage of the break from guiding to start an outdoor technical clothing company.

Since both Tenzeeng and his business partner Pasang Gyeljen are guides, they knew what climbers at high altitudes required. By December of 2020 they had twenty-five different products: hardshell jackets, insulated pants, light jackets, trekking pants. "Our clothes are not as expensive as the big brands, but they have been tested locally in the Himalaya," Tenzeeng said. Their first down suit was worn by Kami Rita Sherpa on his twenty-fifth ascent of Everest. Their second prototype was worn on Manaslu and Dhaulagiri in 2021 by Kami Rita, Phunuru, Pasang Lhamu Sherpa Akita, and Princess Asma Al Thani of Qatar. While Tenzeeng's business is based in Kathmandu, other Nepalis have created successful outdoor companies abroad. The brainchild of UIAGM guide Tendi Sherpa and Dave Schaeffer, HIMALI now includes a number of Nepali climbers as shareholders.

There are other useful and creative ways for Nepali climbers to stay connected to their mountains and their traditions. Tenzing Gyalzen Sherpa is a thirty-one-year-old electrician, mountain guide, and IT specialist from Phortse whose office commute is more unusual than most; he services the highest weather station on Earth at 8,810 meters on Everest. It provides unique and valuable data on wind speeds and direction, temperature fluctuations, and precipitation levels. In the short term, this improves safety for climbers on the mountain, but more critically, it helps scientists respond to climate risks that threaten 53 million people who live in the Himalayan region.

Many wish to give back to their community in some way. As a globally recognized female Sherpa guide and role model, Dawa Yangzum is naturally at the forefront. She routinely trains younger climbers at the Khumbu Climbing Center, and in the fall of 2021, she led a group of six young Nepali women on a climb in Rolwaling, her home valley. She had trained with them for two years before taking them on a proper expedition. Two weeks later she reported on social media: "I was obviously happy to see the mentees becoming technically savvy on the mountains. But more importantly, they grew emotionally, and psychologically. They were no longer shy and timid little girls and had in fact become young and confident women who seemed ready to pursue different adventures in life. This emotional and psychological transformation was not something I had foreseen, and now I realize, this is the most important transition, and I feel, this is the most worthwhile outcome of my efforts, and I truly feel blessed to have the opportunities to make these differences."

Dawa Yangzum isn't alone in giving back to the community. Ang Tshering Lama not only rescued Sange Sherpa from immediately below Everest's summit. He inspired and enabled two climbing widows to climb Everest and boost their self-confidence, and then did the same for a friend struggling with drug addiction.

Wangda Sherpa had recently emerged from rehab and was feeling lost and vulnerable when he first met Ang Tshering. "He said it's okay what you did in your past, but now you can come out with a totally new version of Wangda," he recalled their conversation. Ang Tshering was training Fura Diki and Nima Doma at the time, so he invited Wangda to join them as a porter on a trek to Annapurna. After performing well, Wangda screwed up his courage to ask a favor.

"Ang Tshering, do you think there is any way I could be part of one of your Everest trips?"

Ang Tshering didn't hesitate. "If you wanna climb, join us. I just have to manage a few oxygen bottles and some climbing equipment, which is not a big deal."

Ecstatic, Wangda promised to stay clean and train hard.

"But you have to promise me that if you get to the top, you will do something with your success. You have to make something positive out of it."

Wangda reached the top, as did the two widows, Fura Diki and Nima Doma. At the summit, he unfurled a banner reading "No to Drugs"; he has been sharing his story with schools and rehab facilities ever since. "Ang Tshering was like an Angel for me who came from heaven to lift me up and show me I am capable and of value," Wangda said.

At 7:40 a.m. on May 19, 2013, Samina Baig stepped onto the summit of Everest. She was twenty-two years old. By becoming the first Pakistani woman and the first Ismaili woman to climb the mountain, Samina acquired a public profile that led to expectations of more. Her older brother and trainer, Mirza Ali Baig, probably grasped that future responsibility better than Samina when he began preparing her for this historic moment. But Samina's first thoughts on the summit revealed that she also understood her role. "I was thinking about the women of Pakistan, those who are not allowed to get education, those who are not allowed to do whatever they want to do in their lives." Born and raised in Shimshal, Samina comes from a community of mountaineers. Mirza Ali recognized and nurtured her interest and natural talent. He considers himself an activist for women's empowerment in Pakistan and is using adventure sports to promote gender equality. Samina is leading the way with her performances in the mountains.

Lavish receptions, endless speeches, awards, and parades, even a meeting with the Pakistani prime minister followed her ascent of Everest. And always the same question: What's next? Climbing the Seven Summits, she decided, which she completed two years after Everest. She was clear about the reasons. "I think for me climbing is not just a fun thing. . . . It is to underscore and promote gender equality and women empowerment and . . . to promote this as a sport in Pakistan," she told Pakistani journalist Abdulmalik Merchant. "Once we are done with our main cause to climb mountains for gender equality and women empowerment, I will for sure climb with other girls as well!"

Although the number of women taking up the sport is growing, Samina still has a lot of work to do to raise the awareness and support for young Pakistani women who aspire to climb professionally, as she does. But she has been spectacularly successful at being recognized for what she has done, and for what she plans to do—climb all fourteen of the 8,000ers. She is not in anyone's shadow, including her brother's.

There is room for optimism in Pakistan; mountaineering is starting to be recognized and supported. As in Nepal, however, the recognition often swirls around 8,000 meters. Sirbaz Khan, who is well on his way to climbing all fourteen of them, is well known in Pakistan. He exudes a quiet confidence with his unflinching gaze and effortless gait. Hailing from Hunza, his first mountain experience was in 2004, when he spent his ninth-grade summer holiday trekking to K2. "When I reached base camp, I knew I was hooked to the mountains and nature," he said. Sirbaz continued with his education, but each summer he would return to the Baltoro to work as a kitchen helper for expeditions.

In 2014 he met Mingma G, who advised him to quit cooking. "He was very active and walked faster than anyone else in the team," Mingma G observed.

"Seeing my work and my physicality he encouraged me to shift my focus to mountaineering," Sirbaz said. "In 2016 when he came back, he asked me to climb K2 with him. I did not have much training then, but I had worked with Ali Sadpara, Ali Raza Sadpara, Fazal [Ali] and other notable climbers including foreigners. I knew how to use the equipment, but my experience was little with no proper training."

Still, Mingma G was impressed. "Even on higher altitudes he was stronger than me," he said. "We didn't summit K2 that year, but he made space in my mind and heart." In the fall of 2017, with Ali Sadpara, Mingma G, and others, Sirbaz reached the summit of Nanga Parbat. "It was my first 8,000-meter peak," he said. Wasting little time, he announced his plan to climb all fourteen. As of this book's publication he has climbed thirteen. He supports his passion, in part, by working on Mingma G's rope-fixing team. "Very proud of you, brother Sirbaz," commented Mingma G. "Your nation and people are proud of you."

Sirbaz is breaking new ground for Pakistani climbers, but he is respectful and knowledgeable of those who came before him. He dedicated his Annapurna summit in the spring of 2021 to Ali Sadpara, the man who taught him and climbed with him on many peaks. His Dhaulagiri summit in the fall of 2021 was dedicated to Amir Mehdi, the forgotten hero from the first ascent of K2. And his Makalu summit in 2022 was dedicated to Ali Raza Sadpara, "the teacher of all teachers in our field" who could have "climbed the entire circuit [of 8,000ers] within ten months without any oxygen." Upon hearing of his death, Sirbaz said, "Ali Raza, my friend, thank you for teaching me how to climb and even more importantly for teaching me how to live.... I have rarely loved and respected any Mountaineer as much as I have loved and respected Apo Ali Raza. He was my *ustaad*, my friend, my partner."

Sirbaz is determined to bring the names of his mentors into prominence in the history of climbing. His journey started as a personal goal but evolved into something much greater. "Now there is so much more attached to it and I am fully committed to winning honour and pride for my country, my people, and especially the underprivileged mountaineering community of Pakistan," he said.

He feels responsible to the younger climbers of his country. "The coming period is ours," he says. "We will try our best to leave a better field for the coming generation. I will work for them whether it is insurance, training, or any other way. Our climbing community can go a long way if we work together."

Shehroze Kashif agrees. When he climbed Broad Peak at the age of seventeen, he became known as "The Broad Boy." Tall and slender, topped by an unruly mop of curls, he is convinced that the fourteen 8,000ers are the key to his happiness. The Lahore native has climbed several peaks in the 6,000-meter range with his father. In 2021 he became the youngest Pakistani to summit Everest and K2, and then he extended that record the following year with Kangchenjunga, Lhotse, and Makalu. He is already a national hero in Pakistan.

When Shehroze stood on top of Everest, he was obviously proud, but another Pakistani climber was on his mind. He posted a video with these words to Ali Sadpara, who had disappeared a few months earlier on K2: "Brother, this one is for you, for your legacy, for your memory and for your mission. . . . It will not be Shehroze Kashif alone, but WE all young mountaineers of Pakistan will carry on your legacy and will realize your dream for you. . . . In Shaa Allah!"

Shehroze Kashif. Sirbaz Khan. Samina Baig. Dawa Tenzing. Vinayak Malla. Abiral Rai. Sanduk Tamang. Dawa Gyalje. Tenji Sherpa. Gelje Sherpa. Dawa Yangzum. They are all part of a generation of climbers from Pakistan and Nepal who want to do more than climb simply to pay their bills. They are proud of their achievements and passionate about their mountains. Whether they are making first ascents or opening new routes, guiding 8,000-meter peaks, or climbing to inspire, they are ready to show the world what they can do.

EPILOGUE

Light and Shadow

The mountains are about mutual respect.

—TASHI SHERPA

THE HIMALAYA IS A PLACE OF TERRIFYING BEAUTY. IT INSPIRES BOTH awe and fear. But to focus only on the magnificent landscape diminishes the complexity and humanity of the area; we miss out on the perspective of those who live in the shadows of those towering peaks—the people of Shimshal and Phortse and Na, and many other places—whose lives are shaped by the architecture of their mountains.

When imaginations wander to the giant peaks of the Himalaya, often the images seen and the emotions felt are influenced by earlier Western perceptions and prejudices. Foreign explorers, alpinists, and athletes have all shaped our views of these mountains through their dreams and aspirations as we celebrate their accomplishments and marvel at their curiosity and bravery.

Western recognition and understanding of Pakistani and Nepali climbers have been far less evolved. "We have always been there, even on the first Himalayan expeditions, but the media never gave us a voice," Nimsdai insists. "We were in the shadows, and nobody talked about us." Although Western media hasn't covered the accomplishments of Pakistani and Nepali climbers extensively, some Western, Pakistani, and Nepali alpinists, journalists, and writers have offered nuanced accounts of local mountaineers that are part of the historical record, including those quoted throughout this book. But part of that nuance is how the accounts are received by the general public, and how those stories affect the individuals involved. By now, many people know the name of Lhakpa Sherpa, who is listed in the Guinness Book of Records as the most successful woman on Mount Everest with ten summits. Still, instead of being a celebrated athlete with sponsors vying for her attention, Lhakpa is a single mother of three, a former victim of spousal abuse who is now working for minimum wage in Connecticut. She can't even afford a car.

She isn't sure of her exact age, since no birth certificates were issued to children born at home in Balakharka, a village in the Makalu region. One of eleven siblings, she had no opportunity to attend school. Uneducated, and from the pre-internet generation, Lhakpa would have needed a fairy god-mother not only to launch her story onto the global stage, but to offer her a level of affluence and security commensurate to that of a ten-time Everest summiter.

⋯⋯

Or how about Gyalzen Norbu Sherpa, one of only three mountaineers with two first ascents of 8,000-meter peaks? The other two—Hermann Buhl and Kurt Diemberger—are world-famous mountaineering legends. But Gyal-zen Norbu, who was on the second rope team to make the first ascent of Makalu in 1955 and who made the first ascent of Manaslu in 1956, is virtually unknown.

Ghulam Rassul Galwan, an intrepid Ladakhi explorer who accompanied many important European expeditions and even learned English in order to write his memoir, *Servant of Sahibs*, remains almost completely unknown to this day.

Two pioneering Nepali climbers who did reach a wider audience through their memoirs are Ang Tharkay and Tenzing Norgay, but it's significant that both did so with Western co-authors. They probably intended to tell unfiltered stories, but there are elements of curation and interpretation in the writing. Just as this book is an interpretation of the history of climbers from Pakistan and Nepal seen through the lens of a woman from the Canadian Rockies.

Today's generation of climbers from Nepal and Pakistan have the internet advantage. And because they often speak English, their audience is global.

"We can reach people directly to tell our stories," Nimsdai told journalist Joe Bindloss. "We're not in the shadows anymore." They are speaking to the world in their own unfiltered voices, publishing their work on social media and in international newspapers and magazines.

Within the mountaineering community there is a certain amount of hand-wringing about modern Nepali and Pakistani climbers; they self-promote, collaborate with sponsors, and are constantly on their Instagram accounts posting pictures and videos of themselves doing brave and courageous feats. But this is what Westerners have been doing in one way or another for a very long time; to expect otherwise signals outdated romanticism. It's important to note that on social media announcements of Himalayan summits, it's now standard to see *all* the summit climbers named, not only the clients. And in a significant leap forward, we can also find posts naming the previously unheralded Icefall Doctors and rope-fixing teams.

Jan Morris's editorial about the 1953 Everest expedition for the *Times* expressed concern about the future: "Before long, I am afraid, the Sherpa as we knew him in 1953 will be a figure of the past, obliterated by fame, fortune and foreign innovations; and I am glad to have a caught a glimpse of him first." Any lingering fear of that change is surely a hangover from colonialist attitudes. But however enlightened contemporary climbers and readers think they are, there is still a tendency to define mountaineering in terms of personal fulfillment, self-awareness, and "pure" alpine-style, despite the supersized logos plastered on all of those supersized down suits designed for the supersized 8,000ers. For climbers from Nepal and Pakistan, mountaineering represents something more complex. Even though they are driven by a passion for the sport, they are also motivated by more practical issues such as earning a living and helping other members of their community do so. It seems curious—and a little hypocritical—that getting paid to do what you love is often considered impure or less admirable. Local climbers, whether from Shimshal or Rolwaling, have a vested interest in the financial stability, elements of fame, and above all, respect that comes from the world outside.

Back in the 1930s, German expedition leader Paul Bauer argued money wasn't a motivator for the locals. "With such splendid fellows as these Bhutias [Tibetans] and Sherpas . . . following us to the last man in desperate places, with a trust and enthusiasm beyond rewarding, which had no thought of payment, but sprang purely from ethical motives, from noble natural instincts." He was mistaken. Few locals living in Darjeeling in the 1930s would have willingly left their families for months at a time for "ethical motives" or "noble natural instincts." They did so to earn money to survive. Phurba Tashi Sherpa, one of the most accomplished high-altitude climbers in history, was clear about the importance of making a living from climbing rather than breaking Everest records: "A lot of people tell me I should go one more time to break the record, but it doesn't mean anything to me," he explained to journalist Andrew MacAskill. "Since the earthquake, when I look back at my career, my biggest disappointment is that I am still worrying about my future." Mingma G recently said that he would like to do more Piolet d'Or award-worthy climbs, but he also needs to make a living. And if that means posting triumphant photos of his company's guides leading clients to the top of 8,000ers, then that's what he will do.

Sherpas, as we have seen, have made significant gains in reshaping their relationship with Westerners. In the old days, foreign climbers called the shots. Sherpas were porters, taking orders, humping loads, perhaps learning a few skills, but treated as underlings. Understandable, perhaps, since in those days the Westerners had superior mountain skills and greater exploratory drive. But foreign climbers quickly discovered that their employees could do a lot more than carry heavy loads up steep slopes. They could acclimatize faster than anyone. They could be cultural liaisons, climbing partners, and fearless rescuers. They could acquire the skills to climb high and eventually, to lead high.

Today the situation has almost reversed. One by one, Pakistani and Nepali climbers are emerging into the light. Some are creeping out, painfully slowly. Others explode into the spotlight, an experience that can be harsh for them. Dawa Yangzum is inundated with media questions about her next big project and feels compelled to perform. What if she wants to take a year off? On an upward trajectory, stepping off the curve is difficult for her—not only because of her personal career, but because of the expectations from every Nepali girl who sees her as a role model.

In 1953 the pressure on Tenzing Norgay was even greater. The moment his Everest victory was broadcast, he was hounded, not only by the press, but by the governments of India, Nepal, and Tibet. "For the first thirty-eight years of my life no one cared what nationality I was," he said. "Indian, Nepali, or even Tibetan—what difference did it make? I was a Sherpa, a simple hillman; a man of the mountains, of the great Himalayas. But now everything was pushing and pulling. I was no longer a man, but some sort of doll to be hung from a string."

Nimsdai appears confident enough to handle any amount of pressure the world can throw at him. He enjoys his fame. But he hasn't experienced what Tenzing endured. For a few years, Tenzing was one of the most famous human beings alive. What pressure. Nimsdai, too, has to answer the question "What next?" After climbing the fourteen 8,000ers in short order, K2 in winter, the Seven Summits, and all his other record-breaking feats, he may have to go into space. And climb something. Without bottled oxygen.

At some point, all these men and women must return to their communities, reconnect with their neighbors and their families. Life isn't only about "followers." Fame can be a trap—as Polish alpinist Voytek Kurtyka called it, a "starry destiny"—that can destroy as quickly as it builds. It can become addictive. Or, as the Canadian author Alice Munro wrote, "Fame must be striven for, then apologized for. Getting or not getting it, you will be to blame." Nepali guide Abiral Rai wants to avoid it. "I'm not one of these people who everyone knows. I like staying in the background. I don't even want to be famous."

Sajid Sadpara would probably agree, but as the son of Ali Sadpara and a person who loves to be in the mountains—*on* the mountains—he feels obliged to be in the spotlight. Alex Txikon reflected on his time with Sajid when they traveled to Nanga Parbat base camp in the summer of 2021 to erect a memorial to Ali. "He showed me distressing videos of Ali, scenes of dire suffering. These were heart-wrenching moments. Sajid is strikingly poised and composed. . . . We huddled in conversation past midnight, while the Milky Way and millions of stars sparkled over our heads. A beautiful conversation swollen with much emotion." Strikingly poised—but breaking apart inside.

What would the elders think of this new order? Would Amir Mehdi be proud to know that Shimshali climbers are leading foreigners to the top of *his* mountain—K2—and being paid to do so? That young Shimshali girls are being trained, together with young boys, in the art of mountaineering? That Ali Sadpara transcended local and even national fame to become a global mountaineering icon? What would Pasang Lhamu Sherpa think of Dawa

Yangzum, Nepal's first internationally qualified female mountain guide? Would Pasang Kikuli be thrilled to learn that an all-Nepali team was the first to climb K2—the mountain that claimed his life—in winter? What would Ang Tharkay make of the conga line near Annapurna's summit in the spring of 2021?

Would these mountaineering elders be proud? Envious? Horrified?

Tenzing Norgay's daughter Pem Pem was a keen observer of the transition taking place with local climbers. She and her sister Nima had both been involved in high-altitude climbing in the past, including a women's attempt on Cho Oyu in 1959, and they had a good sense of what their father's reactions might be. Pem Pem shared some of her thoughts just days before she passed away in 2022. "I know my father would be horrified at the *tamasha* (fuss) surrounding Everest these days . . . but later in his life he came to realize what climbing Everest could do for his people. Tenzing was ambitious but he was also humble—not subservient or downtrodden—just humble. But he would be pleased that today's modern climbers are doing so well. They are finally getting the respect they deserve."

Fame and money and the glare of the spotlight all present drawbacks that are not immediately apparent to those seeking them. But there's no downside to respect. Climbers from Nepal and Pakistan deserve all the respect they are finally getting. Respect is worth celebrating.

Acknowledgments

WRITING A BOOK DURING A GLOBAL PANDEMIC WAS LIKE MOST PANDEMIC experiences: new, challenging, and sometimes lonely. I could not have done it without my two trusted partners, Saqlain Muhammad and Sareena Rai. Saqlain and I worked together to create a comprehensive interview schedule for Pakistani climbers. Once that was complete, he hit the road—in some cases very rough and dangerous roads—to mountain villages scattered throughout the Karakoram. He set up his sound and video recording devices in all kinds of locations and weather, diligently recording the stories of Pakistani climbers, many of whom are unknown outside their country. He transcribed those recordings and then translated them from Urdu, Shina, and Balti into English. Sareena brought her extensive knowledge of mountaineering in Nepal to this project, introducing me to climbers and family members I would have had no other way of knowing. She conducted her interviews primarily in Kathmandu in Nepali and Sherpa and later transcribed and translated them into English. Although I was able to remotely conduct many interviews myself, the assistance of these two individuals was crucial to the book and I can't adequately express my gratitude to them.

I received many hours of valuable advice from individuals who have spent years amassing expertise and cultural nuance in the world of mountaineering in Nepal and Pakistan. Many thanks to Janice Sacherer, Pasang Yangjee Sherpa, Frances Klatzel, Nandini Purandare, Ian Wall, Billi Bierling, Lisa Chogyal, Julie Rak, Shae A. Frydenlund, Steve Swenson, Jonathan Westaway, and Nokmedemla Lemtur for sharing their wisdom with me.

Research for this book could have gone on forever, but deadlines are deadlines, so at some point it had to end. Thanks to valued friends and colleagues who helped along the way. Bob A. Schelfhout Aubertijn, Lisa Chogyal, Ian Wall, Nazir Sabir, NamGyal Sherpa, Rodolphe Popier, Eberhard Jurgalski, and Jonathan Westaway all pointed me in some interesting and occasionally obscure directions. But I think it's important to be clear that this is not a complete history of Nepali and Pakistani climbers. I focused on certain characters and climbs rather than trying to cram all of the details of this vast, complex, and impressive history into one volume. As a result, many significant ascents and important characters are not included. I hope I won't be the last author to tackle this fascinating theme.

Firsthand interviews inform much of what appears on these pages. I am deeply grateful for the time and the willingness of the following people to share their stories, opinions, and memories: Mushtaq Ahmed, Fazal Ali, Muhammad Ali, Qudrat Ali, Rosi Ali, Yousuf Ali, Azam Baig, Mirza Ali Baig, Rashid Ullah Baig, Shaheen Baig, Adam Bielecki, Bill Buxton, Doug Chabot, Chhurim Dolma, Ali Durani, Alessandro Filippini, Damien Gildea, Prakash Gurung, Peter Hackett, Al Hancock, Muhammad Hanif, Muhammad Hassan, Cheryl Holman, Tom Hornbein, Little Hussain, Taqi Hushe, Katie Ives, Hassan Jan, Scott Johnston, Abdul Joshi, Little Karim, Meharbin Karim, Muhammad Kazim, Sirbaz Khan, Frances Klatzel, Ang Tshering Lama, Phunjo Lama, Phunjo Jhangmu Lama, Muhammad Ali Machulu, Vinayak Jay Malla, Rita Gombu Marwah, Simone Moro, Amanda Padoan, Suraj Paudyal, Nandini Purandare, Nirmal Purja, Suchi Purja, Abiral Rai, Wilco van Rooijen, Haji Rosi, Louis Rousseau, Nazir Sabir, Jan Sacherer, Ali Musa Sadpara, Ali Raza Sadpara, Dilawar Hussain Sadpara, Hassan Sadpara, Imtiaz Hussain Sadpara, Muhammad Sharif Sadpara, Nisan Sadpara, Sadiq Sadpara, Sajid Sadpara, Sadiq Sadpara, Sadparvi, Ang Dorje Sherpa, Chewang Jangmu Sherpa, Dawa Futi Sherpa, Dawa Gyalje Sherpa, Dawa Sherpa, Dawa Sange Sherpa, Dawa Yangzum Sherpa, Fura Diki Sherpa, Gelje Sherpa, Lakpa Rita Sherpa, Maya Sherpa, Mingma G Sherpa, NamGyal Sherpa, Panuru Sherpa, Pasang Dawa Sherpa, Pasang Lhamu Sherpa Akita, Pasang Tshering Sherpa, Pasang Y. Sherpa, Pemba Sharwa Sherpa, Pertemba Sherpa, PK Sherpa, Tenji Sherpa, Tenzeeng Sherpa, Wangda Sherpa, Wangchhu Sherpa, Yangjee Doma Sherpa, Luke Smithwick, Steve Swenson, Sanduk Tamang, Judy Tenzing, Ian Wall, Freddie Wilkinson, and Peter Zuckerman.

Thank you to everyone who generously contributed images to this project. Not all were used in the final pages of the book, but every one of your photographs was a valuable addition to my understanding of the complex and wonderful stories that fill the chapters. Thank you to Shaheen Baig, Chris Bonington, Sandro Gromen-Hayes, Jackson Groves, Al Hancock, Uta Ibrahimi, Toshio Imanishi, Sirbaz Khan, Gao Li, Vinayak Malla, Simone Moro, Saqlain Muhammad, Peter Müllritter, Nirmal Purja, Abiral Rai Collection, Louis Rousseau, Jan Sacherer, Ali Sadpara Collection, Sajid Sadpara, Dawa Futi Sherpa, Mingma G Sherpa, and Pasang Lhama Sherpa Akita, as well as the archives of the German Alpine Club.

An early reading of a manuscript in progress is a delicate operation. I want to thank those who gave me sensitive and informed advice on my early scribblings: Kate Rogers, Bob A. Schelfhout Aubertijn, Billi Bierling, Steve Swenson, Jochen Hemmleb, Ian Wall, and Philip Henderson.

I was incredibly fortunate to work with some inspired (and inspiring) editors who played an important part in the crafting of this book: Marni Jackson, Beth Jusino, Katie Ives, and Mary Metz. I've worked so often with Marni, Katie, and Mary that they are old friends as well as writing colleagues, but it was my first time working with Beth. They are all treasures. Thank you to the entire Mountaineers Books team, particularly Kate Rogers, who encouraged me from day one to tackle what felt like an impossible task.

And finally, thank you to my friends who supported me throughout this process, some of which was done while lying in bed, my newly minted knee propped high on pillows and encased in ice. Thanks most of all to my husband, Alan, for feeding me, encouraging me, and keeping that ice bucket full.

Notes

AUTHOR'S NOTE

8 *As Shae A. Frydenlund, a scholar who studies*: Shae A. Frydenlund, "Situationally Sherpa: Race, Ethnicity, and the Labour Geography of the Everest Industry," *Journal of Cultural Geography* 36, no. 1 (2019).

INTRODUCTION: ONE SUMMIT—TWO CENTURIES

11 *"My dream, and my only real mission*: Mingma Gyalje Sherpa, "When We Unite, Nothing Is Impossible: My Story on K2," *Outdoorjournal.com*, February 18, 2021.

CHAPTER ONE: TEN RUPEES A DIGIT

19 *"If they are properly taught*: C. W. Rubenson, "Kabru in 1907," *Alpine Journal* 24 (February 1908–November 1909): 310–321.

19 *Back again in 1911, Kellas*: This expedition included what can be considered the first alpine-style ascent of a 7,000-meter peak, Pauhunri (7,128m).

21 *"capricious and temperamental, physically almost*: Elizabeth Knowlton, *The Naked Mountain.*

22 *"The tears were streaming down his cheeks*: Frank Smythe, *Kamet Conquered.*

24 *By late afternoon, Schneider and Aschenbrenner*: Neither Peter Aschenbrenner nor Fritz Bechtold reported the skiing incident in their official reports, nor is there any pictorial evidence in the files of the German Alpine Club that skis were taken on the summit climb. This detail comes from Ang Tsering and was a well-known story among Darjeeling Sherpas.

27 *Ang Tsering later confided*: Tenzing Norgay, as told to James Ramsey Ullman, *Man of Everest.*

28 *"There was mourning and grief*: Tenzing Norgay and Ullman.

CHAPTER TWO: A THIN BLACK WALLET: TRAGEDY ON K2

32 *"did not seem to us a very likable type*: H. W. Tilman, *The Ascent of Nanda Devi.*

33 *"only one worth a place on a serious show"*: Tilman.

34 *"I freely confess that I myself*: Richard Sale, *The Challenge of K2.*

34 *"no other race capable of*: Cited in Sale, *The Challenge of K2.*

35 *"Though slight of build*: Quoted in Ed Viesturs, with David Roberts, *K2: Life and Death on the World's Most Dangerous Mountain.*

35 *"Millionaires' Row in expeditioning*: Charles S. Houston and Robert H. Bates, *Five Miles High.*

35 *"take off his master's marching boots*: Houston and Bates.

39 *Blessed with temperatures above freezing*: This was the hardest piece of high-altitude climbing done before World War II and for many years after, somewhere between climbing grades 5.7 and 5.9.

42 *"After all, a Himalayan mountain*: Letter from Lt. George "Joe" Trench to Clifford Smith, May 16, 1940.

43 *"Pasang wouldn't hear of it*: Herbert Tichy, *Cho Oyu.*

44 *"The story should be about the existence*: Katie Ives, "Between the Lines," *Alpinist* 51 (Autumn 2015): 12.

CHAPTER THREE: DARJEELING TIGERS

46 *"The expedition organizers barely*: Ang Tharkay, with Basil P. Norton, *Sherpa: The Memoir of Ang Tharkay.* All other quotes attributed to Ang Tharkay in this chapter taken from the same source.

46 *"Towering up thousands of feet*: Cecil Godfrey Rawling, *The Great Plateau.*

47 *"The porters had come to have a share*: Charles Granville Bruce, *The Assault on Mount Everest, 1922.*

47 *"Only Sherpas and Bhotias killed*: T. H. Somervell, *After Everest.*

47 *"They have done so splendidly*: Patrick French, *Younghusband: The Last Great Imperial Adventurer.*

48 *"This is going to be more like war*: Maurice Isserman and Stewart Weaver, *Fallen Giants.*

51 *"The Sherpas had the notion*: Sherry Ortner, *Life and Death on Mt. Everest.*

51 *"You have to read between the lines*: Katie Ives, "Between the Lines," *Alpinist* 51 (Autumn 2015).: 11.

51 *"He has been with me*: Eric Shipton, *Upon That Mountain.*

52 *"The Sherpas slept on the floor*: Peter Steele, *Eric Shipton.*

CHAPTER FOUR: FATHER OF THE MODERN SHERPA GUIDE

55 *"They made a strong impression on me*: Ang Tharkay, with Basil P. Norton, *Sherpa: The Memoir of Ang Tharkay.* All other quotes attributed to Ang Tharkay in this chapter taken from the same source.

57–58 *"Tomorrow morning Lachenal Sahib*: Adapted from Maurice Herzog, *Annapurna.*

58 *of the 175 names, "51 have died*: H. W. Tobin, "Himalayan Porters," *Himalayan Journal* 16 (1951): 121.

59 *"Now we were nearing our goal*: Herzog.

60 *"I felt the eyes of the Sherpas*: Herzog.

60 *"A new and splendid life*: David Roberts, *True Summit.*

61–62 *"Hillary is a hero in Nepal*: Roberts, *True Summit.*

62 *"I had not seen him since 1939*: Eric Shipton, *The Mount Everest Reconnaissance Expedition 1951.*

62–63 *"My father was a simple*: Dawa Sherpa, afterword to *Sherpa: The Memoir of Ang Tharkay*, by Ang Tharkay, with Basil P. Norton.

63 *"My father used to tell us*: Dawa Sherpa.

CHAPTER FIVE: THE FIRST SUPERSTAR

65 *"He was so big and fat*: Lhakpa Norbu Sherpa, "Was Tenzing a Tibetan, Nepali or Indian? It Does Not Matter," Nepalitimes.com, May 28, 2021. (From a radio interview for All India Radio Kurseong done in 1985, a year before Tenzing Norgay died.)

65 *"For me it is all right*: Tenzing Norgay, as told to James Ramsey Ullman, *Man of Everest*. All other quotes attributed to Tenzing Norgay in this chapter taken from the same source.

68 *"From a hundred applicants*: Eric Shipton, *That Untravelled World*.

70 *"I remember vividly*: Ian Cameron, *Mountains of the Gods*.

73 *"I always remember with pleasure*: Jan Morris, *Coronation Everest*.

73 *"An oddly assorted pair*: Jan Morris, introduction to *Tenzing: Hero of Everest* by Ed Douglas.

73–74 *"Tenzing sat there inscrutably*: Morris, *Coronation Everest*.

75 *"As the greatest of their little*: Morris, *Coronation Everest*.

75 *"It was 2 June and Mummy*: Tashi Tenzing, *Tenzing Norgay and the Sherpas of Everest*.

76 *"I bought him a present*: Ed Douglas, *Tenzing: Hero of Everest*.

77 *"He is paying the price of fame*: James Ramsey Ullman, introduction to *Man of Everest*, by Tenzing Norgay, as told to Ullman.

78 *"I climbed Everest so that*: Jamling Tenzing Norgay, with Broughton Coburn, *Touching My Father's Soul*.

CHAPTER SIX: FORGOTTEN HERO

80 *"Although the spirit is willing*: Mohammad Ata-Ullah, *Citizen of Two Worlds*.

80 *"The Americans were all for*: Ata-Ullah.

81 *"Those three days never came*: Ata-Ullah.

81 *"This is Camp 8*: Adapted from Ata-Ullah.

81 *"Hello, Base Camp. Hello*: Abridged conversation from Charles S. Houston and Robert H. Bates, *K2: The Savage Mountain*.

82 *"We were witnessing an epic*: Ata-Ullah.

82 *"It was," said Bob Craig,"the deepest experience*: Houston and Bates, *K2: The Savage Mountain*.

83 *"At this point the biggest and strongest*: Abridged conversation from Houston and Bates, *K2: The Savage Mountain*.

83 *"We entered the mountains*: Houston and Bates, *K2: The Savage Mountain*.

84 *"The exuberant eagerness*: Ata-Ullah.

84 *"This man was remarkable*: Walter Bonatti, *The Mountains of My Life*.

84 *"this was a subtle but necessary*: Bonatti, 89.

86 *"It reminded him of his suffering*: Shahzeb Jillani, "Amir Mehdi: Left Out to Freeze on K2 and Forgotten," BBC.com, August 7, 2014.

CHAPTER SEVEN: NOT ALLAH, LITTLE KARIM

89 *"Team members talking*: Galen Rowell, *In the Throne Room of the Mountain Gods.*

91 *"Mountains are my soul*: Graham Zimmerman, "Through the Field," *Alpinist* 51 (Autumn 2015): 83.

91 *"My feet had been burned*: Yasal Munim, "Ali Sadpara's Trainer Was the First Pakistani to Summit K2," Samaaenglish.tv, February 18, 2021.

91–92 *"I was one of the luckiest people*: Sonya Rehman, "Interview: Pakistan's Premier Mountaineer on His Passion for Heights and Homeland," Asiasociety.org, April 29, 2013.

93 *"For the next forty-five minutes*: Richard Sale, *The Challenge of K2.*

93 *"Ohtani wept as he called*: Nazir Sabir, "Dawn on the West Ridge" *Alpinist* 38 (Spring 2012): 51.

93 *"In a way I was paranoid*: Rehman.

95 *"Even back then, I knew*: Obaid Ur Rehman Abbasi, "Adventure: The incredible Tales of Little Karim," Dawn.com, June 22, 2014.

95 *"A group of mountaineers*: Shabbir Mir, "The extraordinary life of Little Karim," *Express Tribune.*Abbasi.

95 *"snuck his head between*: Abbasi.

95 *"The climb with the British*: Abbasi.

96 *"Not Allah, Little Karim*: Ian Welsted, "What Makes a Climbing Hero and the Legendary Little Karim," Gripped.com, March 3, 2021.

97 *"Meeting Little Karim*: Welsted.

CHAPTER EIGHT: TURNING POINTS

100 *"I didn't think about anything*: Kapil Bisht, "The Mountain Lover," *Alpinist* 78 (Summer 2022): 57.

101 *"The boredom, the sheer*: Jimmy Roberts, "The Himalayan Odyssey," Nepalitimes.com, September 12, 2020. (Parts of blog entry originally posted in 1997.)

101 *"The years from 1950 to 1965*: Jimmy Roberts.

102 *"Jimmy Roberts' Mountain Travel Sherpas*: Chris Bonington, *Everest South West Face.*

102 *"We saw a touching, solemn scene*: Chris Bonington, *Everest the Hard Way.*

102–3 *"I consulted Pertemba at each step*: Bonington, *Everest the Hard Way.*

103 *"Would you like to say*: Adapted from Bonington, *Everest the Hard Way.*

104 *"For years after he passed away*: Bisht.

105 *"I'm not going to take anything*: Bisht.

CHAPTER NINE: TOWER OF BABEL

108–9 *"safest climber around*: Peter Zuckerman and Amanda Padoan, *Buried in the Sky.*

109 *"Karim and Jehan became*: Zuckerman and Padoan.

109 *"I asked him to stay in Shimshal*: Zuckerman and Padoan.

112 *"We need flexibility*: Freddie Wilkinson, *One Mountain Thousand Summits.*

113 *"It was unjust*: Zuckerman and Padoan.

118 *"If we die," he said*: Wilkinson.

118–19 *"What's happening?*: Adapted from Wilkinson.

120 *"I took it like a knife*: Zuckerman and Padoan.

120 *Wilco van Rooijen approached Nazir*: Zuckerman and Padoan.

121 *"The mainstream media focused on*: Zuckerman and Padoan.

122 *"I've been cut in half*: Zuckerman and Padoan.

CHAPTER TEN: DAYS OF JOY AND SORROW

124 *"Reportedly, a porter helped*: Angela Benavides, "Broad Peak: New Reports on the Rescue and Kim's Fatal Fall," Explorersweb.com, July 21, 2021.

124 *"After saving the girl*: Kan Hyeong-woo, "Russian Mountaineer Accuses Climbers of Passing by Missing Korean Mountaineer," Koreaherald.com, July 25, 2021.

129 *"I watched busloads*: Steve Swenson, *Karakoram*.

130 *"This includes knowing when*: Kamran Ali, "Shaheen Baig--The Rescuer," Kamranonbike.com, December 22, 2020.

CHAPTER ELEVEN: SADPARA CLIMBERS—MASTERS OF WINTER

137 *"Several hours spent*: Robert Szymczak, "Broad Peak 18.02.2011," Karakorumclimb.com, February 20, 2011.

137 *"We sleep in what is left*: Szymczak.

138 *"The things I experienced*: Adam Bielecki and Dominik Szczepański, *Spod Zamarzniętych Powiek* [Under frozen eyelids], translated by Julia Pulwicki for the author.

140 *"Of course he climbs for money*: "Nisar Hussain," Altitudepakistan.blogspot.com, December 31, 2012.

141 *"We will start at about 3 a.m:* Jochen Hemmleb, *Gerfried Göschl: Spuren für die Ewigkeit* [Gerfried Göschl: tracks for eternity], translated by Hemmleb for the author.

CHAPTER TWELVE: ICE WARRIORS

144 *"I left Camp 4 and when*: Bernadette McDonald, *Winter 8000*.

145 *"Ali worked his heart out*: Alex Txikon, *La Montaña Desnuda: Primera Ascensión Invernal al Nanga Parba* [The Naked Mountain: First winter ascent of Nanga Parbat], translated by Larry Lilue for the author.

145 *Partway up the Kinshofer Couloir*: The more correct, although less well-known name, is the Löw Couloir, named after Sigi Löw, who made the first ascent of the route in 1962 but died on the descent.

146 *"As we closed in on that*: Txikon.

146 *"Just a few minutes before*: Txikon.

148 *"But Ali, twenty minutes ago*: Txikon.

148–49 *"Initially I told them only half-truth*: Raheel Adnan, "Interview with Muhammad Ali Sadpara (Part-2): Winter Climbing and First Winter Ascent of Nanga Parbat," Explorersweb.com, March 8, 2016.

CHAPTER THIRTEEN: DAY JOB ON EVEREST

153 *"[Twenty-fifth] time was fun*: Interview conducted by Bhusan Dahal for *Legends Talk*, Episode 5, August 12, 2021, video.

154 *"Foreigners never find*: Deepak Thapa, "Upwardly Mobile Ang Rita," Himalmag. com, September 1, 1996.

154 *"Ang Rita Sherpa would have*: Thapa.

155 *"Commercial expeditions were very rare*: Mark Pattison, "Lakpa Rita Sherpa," episode 189 of *Finding Your Summit* (podcast), February 5, 2021.

157 *Later, when Canadian mountaineer Roger Marshall*: Roger Marshall, "The King of Everest," *Backpacker Magazine*, May 1986.

157 *When Roger pressed him to explain*: Marshall.

158 *"It was like an exam*: Ed Douglas, "Babu Chhiri Sherpa," *Guardian*, May 3, 2001.

158 *"I remember this guy*: Josh Sens, "Tent-Makers Remember 'King' Climber," SFgate.com, May 11, 2001.

CHAPTER FOURTEEN: BIG MOUNTAINS ARE BIG BUSINESS

159 *"Fixing ropes is a sensitive*: Deepak Adhikari, "The Everest Brawl: A Sherpa's Tale," Outsideonline.com, August 13, 2013.

160 *"I think the leader felt like*: Tim Neville, "Brawl on Everest: Ueli Steck's Story," Outsideonline.com, May 2, 2013.

160 *"Greg knew it was not*: Neville.

160 *"It was natural for Sherpas*: Adhikari.

161 *"That's false," Tashi said*: Adhikari.

161 *"I lost something I really love*: Neville.

161 *"Not a single journalist or blogger*: Adhikari.

161 *"I think the relation between Sherpas*: Adhikari.

161 *"This is not over*: Neville.

161–62 *"Much has been written*: Tashi Sherpa, "Everest Interrupted," *Alpinist* 47 (Summer 2014): 90.

162 *"Himalayan mountaineering was originally*: Sherry Ortner, *Life and Death on Mt. Everest*.

163 *"Climbing Everest is so big*: Neville.

165 *"The strategy doesn't take*: Angela Benavides, "Annapurna, the New 8,000m Business Model," Explorersweb.com, April 25, 2021.

167–68 *"Namche Bazar is among*: Ed Douglas, *Himalaya*.

168 *Anthropologist Pasang Yangjee Sherpa shed light*: Pasang Yangjee Sherpa, "Mountain As Metaphor: A Future of Multiple Worldviews," *Alpinist* 75 (Autumn 2021): 49.

168 *"I could not live with being responsible*: Angela Benavides, "Everest: COVID Parties and Summit Pushes," Explorersweb.com, May 16, 2021.

170 *It's fairly common now*: On July 22, 2022, more than 140 people reached the summit of K2, almost all of them guided by Sherpas from Nepal.

CHAPTER FIFTEEN: GAPS IN THE LINE

171 *"a cross between a medieval assault*: Chris Bonington, *Everest the Hard Way*.

179 *"I picture next year, at gatherings*: Jemima Diki Sherpa, "Three Springs," Alpinist. com, April 25, 2014.

CHAPTER SIXTEEN: THE NIMSDAI EFFECT

181 *In his autobiography*: Nirmal Purja, *Beyond Possible*. All other quotes attributed to Nirmal "Nimsdai" Purja in this chapter taken from the same source, unless credited otherwise below.

181 *"Well, you've got to roll into it*: Stephen Potter, "'I Wanted to Completely Change the Dynamic on 8,000-Meter Peaks': A Q&A with Nims Purja," Climbing.com, November 25, 2021.

184 *"I just said, 'You know, let's climb*: Potter.

185 *"I spent a year fighting*: Potter.

186 *"I carried part of his [Nimsdai's] weight*: Angela Benavides, "Gesman Tamang: The Long, Hard Path from Cook to Elite Guide," Explorersweb.com, August 31, 2022.

192 *"I had so many grey hairs*: Torquil Jones, *14 Peaks: Nothing Is Impossible*.

192 *"With his coolness, he has made himself*: Stephanie Geiger, "Nirmal Purja, the 'Superstar of the Eight-Thousanders': How Cool Is the Nepalese Mountaineer Really?" [in German], Nzz.ch, December 17, 2021.

192 *"The bottom line is, we*: Potter.

192–93 *"What makes the international news*: Joe Bindloss, "The Nepali Mountaineer Reclaiming the Himalaya," Lonelyplanet.com, April 9, 2021.

193 *"It wasn't my project*: Potter.

CHAPTER SEVENTEEN: ROLWALING'S MINGMA G

195 *"Once I began the climb*: Mingma Gyalje Sherpa, "Full Value," *Alpinist* 53 (Spring 2016): 93. All other quotes attributed to Mingma Gyalje Sherpa in this chapter taken from the same source, unless credited otherwise below.

197 *"A beyul is more than just a place*: Stuart Butler, "The Himalaya's Hidden 'Paradise Valleys,'" BBC.com, August 30, 2022.

198 *"the old, the poor, the alcoholic*: Janice Sacherer, "Tsho Rolpa, GLOFS, and the Sherpas of Rolwaling Valley: A Brief Anthropological Perspective," Mountain Hazards, Mountain Tourism e-conference, November 15, 2006.

198 *"For many of the original settlers*: Janice Sacherer, "Rolwaling: A Sacred Buddhist Valley in Nepal," in *Sacredscapes and Pilgrimage Systems*, ed. Rana P. B. Singh:153–174.

198 *"The Nepalese government, unable*: Sacherer, "Rolwaling: A Sacred Buddhist Valley in Nepal."

198 *"It was the men of the poorest*: Ruedi Baumgartner, *Farewell to Yak and Yeti?*

199 *"Even today, we still don't*: Angela Benavides, "Mingma G. Sherpa: The Pawn Who Chose to Be a King," Alpinemag.com, November 9, 2021.

200 *"I left Rolwaling as a student*: Baumgartner.

201   "It was my most dangerous climb: Benavides, "Mingma G. Sherpa: The Pawn Who Chose to Be a King."

202   *"Once I fixed the final anchors*: Angela Benavides, "Interview with Mingma G about Manaslu: 'No Excuses in the Future,'" Explorersweb.com, October 14, 2021.

203   *"There won't be any excuses*: Benavides, "Interview with Mingma G."

CHAPTER EIGHTEEN: K2 IN WINTER

206–7   *"Without risking, I don't think*: Pedro Gil, "Winter Expedition to K2. Day 2. Interview with Sergi Mingote: 'I Am a Risk-Taker Mountaineer,'" Mundo-geo. es/expediciones-extremas, December 20, 2020.

207   *"We spoke for a few minutes only*: Mingma Gyalje Sherpa, "When We Unite, Nothing Is Impossible: My Story on K2," Outdoorjournal.com, February 18, 2021.

207   *"My first attempt failed*: Angela Benavides, "Mingma David Sherpa on Winter K2," Explorersweb.com, November 29, 2021.

207   *"But we got back down*: Natalie Berry, "An Oral History of Winter K2," *Himalayan Journal* 76 (2021): 211.

210   *"Our policy was to make zero contact*: Benavides, "Mingma David Sherpa on Winter K2."

210   *"I cannot describe in words how*: Joe Bindloss, "The Nepali Mountaineer Reclaiming the Himalaya," Lonelyplanet.com, April 9, 2021.

210   *"When Sergi fell*: Alessandro Filippini, "Tamara's Emotions and Thoughts" [in Italian], Alpinistiemontagne.gazzetta.it, February 27, 2021, translated by Filippini for the author.

211   *"We started the ascent at 11*: Isaac Fernández, "Sajid Ali's Experience on Winter K2" [in Spanish], Desnivel.com, February 25, 2021.

212   *"They must have had the accident*: Jerry Kobalenko, "K2: Sajid Speaks," Explorersweb.com, February 7, 2021.

214   *Legendary Himalayan alpinist Denis Urubko*: Angela Benavides, "Exclusive Interview: Denis Urubko on Nims, O2, and the Rules of Winter," Explorersweb. com, February 18, 2022.

215   *"Our plan was to announce this news*: Benavides, "Mingma David Sherpa on Winter K2."

215   *"I seem to have a genetic advantage*: Bindloss.

215   *"Well, that's what he said*: Benavides, "Exclusive Interview: Denis Urubko."

215   *When asked by journalist Thomas Pueyo why K2*: Thomas Pueyo, "Meeting Nirmal Purja, Universal Mountaineer," Alpinemag.com.

216   *"I had one of the most challenging*: Angela Benavides, "Sajid Sadpara on His Return to K2 and What Happened Up There," Explorersweb.com, June, 25, 2021.

216   *"We want to find out what happened*: Benavides.

216   *"That is the last time*: Benavides, "Sajid Sadpara on His Return to K2."

CHAPTER NINETEEN: THE MAOISTS ARE COMING

220 *"They were shy towards me*: Ruedi Baumgartner, *Farewell to Yak and Yeti?*

221 *"When he came home drunk*: Baumgartner.

222 *"If something happens to me*: Frances Klatzel, *Daring to Dream: Sherpa Women Climbing K2.*

225 *"More than anything else*: Leo Montejo, "What Really Happened on the Day That Ueli Steck Fell from Nuptse?," Wicis-sports.blogspot.com, June 21, 2017.

225 *"If you have been to the Himalayas*: Montejo.

233 *"I was thinking about the women*: "Female Ismaili Mountaineer Conquers Everest as an Inspiration to the Women of Pakistan," The.ismaili, June 21, 2013.

233 *"I think for me climbing is*: Abdulmalik Merchant, "Samina Baig and Mirza Ali in Conversation with Simerg," Simerg.com, April 29, 2014.

EPILOGUE: LIGHT AND SHADOW

237 *"We have always been there*: Joe Bindloss, "The Nepali Mountaineer Reclaiming the Himalaya," Lonelyplanet.com, April 9, 2021.

239 *"We can reach people directly*: Bindloss.

239 *"Before long, I am afraid*: Jan Morris, *Coronation Everest.*

240 *"With such splendid fellows*: Paul Bauer, *Himalayan Campaign: The German Attack on Kangchenjunga, the Second Highest Mountain in the World*, trans. Sumner Austin.

240 *"A lot of people tell me*: Andrew MacAskill, "Nepal Climbers Face Ruin after Quake, Blockade Hits Everest Industry," Reuters.com, December 20, 2015.

241 *"For the first thirty-eight years*: Tenzing Norgay, as told to James Ramsey Ullman, *Man of Everest.*

241 *"Fame must be striven for*: Alice Munro, *My Best Stories.*

241 *"He showed me distressing videos*: Alex Txikon, *La Montaña Desnuda: Primera Ascensión Invernal al Nanga Parba* [The Naked Mountain: First winter ascent of Nanga Parbat], translated by Larry Lilue for the author.

Select Bibliography and Sources

I AM DEEPLY INDEBTED TO THE WORK THAT HAS BEEN DONE BEFORE ME by all the writers, journalists, historians, and climbers who have documented the stories of Pakistani and Nepali climbers in the Greater Ranges. Their work has been invaluable for my research for this book. Although I was fortunate to have access to a wide array of published materials, many of the most important sources are not listed in the pages that follow. Hundreds of interviews took place during the writing of this book, many of them in English, but even more in Urdu, Nepali, Sherpa, Shina, and Balti, thanks to my two most valued partners, Saqlain Muhammad in Pakistan and Sareena Rai in Nepal. They not only conducted many of the interviews on my behalf, but taped, transcribed, and translated them. There is always a danger of missing the nuance, the implied meaning, or even the humor in an interview situation, but thanks to Saqlain's and Sareena's care and attention, and the incredible generosity of spirit of all the men and women who were interviewed, I am confident that the firsthand stories and opinions and memories presented in this volume are true representations of their authors, the people I most wanted to honor.

BOOKS

Ata-Ullah, Mohammad. *Citizen of Two Worlds*. New York: Harper & Brothers, 1960.

Band, George. *Everest: Fifty Years on Top of the World*. London: HarperCollins, 2003.

Bauer, Paul. *Himalayan Campaign: The German Attack on Kangchenjunga, the Second Highest Mountain in the World*. Translated by Sumner Austin. Oxford, UK: Basil Blackwell, 1937.

Baumgartner, Ruedi. *Farewell to Yak and Yeti?* Kathmandu: Vajra Books, 2015.

Bielecki, Adam, and Dominik Szczepański. *Spod Zamarzniętych Powiek* [Under frozen eyelids]. Warsaw: Agora, 2017.

Blum, Arlene. *Annapurna: A Woman's Place*. San Francisco: Sierra Club Books, 1980.

Bonatti, Walter. *The Mountains of My Life*. London: Penguin Classics, 1996.

Bonington, Chris. *Ascent*. London: Simon & Schuster, 2017.

———. *Everest South West Face*. London: Penguin Books, 1975.

———. *Everest the Hard Way*. London: Arrow Books, 1977.

Bowley, Graham. *No Way Down: Life and Death on K2*. London: Viking, 2010.

Bruce, Charles Granville. *The Assault on Mount Everest, 1922*. New York: Longmans, Green, 1923.

Cameron, Ian. *Mountains of the Gods*. New York: Facts On File Publication, 1984.

Douglas, Ed. *Himalaya*. London: The Bodley Head, 2020.

———. *Tenzing: Hero of Everest*. With an introduction by Jan Morris. Washington, DC: National Geographic, 2003.

French, Patrick. *Younghusband: The Last Great Imperial Adventurer*. New York: HarperCollins, 1995.

Galwan, Ghulam Rassul. *Servant of Sahibs*. Cambridge, UK: W. Heffer & Sons, 1924.

Hemmleb, Jochen. *Gerfried Göschl: Spuren für die Ewigkeit* [Gerfried Göschl: Tracks for Eternity]. Vienna: EGOTH—Verlag, 2014.

Herzog, Maurice. *Annapurna*. London: Jonathan Cape, 1952.

Holzel, Tom, and Audrey Salkeld. *The Mystery of Mallory & Irvine*. London: Pimlico, 1996.

Horrell, Mark. *Sherpa Hospitality as a Cure for Frostbite*. N.p.: Mountain Footsteps Press, 2022.

Houston, Charles S., and Robert H. Bates. *Five Miles High*. New York: Lyons Press, 1939.

———. *K2: The Savage Mountain*. New York: First Adventure Library Edition, 1994.

Isserman, Maurice, and Stewart Weaver. *Fallen Giants*. New Haven, CT: Yale University Press, 2008.

Jordan, Jennifer. *The Last Man on the Mountain*. New York: W. W. Norton, 2010.

Kauffman, Andrew J., and William L. Putnam. *K2: The 1939 Tragedy*. Seattle: Mountaineers Books, 1992.

Klatzel, Frances. *Daring to Dream: Sherpa Women Climbing K2*. As told by Dawa Yangzum Sherpa, Maya Sherpa, and Pasang Lhamu Sherpa Akita. Kathmandu: Mera Publications Pvt. Ltd., 2020.

Knowlton, Elizabeth. *The Naked Mountain*. New York: G. P. Putnam's Sons, 1934.

Lhamo, Rinchen. *We Tibetans*. London: Seeley Service, 1926.

McDonald, Bernadette. *Brotherhood of the Rope*. Seattle: Mountaineers Books, 2007.

———. *I'll Call You in Kathmandu*. Seattle: Mountaineers Books, 2005.

———. *Winter 8000*. Seattle: Mountaineers Books, 2020.

Moro, Simone. *The Call of the Ice*. Translated by Monica Meneghetti. Seattle: Mountaineers Books, 2014.

Morris, Jan. *Coronation Everest*. London: Faber and Faber, 2003.

Munro, Alice. *My Best Stories*. Toronto: Penguin Random House, 2009.

Neale, Jonathan. *Tigers of the Snow*. New York: Thomas Dunne Books / St. Martin's Press, 2002.

Norgay, Jamling Tenzing, with Broughton Coburn. *Touching My Father's Soul*. San Francisco: HarperCollins, 2001.

Norgay, Tenzing, as told to James Ramsey Ullman. *Man of Everest*. London: The Reprint Society, 1956.

Ortner, Sherry. *Life and Death on Mt. Everest*. Princeton, NJ: Princeton University Press, 1999.

Perrin, Jim. *Shipton & Tilman*. London: Hutchinson, 2013.

Purja, Nimsdai. *Beyond Possible*. London: Hodder & Stoughton, 2020.

Rawling, Cecil Godfrey. *The Great Plateau*. London: E. Arnold, 1905.

Roberts, David. *Limits of the Known*. New York: W. W. Norton, 2018.

———. *True Summit*. New York: Simon & Schuster, 2000.

Rowell, Galen. *In the Throne Room of the Mountain Gods*. San Francisco: Sierra Club Books, 1986.

Sale, Richard. *Broad Peak*. Hildersley, UK: Carreg, 2004.

———. *The Challenge of K2*. Barnsley, UK: Pen & Sword Discovery, 2011.

Schoening, Pete. *K2 1953*. Kenmore, WA: Estate of Peter K. Schoening, 2004.

Sherpa, Pasang Tshering. *Sherpa: The Ultimate Mountaineers*. Kathmandu: Hello Himalayan Homes, 2016.

Shipton, Eric. *Mount Everest Reconnaissance Expedition 1951*. London: Diadem Books, 1985.

———. *That Untravelled World*. Seattle: Mountaineers Books, 2015.

———. *Upon That Mountain*. London: Diadem Books, 1985.

Smythe, Frank. *Kamet Conquered*. London: Victor Gollancz, 1932.

Somervell, T. H. *After Everest*. London: Hodder & Stoughton, 1936.

Steck, Ueli, with Karin Steinbach. *My Life in Climbing*. Translated by Billi Bierling. Seattle: Mountaineers Books, 2018.

Steele, Peter. *Eric Shipton: Everest and Beyond*. Seattle: Mountaineers Books, 1998.

Swenson, Steve. *Karakoram*. Seattle: Mountaineers Books, 2017.

Tenzing, Tashi. *Tenzing Norgay and the Sherpas of Everest*. Camden, ME: Ragged Mountain Press, 2001.

Tharkay, Ang, with Basil P. Norton. *Sherpa: The Memoir of Ang Tharkay*. With an afterword by Dawa Sherpa. Seattle: Mountaineers Books, 2016.

Tichy, Herbert. *Cho Oyu*. London: Methuen, 1957.

Tilman, H. W. *The Ascent of Nanda Devi*. London: Diadem Books, 1983.

Txikon, Alex. *La Montaña Desnuda: Primera Ascensión Invernal al Nanga Parbat* [The Naked Mountain: First winter ascent of Nanga Parbat]. Bilbao: Sua Edizioak, 2021.

Viesturs, Ed, with David Roberts. *K2: Life and Death on the World's Most Dangerous Mountain*. New York: Broadway Books, 2009.

Wilkinson, Freddie. *One Mountain Thousand Summits*. New York: New American Library, 2010.

Zuckerman, Peter, and Amanda Padoan. *Buried in the Sky*. New York: W. W. Norton, 2012.

JOURNALS, THESES, CHAPTERS, NEWSPAPERS, AND MAGAZINES

Berry, Natalie. "An Oral History of Winter K2." *Himalayan Journal* 76 (2021): 204–220.

Bisht, Kapil. "The Mountain Lover." *Alpinist* 78 (Summer 2022): 54–71.

Douglas, Ed. "Babu Chhiri Sherpa." *Guardian*, May 3, 2001.

———. "The Mirror Cracked." *Alpinist* 51 (Autumn 2015): 87–91.

Frydenlund, Shae A. "Situationally Sherpa: Race, Ethnicity, and the Labour Geography of the Everest Industry." *Journal of Cultural Geography* 36, no. 1 (2019): 1–22.

Ives, Katie. "Between the Lines." *Alpinist* 51 (Autumn 2015): 11–12.

MacDiarmid, Campbell. "Who Carries the Load." *Alpinist* 42 (Spring 2013): 93–96.

Marshall, Roger. "The King of Everest." *Backpacker Magazine*, May 1986, 26–33.

Oh, Young Hoon. "Sherpa Intercultural Experiences in Himalayan Mountaineering: A Pragmatic Phenomenological Perspective." UC Riverside Electronic Theses and Dissertations, 2016.

Oppitz, Michael. "Myths and Facts: Reconsidering Some Data Concerning the Clan History of the Sherpa." *Kailash—Journal of Himalayan Studies* 2, no. 1 and 2 (1974): 121–31.

Rak, Julie. "Mediation, Then and Now: Ang Tharkay's *Sherpa* and *Memoires d'un Sherpa*." *Primerjalna Književnost* 45, no. 3 (2022): 125–44.

Rubenson, C. W. "Kabru in 1907." *Alpine Journal* 24 (February 1908–November 1909): 310–21.

Sabir, Nazir. "Dawn on the West Ridge." *Alpinist* 38 (Spring 2012): 50–51.

Sacherer, Janice. "The Recent Social and Economic Impact of Tourism on a Remote Sherpa Community." In *Asian Highland Societies in Anthropological Perspective*, edited by Christoph von Fürer-Haimendorf. New Delhi: Sterling; Atlantic Highlands, NJ: Humanities Press, 1981.

———. "Rolwaling: A Sacred Buddhist Valley in Nepal." In *Sacredscapes and Pilgrimage Systems*, edited by Rana P. B. Singh, 153–74. Planet Earth & Cultural Understanding Series, no. 7. New Dehli: Shubhi Publications, 2011.

———. "The Sherpas of Rolwaling: A Hundred Years of Economic Change." In *Himalaya: Écologie-Ethnologie*. Paris: Éditions du Centre Nationale de la Recherche Scientifique, 1977.

———. "Sherpas of the Rolwaling Valley: Human Adaptation to a Harsh Mountain Environment." Special issue on Nepal, *Objets et Mondes: La Revue du Musée de l'Homme* 14, no. 4 (1974): 317–24.

———. "Tsho Rolpa, GLOFS, and the Sherpas of Rolwaling Valley: A Brief Anthropological Perspective." Mountain Hazards, Mountain Tourism e-conference, November 15, 2006.

Sherpa, Jemima Diki. "Two Thoughts." *Alpinist* 47 (Summer 2014): 90.

Sherpa, Mingma Gyalje. "Full Value." *Alpinist* 53 (Spring 2016): 91–94.

Sherpa, Nima Tenji. "Yak Boy to IFMGA Guide." *Alpinist* 74 (Summer 2021): 30–36.

Sherpa, Pasang Yangjee. "Community and Resilience among Sherpas in the Post-Earthquake Everest Region." *HIMALAYA* 37, no.2 (December 2017): 103–12.

———. "Mountain As Metaphor: A Future of Multiple Worldviews." *Alpinist* 75 (Autumn 2021): 49–50.

Sherpa, Tashi. "Everest Interrupted." *Alpinist* 47 (Summer 2014): 89–94.

———. "From Rolwaling to Denali." *Alpinist* 61 (Spring 2018): 37–42.

Tobin, H. W. "Himalayan Porters." *Himalayan Journal* 16 (1951): 121.

Unsoeld, Willi. "Masherbrum—1960." *American Alpine Journal*, 1961.

Ward, Michael. "The Great Angtharkay: A Tribute." *The Alpine Journal* 101 (1996): 182–86.

Zimmerman, Graham. "Through the Field." *Alpinist* 53 (Spring 2016): 74–83.

FILMS

Adhikari, Rojita, and Sreya Banerjee. "The Widows of Everest." *101 East*. Qatar: Al Jazeera. Aired July 15, 2021.

Carpenter, Sue, and Belmaya Nepali. *I Am Belmaya*. London: Dartmouth Films, 2021.

Chapman, Bev, and Mele Mason. *Nawang Gombu: Heart of a Tiger*. Omaha: Mason Video, 2012.

Crowell, Cira, and Kyle Ruddick. *Dream Mountain*. InLightWorks Productions, 2021.

de Gerlache, Henri. *Les regards de Sagarmatha*. Levallois-Perret, France: AlloCiné, 2003.

Else, Richard, James Lamb, and Meg Wicks. *Sherpas Speak*. Dunkeld, Scotland: The Little Sherpa Foundation, 2019.

Jones, Torquil. *14 Peaks: Nothing Is Impossible*. London and New York: Noah Media Group and Little Monster Films, 2021.

Lassche, Geertjan, and Jangmu Sherpa. "Schone Bergen" [Clean mountains]. *2DocKort.* The Netherlands: 2Doc, Nederlandse Publieke Omroep, 2022.

Lee, Iara. *K2 and the Invisible Footmen.* USA/Pakistan: Caipirinha Productions, 2015.

Peedom, Jennifer. *Sherpa.* London and Sydney: Arrow International Media and Felix Media, 2015.

Ryan, Nick. *The Summit.* Dublin: Image Now Films, 2012.

Sharif, Jawad. *Beyond the Heights.* Wembley Park, UK: Karakorum Films, 2015.

Svendsen, Nancy. *Pasang: In the Shadow of Everest.* Ross, CA: Follow Your Dream Foundation, 2022.

ONLINE

Abbasi, Obaid Ur Rehman. "Adventure: The Incredible Tales of Little Karim." www.dawn.com, June 22, 2014.

Adhikari, Deepak. "The Everest Brawl: A Sherpa's Tale." www.outsideonline.com, August 13, 2013.

Adnan, Raheel. "Interview with Muhammad Ali Sadpara (Part-2): Winter Climbing and First Winter Ascent of Nanga Parbat." https://explorersweb.com, March 8, 2016.

Altitudepakistan.blogspot.com. "Nisar Hussain." December 31, 2012.

Benavides, Angela. "Annapurna, the New 8,000m Business Model." https://explorersweb.com, April 25, 2021.

——. "Broad Peak: New Reports on the Rescue and Kim's Fatal Fall." https://explorersweb.com, July 21, 2021.

——. "Everest: COVID Parties and Summit Pushes." https://explorersweb.com, May 16, 2021.

——. "Exclusive Interview: Denis Urubko on Nims, O2, and the Rules of Winter," https://explorersweb.com, February 18, 2022.

——. "Gesman Tamang: The Long, Hard Path from Cook to Elite Guide." https://explorersweb.com, August 31, 2022.

——. "Interview with Mingma G about Manaslu: 'No Excuses in the Future.'" https://explorersweb.com, October 14, 2021.

——. "Mingma David Sherpa on Winter K2." https://explorersweb.com, November 29, 2021.

——. "Mingma G. Sherpa: The Pawn Who Chose to Be a King." https://alpinemag.com, November 9, 2021.

——. "Sajid Sadpara on His Return to K2 and What Happened Up There." https://explorersweb.com, June 25, 2021.

Bindloss, Joe. "The Nepali Mountaineer Reclaiming the Himalaya." www.lonelyplanet.com, April 9, 2021.

Butler, Stuart. "The Himalaya's Hidden 'Paradise Valleys.'" www.bbc.com, August 30, 2022.

Fernández, Isaac. "Sajid Ali's Experience on Winter K2." [In Spanish.] www.desnivel.com, February 25, 2021.

Filippini, Alessandro. "Tamara's Emotions and Thoughts." [In Italian.] https://alpinistiemontagne.gazzetta.it, February 27, 2021.

Geiger, Stephanie. "Nirmal Purja, the 'Superstar of the Eight-Thousanders': How Cool Is the Nepalese Mountaineer Really?" [In German.] www.nzz.ch/reisen, December 17, 2021.

Gil, Pedro. "Winter Expedition to K2. Day 2. Interview with Sergi Mingote: 'I Am a Risk-Taker Mountaineer.' " [In Spanish.] www.mundo-geo.es/expediciones-extremas, December 20, 2020.

Jillani, Shahzeb. "Amir Mehdi: Left Out to Freeze on K2 and Forgotten." www.bbc.com, August 7, 2014.

Kan, Hyeong-woo. "Russian Mountaineer Accuses Climbers of Passing by Missing Korean Mountaineer." www.koreaherald.com, July 25, 2021.

Kobalenko, Jerry. "K2: Sajid Speaks." https://explorersweb.com, February 7, 2021.

MacAskill, Andrew. "Nepal Climbers Face Ruin after Quake, Blockade Hits Everest Industry." www.reuters.com, December 20, 2015.

McKerrow, Bob. "Ang Tharkay—the Father of Modern Sherpa Climbers." https://bobmckerrow.blogspot.com, September 12, 2010.

Merchant, Abdulmalik. "Samina Baig and Mirza Ali in Conversation with Simerg." https://simerg.com, April 29, 2014.

Mir, Shabbir. "The Extraordinary Life of Little Karim." https://tribune.com.pk, February 8, 2020.

Montejo, Leo. "What Really Happened on the Day That Ueli Steck Fell from Nuptse?" https://wicis-sports.blogspot.com, June 21, 2017.

Munim, Yasal. "Ali Sadpara's Trainer Was the First Pakistani to Summit K2." www.samaaenglish.tv, February 18, 2021.

Neville, Tim. "Brawl on Everest: Ueli Steck's Story." www.outsideonline.com, May 2, 2013.

Pakistan-explorer.com. "Interview with Gerfried Goschl: Leader of the Gasherbrum-1 Winter Expedition." January 31, 2012.

Pattison, Mark. "Lakpa Rita Sherpa." Episode 189 of *Finding Your Summit* (podcast). Audio, 36:04. www.markpattisonnfl.com, February 5, 2021.

Potter, Steven. " 'I Wanted to Completely Change the Dynamic on 8,000-Meter Peaks': A Q&A with Nims Purja." www.climbing.com, November 25, 2021.

Prasain, Sangam. " 'My Body Was Freezing. I Told My Teammates I Couldn't Move.' " https://kathmandupost.com, January 20, 2021.

Pueyo, Thomas. "Meeting Nirmal Purja, Universal Mountaineer." https://alpinemag.com, February 8, 2022.

Rehman, Sonya. "Interview: Pakistan's Premier Mountaineer on His Passion for Heights and Homeland." https://asiasociety.org, April 29, 2013.

Roberts, Jimmy. "The Himalayan Odyssey." www.nepalitimes.com, September 12, 2020. (Parts of blog entry originally posted in 1997.)

Sens, Josh. "Tent-Makers Remember 'King' Climber." www.sfgate.com, May 11, 2001.

Sherpa, Jemima Diki. "Three Springs." www.alpinist.com, April 25, 2014.

Sherpa, Lhakpa Norbu. "Was Tenzing a Tibetan, Nepali, or Indian? It Does Not Matter." www.nepalitimes.com, May 28, 2021.

Sherpa, Mingma Gyalje. "When We Unite, Nothing Is Impossible: My Story on K2." *Outdoor Journal*, February 18, 2021. www.outdoorjournal.com/featured/when-we-unite -nothing-is-impossible-my-story-on-k2/.

Szymczak, Robert. "Broad Peak 18.02.2011." https://karakorumclimb.wordpress.com, February 20, 2011.

Tahir, Nabil. "Shehroze Kashif: In Pursuit of the Tallest Peaks." www.redbull.com/pk-en/, June 9, 2021.

Thapa, Deepak. "Upwardly Mobile Ang Rita." www.himalmag.com, September 1, 1996.

The.ismaili. "Female Ismaili Mountaineer Conquers Everest as an Inspiration to the Women of Pakistan." June 21, 2013.

Welsted, Ian. "What Makes a Climbing Hero and the Legendary Little Karim." https://gripped.com, March 3, 2021.

Index

Giving Back

Bernadette McDonald and Mountaineers Books believe it's important to support organizations working to support and teach new generations of local climbers in the Greater Ranges. They've partnered to contribute a share of the proceeds from sales of *Alpine Rising* to two organizations based in the region.

The nonprofit Khumbu Climbing Center in Phortse, Nepal, was founded in 2003, with a mission to increase the safety margin of Nepali climbers and high altitude workers by encouraging responsible climbing practices in a supportive and community-based program. In addition to offering classes, it provides gear and serves as a community center for the region, with an earthquake-safe facility that includes climbing walls, a library, and a medical clinic. KCC operates in cooperation with the Alex Lowe Charitable Foundation. Learn more at www.alexlowe.org.

Ascend is an international not-for-profit organization that offers programs in Pakistan and Afghanistan designed to empower young women through mountaineering-based leadership, training, and community service. Its two-year holistic leadership development program is based on sport and civic engagement. ASCEND believes that when women play leadership roles in societies, there are better outcomes for family health, personal and societal wealth, and lasting peace. Learn more at www.ascendathletics.org.

About the Author

Bernadette McDonald is the author of twelve books on mountaineering and mountain culture including *Winter 8000* and *Brotherhood of the Rope: the Biography of Charles Houston*. In 2017, her biography of Voytek Kurtyka, *Art of Freedom*, won both the Boardman Tasker Prize and the Banff Mountain Literature Award, while her history of Polish climbers was awarded the Boardman Tasker Prize and the Banff Mountain Book Festival Grand Prize in 2011. She has twice won Italy's ITAS Prize for mountain writing (2010 and 2020) and is a three-time winner of India's Kekoo Naoroji Award for Mountain Literature.  In 2011 the American Alpine Club awarded her their highest literary honor for excellence in mountain literature. Her books have been translated into sixteen languages.

Bernadette was the founding Vice President of Mountain Culture at The Banff Centre and director of the Banff Mountain Festivals for twenty years. She has received the Alberta Order of Excellence (2010), the Summit of Excellence Award from The Banff Centre (2007), the King Albert Award for international leadership in the field of mountain culture and environment (2006), the Queen's Golden Jubilee Medal (2002), and the Queen's Platinum Jubilee Medal (2022). She is an honorary member of the Himalayan Club and the Polish Mountaineering Association, and has been appointed a Fellow of the Explorers Club.

Bernadette has degrees in english literature and music, with specialization in performance and analytical theory. When not writing, she climbs, hikes, skis, paddles, and grows grapes.

MOUNTAINEERS BOOKS including its two imprints, Skipstone and Braided River, is a leading publisher of quality outdoor recreation, sustainability, and conservation titles. As a 501(c)(3) nonprofit, we are committed to supporting the environmental and educational goals of our organization by providing expert information on human-powered adventure, sustainable practices at home and on the trail, and preservation of wilderness.

Our publications are made possible through the generosity of donors, and through sales of 700 titles on outdoor recreation, sustainable lifestyle, and conservation. To donate, purchase books, or learn more, visit us online:

MOUNTAINEERS BOOKS
1001 SW Klickitat Way, Suite 201 · Seattle, WA 98134
800-553-4453 · mbooks@mountaineersbooks.org · mountaineersbooks.org

An independent nonprofit publisher since 1960

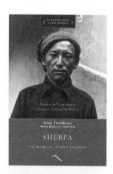
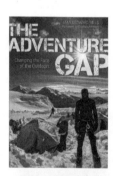

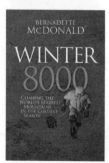